Praise for

M000205071

"The ability to focus on your sity!—is the key to success ir Williams has nailed it in his ~~book Extreme Focus. He breaks the~~ issue of focus down into its component parts, and shows you, step by step, how to bring a new sense of intensity and direction to your life. It's a great book! Read it, live in it—then go for your dreams!"

—**Bobby Petrino**, Head Football Coach, University of Arkansas

"*Extreme Focus* is must reading for anyone in my profession! This book will help you lock into what's important and empower you to achieve your full potential."

—**Gene Chizik**, Head Football Coach, Auburn University

"Focus is a term used by every coach in every sport. Pat Williams provides a perfect blueprint for all of us on how to achieve your dreams and goals with Extreme Focus. This book is a must-read for anyone who aspires to be successful."

—**Pat Fitzgerald**, Head Football Coach, Northwestern University

"This is another outstanding book from the fertile mind of my friend, Pat Williams. The premise of *Extreme Focus* is topical, timely and very important to all successful endeavors."

—**Rod Thorn**, President, Philadelphia 76ers

"Focus was the key to my career. I had the ability to block out the distractions and really concentrate on what was important. Pat Williams has captured that concept brilliantly in *Extreme Focus*. He breaks down the dynamic power of focus into a series of workable, learnable steps. I recommend this book to everyone who is committed to success in life."

—**Brooks Robinson**, Baseball Hall of Famer

"I preach focus to my team constantly, so I'm thrilled to have this valuable new resource from the prolific pen of Pat Williams. No matter your field of endeavor, this book will impact you deeply."

—**Steve Alford**, Head Basketball Coach, University of New Mexico

"Pat Williams once again gives us the blueprint for a life of success with this valuable new book. Pat is one of America's top motivational speakers and writers, and this might be his finest work to date."

—**Brian Kilmeade**, Cohost, FOX News' *Fox & Friends*

"The man who turned a dream into a multimillion dollar NBA franchise has written a powerful, practical manual for making dreams come true. Pat Williams's *Extreme Focus* is such a fun read, you'll hardly be aware of how much you are learning—and how radically your life is changing. Read it—then focus on its truths. This is your guidebook to an exciting future!"

—**Jack Canfield**
Coauthor of *The Power of Focus* and
the Chicken Soup for the Soul series

"Pat has really captured the importance and value of intense focus. In the sport of basketball, focus is everything. Ignoring the noise and blocking out all distractions is paramount to success. As someone who has been fortunate enough to play and coach at the highest of levels, I have witnessed firsthand the tangible power of focus."

—**Scott Brooks**, Head Coach, Oklahoma City Thunder

"This book will change your life for the better. I've known Pat Williams for many years and have admired his work greatly. *Extreme Focus* will touch you deeply, and help put shoe-leather to your dreams!"

—**Zig Ziglar**, Author of *See You at the Top* and *Better Than Good*

"This powerful, practical book shows you how to focus your energies and talents, concentrate single-mindedly on your goals, and achieve greater success—faster than you ever thought possible."

—**Brian Tracy**, Author of *Goals!*

"Focus will get you where you want to go. *Extreme Focus* will help you get there easier, faster and more profitably, with you in your heart. Read this book and use it."

—**Mark Victor Hansen**, Cocreator of
the Chicken Soup for the Soul series

EXTREME
FOCUS

EXTREME FOCUS

Harnessing the Life-Changing Power to Achieve Your Dreams

PAT WILLIAMS & JIM DENNEY

Health Communications, Inc.
Deerfield Beach, Florida
www.hcibooks.com

Library of Congress Cataloging-in-Publication Data

Williams, Pat, 1940-
  Extreme focus : harnessing the life-changing power to
achieve your dreams / by Pat Williams, with Jim Denney.
      p. cm.
  Includes bibliographical references and index.
  ISBN-13: 978-0-7573-1562-6
  ISBN-10: 0-7573-1562-3
  ISBN-13: 978-0-7573-9195-8 (e-book)
  ISBN-10: 0-7573-9195-8 (e-book)
  1. Attention.   2. Distraction (Psychology)   3. Success.
I. Denney, Jim, 1953–   II. Title.
  BF321.W55 2011
  650.1—dc22
                                                            2010050869

Publisher: Health Communications, Inc.
3201 S.W. 15th Street
Deerfield Beach, FL 33442–8190

Cover design by Justin Rotkowitz
Inside design by Dawn Von Strolley Grove

This book is dedicated
to my friend Jim Denney,
who has taught me more
about focus than anybody
I've ever met.

CONTENTS

PREFACE

My first book with Health Communications, Inc., was *How to Be Like Mike*, all about the success secrets of Michael Jordan, the greatest basketball player of all time. Published in 2001, that book is still in print a decade later—and I have followed that book with more than a dozen additional titles for HCI, including *How to Be Like Coach Wooden, How to Be Like Walt Disney, The Three Success Secrets of Shamgar*, and many more.

Over the years, Peter Vegso, the president and publisher of HCI, has become a great friend—but Peter never lets friendship cloud his business judgment. If I pitch him a book idea, he lets me know straight-up whether he thinks it's a homer, a base hit, or a strikeout. His instincts are unerring.

Whenever I get down to South Florida, Peter takes me to lunch at his favorite sushi place and we talk about book ideas. One time, a couple of years ago, I spread out ten book proposals for him. He skimmed through each one, then said, "Pat, you don't have ten *book* ideas here. You have ten *chapter* ideas for *one* book. In fact, this could be the ultimate self-help book if you could pull this thing together."

So I went home to Orlando and combined those ten book proposals into one. Then I took that proposal to Peter's horse farm in Ocala and personally placed it in his hands. I waited in suspense as he read the proposal.

Finally, Peter smiled at me and said, "All right, Pat, write this book—but with one proviso: I don't want a lot of razzle-dazzle, motivational fluff. I want a book that gives readers practical, realistic insight on how they can achieve their dreams of success. Give them *specific steps* they can instantly put into practice.

Write a book that will change people's lives. Can you do that?"

"Peter," I said, "that's exactly the book I had in mind."

"Good," Peter said, "because if this book doesn't deliver on that promise, then there's no need for you to write it and no need for me to publish it."

Well, the book Peter and I discussed that day is the book you hold in your hands—*Extreme Focus*. And I'm happy to report that when Peter read the manuscript, his response to me was, "Pat, you nailed it." Those were the words I'd been waiting to hear.

The insights I share in these pages are real and practical. I feel I can say that with authority, because these are the principles I've lived by throughout my career. These are the success principles that guided me while I assembled an NBA championship team as general manager of the Philadelphia 76ers. They're the success principles I lived by while my associates and I were building the Orlando Magic out of dreams and pixie dust. They're the principles I focused on while raising a family of nineteen kids (four birth children, fourteen by international adoption, and one by remarriage). They're the principles I still live by today as I give more than one hundred speeches a year, host three local radio shows, and write several books a year.

Whatever your dreams, whatever your goals, *Extreme Focus* is the key to your success. To prove it to you, I have packed this book with scores of real-life stories from my own experience and from the lives of people who have achieved great things through the power of *Extreme Focus*.

I would encourage you to read this book together with your family, or read it in a discussion group with other success-minded friends. Underline and highlight these pages. Write notes in the margins. Interact with these principles in a personal way—and let these insights work the same magic in your life that they have in mine.

After you've read this book and begun applying these principles to your own life, send me an e-mail or a letter (my contact information is in the back of the book). Let me know about your experiences in putting the power of *Extreme Focus* to work in your life.

Start reading, start dreaming, and start achieving great things—then write and tell me how your grandest dreams came true!

Pat Williams
Orlando, Florida

INTRODUCTION: FOCUS! FOCUS! FOCUS!

Midway through the 2008–9 NBA season, the world champion Boston Celtics came to Orlando to play the Magic. The Celts and the Magic had nearly identical records, and it was a nationally televised game, so the pressure was intense.

I went to the locker room before the game to talk to Celtics power forward Kevin Garnett. I wanted to give Kevin a signed copy of my most recent book, and I wanted him to autograph his picture on the new Wheaties box so we could auction the box for charity. I had often heard of Kevin's intensity as a player, but until I saw him in the locker room that night, I had no idea how intensely focused he was.

He sat staring straight ahead while one of the Celtics trainers taped his ankles. It was at least an hour and a half before tip-off, but he already had his game face on. I could see the intensity in his eyes—in fact, I could feel it in the room like static electricity. He was in a "zone" all his own. His gaze was so intimidating I was tempted to take my book and my Wheaties box and quietly tiptoe out of the room.

But I gathered up my courage, cleared my throat, and said, "Kevin, I have a book for you and a Wheaties box I'd like you to sign—"

Kevin looked up as if noticing me for the first time. "Mr. Williams," he said, "I don't *sign* anything, I don't *look* at anything, I don't *do* anything before a game."

Then he put his right hand up before his face as if it were an ax with the blade pointing straight out in front of him, and he made a chopping motion. "Focus! Focus! Focus!" he said. "I don't want any distractions. After the game, I'll sign the box, but right now I'm focused on the game."

Then his face again became a mask of intense focus.

That's why Kevin Garnett is a champion: Focus! Focus! Focus!

How would your life change if you lived your life in an intensely focused way, like Kevin Garnett? What would your family relationships be like if you became a husband, a wife, or a parent who practiced *extreme focus* in your family life? What dreams could you achieve in your career if you maintained an intense focus on your most important dreams and goals?

From "Zoned Out" to "In the Zone"

In 1998, Michael Jordan led the Chicago Bulls to their sixth championship of the decade with a pulse-pounding victory over Utah in the NBA Finals. Like all sports fans at that time, I was riding an emotional roller coaster. I felt the excitement of watching Michael play at the top of his game, mingled with the sadness of knowing that he was probably going to leave the Bulls at the end of that season—which, of course, he did. I had been a witness to an era of pure athletic genius, and it was coming to an end.

During that time, I had a busy speaking schedule, and I started giving talks on Michael Jordan's character traits and the leadership and success lessons we could learn from him. Out of this ten-point talk, which I delivered at corporate conventions and basketball camps, came the idea for a book that I called *How to Be Like Mike*. As soon as my friends at Health Communications agreed to publish the book, I got right to work and began researching the life of Michael Jordan. I was determined to interview everyone I could find who knew Michael in a personal or professional way. I didn't want to miss a single insight that might hold the key to Michael's greatness.

Around that time, the Magic picked up one of Jordan's former teammates from Chicago, B. J. Armstrong. He was a veteran guard who had played with Michael during the era of those first three Bulls championships, 1990 through 1992. On one occasion, I accompanied the team to New York, and I sat on the bus with B. J. After explaining the book project to B. J., I said, "Take a look at my outline for the book. I've tried to list all the traits that have made Michael so successful. What do you think? Have I captured the man?"

B. J. looked at my ten-point outline and said, "Yeah, it looks good. It looks like you captured it all, except—" he paused, "except you've forgotten the most important thing that makes Michael who he is."

I almost choked. "B. J.," I said, "I am all ears."

"Focus," he said. "That's what sets Michael apart. He has an almost superhuman ability to focus on *this* moment, *this* task, *this* goal. His head is totally in the game—no distractions. When the game is on, he's not thinking about last night's game or tomorrow night's game. He is totally in the moment, and nothing interferes with his focus. That's what sets him apart."

Focus! That's the key to Michael Jordan's greatness, and that's the key to Kevin Garnett's greatness. Total, concentrated focus.

Now, you might be thinking, "But I'm not a basketball player. I'm not an athlete. I'm an artist," or, "I'm a lawyer," or, "I'm a politician," or, "I'm an entrepreneur." You may be asking, "What can the power of extreme focus do for *me*?" Answer: It doesn't matter what your career path might be. It doesn't matter what your dreams might be. Whether you dream of success in business, science, the arts, or any other field of endeavor, the power of extreme focus is the life-changing power to achieve your dreams.

Stanford business professor Michael L. Ray, author of *Creativity in Business*, expressed the importance of extreme focus in the world of entrepreneurship and business leadership: "If you pay attention at every moment, you form a new relationship to time. In some magical way, by slowing down, you become more efficient, productive, and energetic, focusing without distraction directly on the task in front of you. Not only do you become immersed in the moment, *you become that moment*."[1]

Let's face it: Most of us live highly unfocused lives. Our daily routines are governed by habits that have become chronic and purposeless. We are constantly in motion—but we are moving on a treadmill, not a journey to a destination. We get up in the morning, move aimlessly through the workday, come home, settle back in front of that high-definition flat-screen time-waster—and that is our life, day after day, night after night, until it's time to collect Social Security. We reach a certain age and look back, wondering, "Where did my life go? What happened to all the dreams and ambitions I once had? Was I 'zoned out' throughout my whole life? What do I have to show for my life?"

My friend, I don't want you to live like that. More important, *you* don't want to live like that. You want more out of life than a "zoned out" existence. You want to "zone in" on the challenging, meaningful dreams and goals in your life.

This book will give you the practical tools to transform every aspect of your life, from the outermost reaches of your career to the innermost chambers of your soul and spirit. You will be able to build these principles into your own life—then teach them to your children, so that you can give your kids a foundation for a successful, satisfying, high-achieving life.

It's time to stop "zoning out." It's time to get "in the zone" and start living by the power of extreme focus. It's time to turn your dreams into reality.

So turn the page with me. Let me show you how you can harness the life-changing power of extreme focus to achieve your dreams.

1

Turning
Dreams
into
Reality

'll never forget where I was and what I saw the night of April 8, 1974. I was living in Atlanta, working as the general manager of the Hawks. It was the night of the Atlanta Braves' home opener against the Dodgers, and the legendary Henry "Hank" Aaron was chasing Babe Ruth's career home-run record, which had stood unchallenged for nearly four decades.

The Braves had begun the season with a three-game road trip. Aaron had played in two of those games, tying Ruth's 714-homer record. So that night I was in the stands at the Atlanta–Fulton County Stadium, along with 53,774 other cheering fans. It was humid and overcast when the game began, but nobody gave a thought to the weather. We were all thinking about being witnesses to history.

Dodgers pitcher Al Downing walked Aaron on his first at bat. Aaron's next chance came in the fourth inning. Downing threw his first pitch too low, into the dirt. His second delivery was right down the middle of the plate—right in Aaron's sweet spot. Aaron took his first swing of the evening—and in my memory, I can still hear the sound of the bat and ball connecting.

The ball went sailing, and Aaron took off running. The ball made a high arc, cleared the glove of Dodgers outfielder Bill Buckner—then cleared the left center field fence. The crowd roared and fireworks exploded. A couple of overeager fans clambered over the wall and onto the field, cheering Aaron on his way around the bases. As he came toward home, his teammates poured out of the dugout and surrounded him, whooping and hollering. Even Aaron's own mother ran onto the field and hugged him.

Few people realize the enormous obstacles and distractions Henry Aaron faced on his way to breaking Babe Ruth's home-run record. In those racially turbulent times, there were some white sports fans who resented the attempt by an African American to break Babe Ruth's record, so he received hate mail and death threats. At the same time, Aaron was also troubled by a painful sciatic nerve condition. But he remained focused on his dream, and he refused to let pain or the hatred of small-minded people stand in his way.

His teammate Dusty Baker (now the manager of the Cincinnati Reds) was watching from the on-deck circle when home-run number 715 exploded off of Aaron's bat. Baker recalled that Aaron had an almost superhuman ability to focus on his goals and block out distractions. Baker added that Aaron could "think away the pain" and "condition himself like no other baseball player of his time."

Aaron's focus on excellence involved a grueling, year-round

workout regimen. "Ralph Garr and I went to work out with Hank during the off-season," Dusty Baker told the *New York Times,* "and we thought that meant playing a little basketball. We saw him run, run, run with that medicine ball, play racquetball and tennis, eat his meals at the same time every day."

We tend to use the word "focus" in a metaphoric sense, meaning a mental concentration on a task or a goal. But Aaron's focus on being the best in the game of baseball involved a literal ability to *visually focus* on his opponents. When you were in school, you may have experimented with a "pinhole lens." By looking through a tiny hole, you can actually focus an image with the clarity of a polished glass lens—and that's what Aaron used to do. "Nobody had concentration like he did," Baker recalls, adding that Aaron would sit in the dugout, "looking at the pitcher through the little hole in his cap to focus on the release point. Never saw anyone do that before Hank."[1]

Why was Henry Aaron the greatest home-run hitter of the pre-steroids era? In a word: *focus.*

In the late 1990s, I flew into O'Hare International Airport in Chicago. A limo driver picked me up and drove me to Lake Geneva, Wisconsin, for a speaking engagement. The driver, Joe Curtis, was a Chicagoan in his seventies, a big man with a white flattop haircut. I often ask my limo drivers about their favorite passengers.

Joe told me, "One of my favorite passengers was Don Keough, the former CEO of Coca-Cola. I got to chauffeur him a number of times, and we talked about a lot of things. Mr. Keough told me about the two great passions in his life—Coca-Cola and Notre Dame. He told me that one time he went to a party and was introduced to the actress Kim Basinger. Mr. Keough didn't know her, even though she had been a major star for years. He thought she was just another Hollywood starlet. He said, 'Nice to meet you,

Miss Basinger. I wish you well in your career.' Later, he found out who Kim Basinger was, and he got all embarrassed. He went back to her, apologized for not recognizing her, and explained, 'I'm so focused on Coca-Cola and Notre Dame that I don't really have time to concentrate on the rest of the world.'"

Don Keough was one of the most successful executives in the world—yet to him, the Oscar-winning star of *L.A. Confidential* was just another pretty face. Did his ability to focus so single-mindedly on his two great passions in life contribute to his success? What do *you* think?

Some years back, I was talking to Charlie Morgan, an old friend of mine who is also the attorney of former Miami Dolphins head coach Don Shula. Charlie told me that after Shula retired, he sat in the stands to watch his first Dolphins game as a mere spectator.

Between the third and fourth quarters, the team-owner's wife honored some inner-city kids in front of the Dolphins bench. Shula was impressed. "What a great idea! How long has that been going on?"

"Don," said Charlie, "it's been going on at every game throughout your entire coaching career."

Shula's jaw dropped. "I didn't know that!"

Charlie laughed. "Of course you didn't. You were totally focused on the game."

To those who are truly focused, the rest of the world disappears. Time ceases to exist. There are no distractions. All they can see is the goal. That is why they succeed.

Janet Guthrie is a retired professional race car driver and the first woman to compete in both the Indianapolis 500 and the Daytona 500. She is also a flight instructor and aerospace engineer. Her helmet and racing suit are on display at the Smithsonian Institution. I once interviewed Janet on my Orlando sports talk radio show and asked her if she could give me the secret of her success in one word.

"Focus," she replied. "When I was racing, I was so intensely focused that if all four hundred thousand fans had stood up and left in the middle of the race, I never would have known. I was totally focused on the track and on winning."

Opera singer Luciano Pavarotti once put it this way: "On the day I'm performing, I don't hear anything anyone says to me."[2] Have you ever been that focused? Have you ever concentrated on a challenge or a performance with such intensity that you were unaware of your surroundings, unconscious of the people and events around you? When you experience that level of mental, emotional, and spiritual focus, you can harness the life-changing power to achieve your dreams.

The Million-Dollar Proof

The power of *extreme focus* is the power to enhance your creativity, insight, and intuition. The ability to focus with intensity is a key to success, not only for athletes, executives, and performers, but even for mathematicians. *Extreme focus* can enable anyone to experience that sudden flash of insight that we call "inspiration," "enlightenment," or even simply, "aha!"

Let me tell you a story that was nearly four centuries in the making—and that turned a Princeton mathematics professor into a millionaire. The story began in 1637, when a French mathematician, Pierre de Fermat, was studying an ancient Greek book of mathematics, the *Arithmetica*, written around AD 250 by Diophantus of Alexandria. As Fermat read, he experienced a moment of revelation, a concept that became known among mathematicians as Fermat's Last Theorem.

Now, I don't claim to be a mathematician. In fact, if I ever lost a finger, I couldn't count to ten. So I can't begin to tell you what Fermat's

Last Theorem is all about. But I can tell you this: Pierre de Fermat not only came up with a theorem that astonished generations of brilliant mathematicians, but he also claimed to have proof that demonstrated his theorem to be true in all cases. In fact, in the margin of his copy of the *Arithmetica*, he wrote in Latin, *Hanc marginis exiguitas non caperet*, which translates to, "I have a truly marvelous demonstration of this proposition which this margin is too narrow to contain."

When historians and mathematicians discovered Fermat's claim in the margin of the book, they wept in dismay. What was Fermat thinking? If he could prove his theorem, why didn't he write the proof down someplace—on the title page, on the back of an envelope, on a lavatory wall, someplace! But no! He just left a tantalizing claim that he could prove his Last Theorem . . . and no proof.

Years turned into decades, and decades into centuries. Great mathematical minds tried to discover their own proof for Fermat's Last Theorem, but without success. The French Academy of Sciences, the Academy of Brussels, and the Göttingen Academy of Sciences all offered cash prizes for anyone who could submit a general proof of the Last Theorem. Thousands of supposed "proofs" were submitted by professional and amateur mathematicians, but all were proven to be flawed.

In the early 1960s, a ten-year-old English lad named Andrew John Wiles encountered the mystery of Fermat's Last Theorem in a school science book. He was captivated by this enigma, which had puzzled the world's greatest mathematical minds. He studied mathematics at Oxford and Cambridge and became a professor of mathematics at Princeton University. Throughout his career, he remained fascinated by the Last Theorem. Finally, in 1993, he was sure he had found the proof. So he began writing a paper to be published in a peer-reviewed journal of mathematics. As he wrote the paper, he discovered a fundamental error in his thinking. His "proof" was fatally flawed.

Wiles continued focusing on the problem—and on September 19, 1994, the answer came to him. Assisted by a former student, Richard Taylor, Wiles wrote a new paper that claimed to be the long-sought-after proof of Fermat's Last Theorem. He submitted his findings to the *Annals of Mathematics*, which accepted and published the paper in 1995. Wiles's proof was subjected to the most exacting scrutiny by the world's leading mathematicians—and it passed every test.

Two years after the paper was published, Wiles received the $50,000 Wolf Prize in Mathematics. He also received a MacArthur Fellowship and the 2005 Shaw Prize in Mathematical Sciences. The Shaw Prize alone carried a cash award of $1 million.[3] In his book *Psychology*, Michigan psychologist David G. Myers tells the story of Wiles's discovery:

> Like countless others, Princeton mathematician Andrew Wiles had pondered the problem for more than 30 years and had come to the brink of a solution. Then, one morning, out of the blue, the "incredible revelation"—the fix to the one remaining difficulty—struck him. "It was so indescribably beautiful; it was so simple and so elegant. I couldn't understand how I missed it and I just stared at it in disbelief for 20 minutes. Then during the day I walked around the department, and I'd keep coming back to my desk looking to see if it was still there. It was still there. I couldn't contain myself, I was so excited. It was the most important moment of my working life." . . .
>
> Andrew Wiles says he labored in isolation from the mathematics community partly to stay focused and avoid distraction . . . Asked how he solved such difficult scientific problems, Isaac Newton reportedly answered, "By think-

ing about them all the time." Wiles concluded: "I was so obsessed by this problem that for eight years I was thinking about it all the time—when I woke up in the morning to when I went to sleep at night."[4]

Now, that's three long decades of *extreme focus!*

No matter what your field of endeavor, the life-changing power of extreme focus is the power to achieve your dreams. These principles are truly universal. Henry Aaron and Michael Jordan used the power of *extreme focus* to achieve their dreams in the realm of athletic competition. Coca-Cola's Don Keough practiced extreme focus to reach the pinnacle of the corporate world. Don Shula's extreme focus as coach of the Miami Dolphins made him the only NFL coach to have an undefeated season. Luciano Pavarotti used the power of extreme focus to amplify his creative and performance abilities. And Andrew Wiles used the power of extreme focus over a period of decades to solve one of the most perplexing intellectual puzzles of all time (and, incidentally, achieve wealth and fame as a byproduct).

Extreme focus is the key to mental and physical endurance, as marathon runner Joan Benoit Samuelson discovered. She won the gold medal at the 1984 Summer Olympics in Los Angeles, the year the women's marathon first became an Olympic event. "My body may fail me," she once said, "but my head never has. There's a switch I can throw that puts me into high concentration: I focus 100 percent on the immediate goal; I forget I have a body; I don't feel pain."[5]

I once heard Bobby Murcer, the late, great Yankees outfielder, talk about the time he ran in the 1988 New York Marathon. He described riding to the starting line on a bus with some of the elite long-distance runners of the world over the Verrazano-Narrows Bridge to Staten Island. On the bus, he sat across from Grete

Waitz, one of the greatest women distance runners of all time. Waitz, a Norwegian, had already won eight of the previous nine New York City Marathons in the women's division—and she was destined to win her ninth that day. She had also taken the silver at the 1984 Summer Olympics.

Bobby recalled that Waitz got on the bus, sat across the aisle from him, and didn't look right or left, just straight ahead. "She was totally focused," he said. "She didn't say a single word to anybody. From the look on her face, I don't think she heard a word anyone said to her. I wanted to say hi to her and wish her well, but she didn't see me. She was totally focused on what she was going to do that day. And when the time came, she went out and did it."

In his book *The Fifth Season*, sportswriter Donald Honig wrote about baseball in the post–World War II era, including the 1955 World Series. In that series, the Brooklyn Dodgers defeated the New York Yankees for their only World Series win before moving to Los Angeles in 1958. One of the players who stands out in Honig's book is Dodgers outfielder Pete Reiser. Honig interviewed a number of players who knew Reiser, including longtime Pirates first baseman Elbie Fletcher, who had played against Reiser many times. Fletcher recalled, "A lot of times a fellow would get a base hit, and we'd stand on first and shoot the breeze a little. I was a friendly sort of guy. But Reiser wouldn't talk. Never say a word. He'd get on base, and he'd be all concentration. And you just *knew* what he was thinking about. How am I going to get to second? How am I going to get to third? How am I going to score?"[6]

Extreme focus is also the key to achieving peak mental and physical performance, as NFL veteran Kendall Gammon can testify. His specialty in pro football (with the Steelers, Saints, and Chiefs) was long-snapping. As the center, his job was to snap the ball quickly and accurately during field goals, extra point attempts, and punts. He had to be extremely accurate over a long distance and under extreme pressure—and Gammon gives credit for his success to the power of extreme focus.

"I can focus when I need to and block out all the distractions," Gammon explains. "It's like the baseball pitcher played by Kevin Costner in the movie *For the Love of the Game*, who tells himself 'clear the mechanism' when he really needs to concentrate on the task. I'm certain that's why I'm successful at snapping, because I can focus. In a game, I might do only ten or twelve plays, but they are important plays. With every snap, I'm quite literally holding the fate of the team in my hands. I encourage anyone to develop the skill. Can you concentrate on the moment? Snapping a football is just like many other jobs, because it demands a concentrated focus on the task."[7]

Extreme focus is not merely the ability to think the right thoughts, but the ability to screen out the wrong thoughts—the distractions, doubts, and fears, and the mental cross-talk that interferes with our best performance. As former Reds and Mets third baseman Ray Knight once said, "Concentration is the ability to think about absolutely nothing when it is absolutely necessary."[8] The rest of the universe, with its worries and distractions, fades from our thoughts. Nothing exists except the goal, the performance, the task at hand. When we are able to screen out both doubts and distractions, we empower ourselves to perform to the absolute best of our ability.

Turning Dreams into Reality

The poet Carl Sandburg once wrote, "Nothing happens unless first a dream."[9] And H. Jackson Brown Jr. author of *Life's Little Instruction Book*, once observed, "You can't stuff a great life into a small dream."[10] What are your big dreams? What is the vision that fires you up inside? What is the one great thing you would like to accomplish before you leave this world? Do you want to write the great American novel? Start a new business? Design your dream house? Build a park for the kids in your neighborhood? Run for public office? Launch a spaceship to Mars? How far and how high can your imagination take you?

Let me tell you about some of my dreams—and how extreme focus enabled me to turn those dreams into a reality. In the late 1970s and early '80s, when I was general manager of the Philadelphia 76ers, I dreamed of an NBA championship. Achieving that dream became my extreme focus.

When I heard that a phenomenal talent named Julius Erving— a.k.a. "Dr. J"—had become available, I contacted the general manager of the New York Nets to find out what it would cost to buy out Doc's contract. Answer: $3 million for the Nets and $3 million for Erving himself. That was a record sum to pay for an NBA player in those days. So I went to our owner, Fitz Dixon, and explained the situation. I told him that Dr. J was the top talent in the NBA, "the Babe Ruth of basketball," and worth every cent of $6 million.

Fitz leaned back in his chair and said, "Fine and dandy." He had just made a $6 million decision with those words— and I had just taken a giant leap toward my dream of an NBA championship.

Over the next few years, I focused on recruiting top talent to our team while dealing away players who didn't fit our team chemistry. Working closely with head coach Billy Cunningham, I searched for the perfect balance of talent, temperament, and character. Our team kept improving, and year after year, we made it to the play-offs—only to be disappointed in the end.

In 1981, the 76ers were bought by a new owner, Harold Katz,

and he forked over a cool $13.2 million to sign a powerful new center, Moses Malone. With his fierce rebounding and contagious intensity, Moses became the emotional sparkplug of the team. And that was just what we needed. We ended the 1982–83 regular season with a fantastic record of 65–17. Heading into the playoffs, the 76ers were like a buzz saw. We demolished the New York Knicks in the quarterfinals in four straight games, then defeated the Milwaukee Bucks in five. We faced the reigning NBA champions in the finals—Magic Johnson, Kareem Abdul-Jabbar, and the Los Angeles Lakers—and we swept them in four straight!

The celebration in the locker room on that final night was one of the sweetest moments I've ever experienced, complete with shouting, whooping, and fountains of champagne drenching basketball jerseys and business suits alike.

The City of Brotherly Love gave us a victory parade through the city, all the way to Veterans Stadium. We passed through a snowstorm of confetti and a thunderstorm of cheers. At the stadium, Dr. J stepped up to the microphone and said, "I've been trying to get here for seven years." I could identify with those words. I had been chasing that rainbow and trying to assemble a championship team for even longer.

Once we had achieved that dream, I set my sights on an even bigger, bolder, more improbable goal: I dreamed of building an NBA expansion team from the ground up. The average sports fan has no idea what's involved in creating a brand-new NBA franchise. You have to raise millions of dollars, meet with hundreds of civic and business leaders, market the idea to the community, assemble an ownership group, build an arena, and much more. It's about as big a challenge as running for president.

But once that dream had taken shape in my brain, it grabbed me and wouldn't let go. I had originally thought of locating the new team in Tampa or Miami, but during a speaking trip to Florida, two Orlando civic leaders, John Tolson and Jimmy Hewitt, convinced me that Orlando was the place to be, even though the city had no arena and no history of pro sports. Long story short, I moved my family to Florida in June 1986, and we began building that dream. There were no guarantees that the NBA would grant us the franchise, but we were totally focused on making it happen. Even before we had a name for the team or an arena to play in, we began selling season tickets and skyboxes. We got lots of help from the chamber of commerce and from local marketing and finance wizards. By early 1987, we had assembled an ownership group led by Bill DuPont of the DuPont chemical clan, and we had a name for the team: the Orlando Magic. A short time later, the NBA brass rendered their decision: the Orlando Magic was officially an NBA franchise, scheduled to open its first season in 1989.

From the time I left Philadelphia with a dream between my ears until our inaugural tip-off was a span of more than four years. It was four years of long hours, thousands of handshakes and speeches, countless rubber-chicken dinners, and many, many frustrations and disappointments. There were dozens of times I wondered why I was wasting my life on a hopeless quest.

Today, my dream is a reality. The Orlando Magic is one of the elite teams in the NBA and a major force in the economy of central Florida. As I write these words, the Magic has made twelve play-off appearances in twenty-one years, including two conference titles and five division titles. We just moved into the Amway Center—our new $480 million arena, perhaps the finest indoor sports facility in the world. It seems like it was just yesterday when we broke ground on our first arena.

On the concourse of the new arena is a display that takes you back through the entire history of the Orlando Magic. The first time I walked through that display of memorabilia and photos, I was overwhelmed with memories and emotions of those early days when we were just getting this magical dream off the ground. It's literally the history of a dream come true—and it all happened through the power of *extreme focus*.

If you wonder if *extreme focus* is as powerful as I say it is, and if it is truly the life-changing power to achieve *your* dreams, then come to Orlando, my friend. Take in a Magic game—and *believe*!

Harness the Power!

As I've looked back over my career, I've asked myself: Where does success come from? What is the key to turning dreams into reality? There was a time when I would have chalked it all up to hard work, a team of talented associates, and a fortunate break or two—and that would be true, as far as it goes. But I don't think I was aware until recently of a gift that God has given me, a gift that has always served me well in every venture I've been involved with. That gift is a relentless, persistent, *extreme focus* on my goals.

When I sink my teeth into a dream, I'm like a dog with a bone—I refuse to let go! I focus all my thoughts and energies on achieving that goal. I don't know if I was born with this ability or if it was taught to me at an early age. I only know that, for me, there was never any other way to live.

Only recently have I begun to realize that this ability, which I call *extreme focus*, is not naturally common to us all. Many people have unfulfilled dreams and goals because they have never learned the power of *extreme focus*. Their minds are distracted, their energies are scattered, and their time is squandered on trivialities.

We only get one life to live, my friend. What a tragedy that so many people never achieve their dreams and their true potential—*and many never even get started reaching for their dreams*—all because they have never learned the power of extreme focus.

The good news is that even if you weren't born with a natural gift of extreme focus, you can acquire it. The ability to focus on our dreams and goals is a *learnable skill*—and this book will reveal all the secrets to attaining and exercising this all-important skill.

Every chapter in this book will close with a section of advice—practical, workable insights you can put to use right now. My goal in writing this book is not to dispense information but to *change your life*. I hope and pray that you will be motivated, inspired, and energized to go out and begin building your wondrous, amazing dreams, using the power of *extreme focus*. So here are some closing thoughts for this chapter to speed you on your journey of turning your dreams into reality:

1. Get Started

I once interviewed fantasy writer Ray Bradbury for my motivational biography of Walt Disney, *How to Be Like Walt*. Ray knew Walt well, and he explained to me the central lesson of Walt Disney's life: "Walt teaches us that if you really want to accomplish something big in life, don't hesitate. Go to the edge of the cliff and jump off. Then build your wings on the way down. That's what Walt did. If he had waited for every condition to be perfect, he wouldn't have done anything. The world would have been deprived of so much joy, and we would have never heard of Walt Disney."

That's excellent advice for any endeavor. Whatever you dream of doing, get started! Don't wait until conditions improve. Don't wait until you get "around to it." Don't wait until you feel inspired or motivated or energized. Just do it!

Most of us feel stuck, sluggish, or unmotivated most of the

time. We get up in the morning and we feel like we can't do a thing without our morning coffee . . . and, of course, the coffee isn't right unless it comes from Starbucks . . . and once we get our cup of Starbucks, we don't feel like jumping right in and getting to work, so we check our e-mail, or surf the Internet, or make paper airplanes . . . until it's time for another coffee break. And so it goes . . .

How much of our lives are simply eaten up by procrastination? I think if we knew the answer to that question, we would be horrified. So what is the cure for procrastination? The cure consists of three simple steps:

- *Make a commitment to yourself.* Promise yourself that, starting today, you are through procrastinating. Immediately, now, right this very moment, you are going to get started building your dreams. And once you have made that promise to yourself, keep it. Honor it. Keep faith with the pledge you have made to yourself.

- *Make a plan.* Set aside a specific time for working on your dreams and goals. Make an appointment with yourself and then keep that appointment. Do this every day, and it will automatically lead to the next step.

- *Build a habit.* If you are consistent over a period of days and weeks in keeping that commitment to yourself and sticking to that plan, you will build a habit of working every day toward the realization of your dreams and goals. For example, if you want to run a marathon, then you must start a daily exercise regimen and condition yourself physically and mentally for a marathon. If you want to write a novel, set aside time every day to write. If you want to play lead guitar in a heavy metal band, then dust off that Stratocaster and start learning those licks. Once you build a habit of working on your dreams, that habit becomes hard to break. Good habits enable you to focus intensely on your most important goals. Habits take on a life of their own—and soon you are well on your way to achieving your dreams.

By the time this book comes off the press, I will have run sixty marathons. People ask me, "How do you do it?" Answer: "A little bit each day." I have to do a little bit of work every single day in order to be ready on the day of the race. Each day, I strap on my shoes and go out and get some more mileage in. Each day, I go into the weight room and get on the stair stepper. Running a marathon is purely a matter of habits that I keep every single day.

When this book comes out, it will be my seventieth book. People ask me, "How do you write so many books?" Answer: "A little bit each day." I'm constantly reading, grabbing a story here, a brilliant insight there, a profound quotation someplace else, and I'm writing down the things that have happened to me and the people I've met. I keep all of these items cataloged and categorized and handy for use in my books—literally thousands of items collected one at a time, a little bit each day.

2. Stay Focused Until You Finish

Two of my sons, David and Peter, both graduated from the U.S. Marine Corps basic training at Parris Island, South Carolina. I sat in the reviewing stands with tears of pride rolling down my cheeks, watching the graduation ceremony. There's something very special about watching a son finish his basic training at Parris Island.

Major Stephen Davis, the longtime director of Parris Island's Drill Instructor School, had a succinct way of explaining the U.S. Marine Corps way of getting things done: "Concentrate on doing a single task as simply as you can, execute it flawlessly, take care of your people, and go home."[11] That is excellent advice—and it's another way of saying "stay focused until you finish." Concentrate on the task until you have executed it flawlessly. Don't let distractions pull you off-task. Don't let interruptions prevent you from finishing. Maintain extreme focus until you have completed the task before you. That's how you make progress toward your dreams.

3. Say Yes to the Best and No to the Rest

Many bright, energetic, creative people are thwarted by an overabundance of interests and choices. There are so many things we love to do that we want to do them all! The problem is that when we try to do everything, we end up accomplishing nothing. There's an old saying, "If you chase two rabbits, both will get away." You have to decide which rabbit you're going to chase, then focus on that rabbit with all your might.

Apple CEO Steve Jobs put it this way: "People think focus means saying yes to the thing you've got to focus on. But that's not what it means at all. It means saying no to the hundred other good ideas that there are. You have to pick carefully. I'm actually as proud of many of the things we haven't done as the things we have done."[12]

A lot of people today take pride in their ability to "multitask." But multitasking isn't focusing. In fact, it's the opposite of focusing. Multitasking involves fragmenting your attention and spreading it out over a number of different tasks. The consequences can be fatal.

Fifty-year-old celebrity plastic surgeon Dr. Frank Ryan was in his Jeep on California's winding Pacific Coast Highway, not far from his ocean-side home in Malibu, near Los Angeles. On the seat next to him was his border collie, Jill. One hand gripped the steering wheel while the other held a cell phone as he tapped out a text message to his brother. The road turned—but Ryan didn't. The Jeep went off the edge of the road, over a cliff, and was smashed to a mangled heap on the rocks below. When a fire department rescue team reached him, Ryan was still breathing but trapped in the Jeep with serious head injuries. Before a rescue helicopter could airlift him from the scene, Ryan died from his injuries. The dog suffered injuries to her head and paws, but she lived.[13]

My advice to you is focus, don't multitask—especially when driving. A very wise man, Albert Einstein, put it this way: "Any man who can drive safely while kissing a pretty girl is simply not giving the kiss the attention it deserves."[14] When you're driving, focus on driving.

4. Eliminate Distractions

We all know that distractions are focus-killers. Distractions come in many forms, from phone calls to visitors to headaches, to emotional upset to street noises to a neighbor's blaring TV. We can't always eliminate distractions from our surroundings, so we need to learn to screen them out and eliminate them from our consciousness.

Hall of Fame pitcher Bob Gibson, who played his entire seventeen-season career with the St. Louis Cardinals, was a fierce competitor known for his intense and focused demeanor. Maintaining his mental concentration was half of his game. Gibson once observed:

> I knew it was time to quit when I'd be out on the mound thinking about something else, some nonsense that was going on off the field. I'd be out there rehashing something that my wife had said to me and there is Willie Mays standing up at the plate . . . You can't pitch successfully in the Major Leagues without the ability to block out everything else. That's essential. If you can't do that, you don't belong

on the field. You cannot let your personal life interfere with the job you have to do for two and a half hours. Great players all have the ability to shut out any distractions. For most of my career, I could focus, no matter what. If I was angry about something going on at home, all the better. Once, on Father's Day in St. Louis, I had the biggest, nastiest argument with my wife that I'd ever had, went to the ballpark, pitched a shutout and, when I got home, we took up right where we left off. That's the way it has to be.[15]

Former Supreme Court Justice Sandra Day O'Connor learned at an early age to screen out distractions and focus on the task before her. At age five, she went to live with her grandmother in El Paso, Texas, where she went to a private girls' school. Unfortunately, young Sandra's grandmother was a nonstop talker. She even had a habit of jabbering while young Sandra was trying to do her homework. O'Connor later recalled, "I learned to just automatically respond to what she might be saying at the appropriate intervals, but never let it deter me from concentrating on what I was doing."[16]

Prolific writer Isaac Asimov also learned at an early age how to screen out distractions and maintain his focus. As a teenager, he tended counter in his parents' New York City candy store. He kept his typewriter behind the counter and pounded out stories while things were slow in the store. If a customer came to the counter, he would jump up, ring up the sale, then go right back to writing.

There were as many distractions at home as in the store. The Asimov family lived in a "railroad apartment," a series of rooms without a hallway. Because young Isaac's room was in the middle of this arrangement, there was constant foot traffic and noise all around him. "My apprenticeship as a writer," he later recalled, "took place in a boiler-factory under conditions of constant enforced interruption. I doubt if I ever had fifteen straight minutes of peace. Naturally, the fact that I continued to write meant that I had learned to withstand incredible noise and interruption. . . . I was undistractable."[17]

As I've studied the biographies of high-achieving people, I have found, again and again, that *extreme focus* is the *one* ability that *all* successful people have in common. The truly great names in sports, business, entertainment, the arts, religion, and politics have not always been the best educated or the most talented. But all, without exception, have had the ability to focus single-mindedly on their dreams and goals.

Once you have harnessed the power of *extreme focus*, you *will* be able to hammer your dreams into reality.

2

Focus
on Your
Passion
in
Life

Katharine Hepburn starred in fifty-two films and thirty-three plays and was nominated twelve times for an Academy Award. She won the Oscar four times—more than any other actor or actress. She made her Broadway debut in 1928 with her first film in 1932 and her final film in 1994, enjoying one of the longest acting careers on record.

Yet there was a time in 1937, after she had made four consecutive box office flops, when theater owners labeled Katharine Hepburn "box office poison." Everyone in the motion picture industry thought her Hollywood career was over just a few years after it began. If Katharine Hepburn had simply given up on herself and gone back into seclusion in Connecticut, no one would have blamed her.

But she was made of tougher stuff than that. And besides, acting was her *passion*. She refused to give up on her career. She once summed up her attitude this way: "If you always do what interests you, at least one person is pleased."

Katharine Hepburn was a unique personality. Independent, strong-willed, and athletic, she could hold her own opposite any male lead. Yet she managed to project a luminous femininity that audiences found appealing. She loved to do her own stunts and physically threw herself into every role.

In her first starring role on Broadway in *The Warrior's Husband*, she made a sensational entrance. Wearing a short, loose-fitting tunic, she appeared onstage with a deer's carcass slung over her shoulder, bounded down the staircase, took the final four steps in a single leap, and landed on one knee, flinging the deer on the stage before her.

Audiences loved her brash, confident style. But what few people knew at the time was that her outward confidence was an actor's mask. Inside, she dealt with the same insecurities we all feel. "Everyone thought I was bold and fearless and even arrogant," she once said, "but inside I was always quaking."

Katharine Hepburn preferred comfortable slacks and sneakers rather than frilly dresses and high heels—often over the objections of studio executives. Once, while filming at the RKO studio, an executive ordered that her slacks be removed from her dressing room in order to force Kate to put on a skirt or a dress. So she came out of her dressing room and lounged around the set in her underwear, causing an uproar throughout the studio. Within the hour, the RKO executive had her slacks returned to her.

When the major studios would no longer offer film roles to her after the box office flops that she'd performed in, she took matters into her own hands. She bought out her studio contract and began searching for just the right script to put her on top again.

She was dating industrialist Howard Hughes at the time, and Hughes lent her the money to purchase the film rights to Philip Barry's play *The Philadelphia Story*.

The play opened to rave reviews in 1938, and when MGM wanted to buy the film rights, they had to deal with Katharine Hepburn—and she demanded control of casting and production. When the film version of *The Philadelphia Story* was released in 1940, starring Hepburn, Cary Grant, and Jimmy Stewart, it was an instant hit—and Katharine Hepburn was once again the toast of Hollywood.

In 1942, Hepburn starred in *Woman of the Year*, the first of many successful screen pairings with actor Spencer Tracy. She continued to dominate the screen in the 1950s and 1960s with films like *The African Queen, Guess Who's Coming to Dinner*, and *The Lion in Winter*. Though she made fewer films in the 1970s and 1980s, her performance in *On Golden Pond* with Henry Fonda (1981) earned her the fourth and final Oscar of her career. Though she earned countless honors and awards as an actress on the stage, big screen, and small screen, she once said, "Prizes are nothing. My prize is my work." Those are the words of an actress who is passionate about acting.

When Katharine Hepburn died at her home in Old Saybrook, Connecticut, in 2003, the theaters on Broadway dimmed their lights in her honor. She lived by a philosophy that was taught to her by her mother and grandmother: "Don't give in. Fight for your future. Women are as good as men. Make your own trail." She once expressed her passion for acting this way: "Life is to be lived. If you have to support yourself, you had bloody well better find some way that is going to be interesting. And you don't do that by sitting around wondering about yourself."[1]

The Power of Passion

Real estate developer, business magnate, and TV personality Donald Trump once said, "Without passion, you don't have energy; without energy, you have nothing. Nothing great in the world has been accomplished without passion."[2]

What is this thing called *passion*? It's more than just a sense of eagerness or desire for a goal. It's more than enthusiasm. Passion is an intense and compelling emotional drive. To be passionate is to have intense, driving, motivating feelings. If you want to achieve your dreams and live an exciting life, then *follow your passions*—don't follow the pack. That's the advice a young Eileen Collins received from her Irish immigrant father—and she followed that advice all the way to the stars.

Eileen Collins is an American astronaut and a retired colonel in the U.S. Air Force. She is the first woman commander of a space shuttle, and she has logged thirty-eight days, eight hours, and ten minutes in orbit. Does that mean that she has missed out on life here on Earth? Not at all. Eileen Collins is happily married and the mother of two children.

She became the first woman space shuttle pilot in 1995 when she piloted *Discovery* through a complex maneuver around the Russian space station, Mir. In all, she has flown four shuttle missions, once each on *Columbia* and *Atlantis*, and twice aboard *Discovery*. She commanded the mission in 1999 that deployed the Chandra X-Ray Observatory satellite, which has greatly expanded our understanding of the universe.

In 1997, her achievements were recognized with the prestigious Harmon Trophy, which is awarded to outstanding aviators and aeronauts. She retired from NASA in 2006 and now lends her expertise to television coverage of space shuttle launches and landings.

When *Fortune* magazine asked Colonel Collins to recall the best advice she ever got in life, she replied, "When I was a young child and teenager, my father drilled one thing into my head over and over again: . . . Don't follow the pack. That's tough advice for a teenager, but it's what made me take flying lessons when I was nineteen. No one gave me advice to go fly. No one. I just did it because I wanted to. And those flying lessons are what got me interested in the air force. I've never really wondered what my father's motivation was. I think he didn't want me to be a follower. He wanted me to be a leader. I do know that he was astonished that I went into the military to fly airplanes and became an astronaut."[3] That is excellent advice for any endeavor, whether you dream of being an actor, an author, or an astronaut. Follow your passion—don't follow the pack.

I once had a speaking engagement in Fayetteville, Arkansas. The event was hosted by an Arkansas bank founded by the Walton family (of Walmart fame). I delivered a talk on teamwork to members of the banking community. After my talk, I went to the back of the room and sat down. A man approached me, dressed in khaki pants and a golf shirt. "Nice job!" he said. "I'm Jim Walton."

It was Sam Walton's son, one of scions of the Walmart empire. We chatted for a few moments, then Jim said, "Why don't you join me for lunch?"

I said, "That would be great!" I imagined that the Walton family lunched in grand style—pheasant under glass, caviar, soufflé Rothschild . . . ! Well, it was turkey on rye, and it was very good. That's the way they do things in northwest Arkansas.

So as Jim Walton and I sat at the table, I said, "Jim, tell me something about your dad. What was Sam Walton's greatest strength as a leader?"

He said, "You know, it's interesting, I've never been asked that. His greatest strength? It would have to be his passion. He was passionate about life, and he was passionate about the merchandise. He loved to travel around and see the latest things he could sell in his stores. He was always trying to get the best price on the best merchandise, so he could pass the savings on to his customers. He was absolutely passionate about the merchandise."

I was wearing a Hawaiian shirt that day. (The reason I like Hawaiian shirts is simple: have you ever seen anyone wearing a Hawaiian shirt who was having a bad day?)

Jim pointed to my shirt and said, "Dad would have been fascinated by your shirt. He would have wanted to touch it and examine the weave of the material. He would have wanted to know where it came from, and he would have turned the sleeve inside out and looked at the stitching. Dad was simply passionate about the merchandise."

"Jim," I said, "I can see why Walmart did so well. If the founder would have been passionate about the stitching on the sleeve of my shirt, I think that company just might experience some success along the way."

Passion can take many forms. We can express our passion for success in our tone of voice, our facial expressions, and we can even wear our passion on our skin.

I had dinner with Jay Bilas at an NBA function a few years back. Jay is an ESPN college basketball analyst. He was in Mike Krzyzewski's first big recruiting class at Duke in the early 1980s. I asked him, "Jay, what's your most vivid memory of playing for Coach K?"

He said, "My freshman year, we were practicing for a big game the next night. As we finished up practice, Coach talked to us about the upcoming game. He had on his blue Duke coaching shorts and a golf shirt. And as he talked about the game in that impassioned way he has, wanting to fire us all up, I noticed he had goose bumps on the skin of his legs, along his arms, and down his neck. Everywhere you saw skin, he had goose bumps."

I thought, *Isn't that amazing? That was twenty-five years*

ago—yet Jay vividly remembered his coach having goose bumps as he talked to his players about the big game. When you are passionate about what you do, you get goose bumps—and so do the people around you. Your passion elevates the emotions of the entire team, and that's the kind of passion that turns dreams into reality.

Dwight Stephenson was an All-American center at the University of Alabama and later played for the Miami Dolphins. He played under two legendary coaches, Paul "Bear" Bryant and Don Shula. I once asked Dwight if these two coaches had one great quality in common. He said, "Actually, they had two—intensity and passion. I was always impressed and inspired by the intensity and passion they both had for every practice, every meeting, and every game."

All great achievements begin with *passion*—an intense, all-consuming desire to dare and to do something on a grand scale. Great business leaders have a passion for building industrial or financial empires. Great writers and artists have a passion for expressing their imagination and creativity with a magnificent flourish. Great humanitarians have a passion for meeting the human needs that cry out all around us.

When I was a boy, my passion was sports. I learned to read and write by devouring books about my baseball heroes. I learned arithmetic from checking the box scores and keeping tabs on batting averages. My mother called me a "monomaniac." I didn't know what that word meant, but I had a vague idea that it had something to do with my single-minded passion for sports. Years later, I learned that "monomaniac" is the word novelist Herman Melville repeatedly used to describe Ahab, the peg-legged, mega-obsessed captain of the whaling ship *Pequod*, who was driven by a single-minded passion for hunting down the great white whale. And you know what? That word described me perfectly! I was

Ahab, relentlessly pursuing a career in professional sports. That's how I have lived my life, boy and man—with a single-minded passion for sports.

My passion kept me focused throughout my boyhood, then through college, and throughout my adult career. Everything I've ever accomplished can be traced to my monomania for sports. As a boy, I had filing cabinets that bulged with sports memorabilia, autographs, and baseball cards. When I read in a sports magazine that Don Mueller of the New York Giants would practice hitting curveballs by swinging at corncobs with a broomstick, I dragged my dad into the backyard and had him pitch corncobs over the plate. He must have thought I was out of my flippin' mind—but he humored me and pitched me those corncobs.

When I realized that my career as a professional athlete was coming to an end, I turned to sports management and pursued success in that field with the same monomaniac passion that I had once poured into my athletic pursuits. Over the course of my executive career, I've had the thrill of winning an NBA championship, resuscitating franchises in Philadelphia, Chicago, and Atlanta, and building a team out of dreams and pixie dust in Orlando.

Though I'm still involved with the Magic, speaking and writing have become an enormous passion for me—a second and third career. I want every speech I deliver to be better than the one before. As for my books, I'm still looking to write the bestselling book of all time. I have fifty books in the pipeline and fifty dreams that I want to get into print during the next thirty years.

Some people lack the flexibility and imagination to pursue new dreams. They hit a wall in their chosen career and never realize that they can *choose* to reinvent themselves and reimagine their dreams! New dreams are all around us—new adventures and opportunities to explore. If one dream dies, dream a *new* dream, then make that dream come true through the power of extreme focus.

If you want to have an exciting, meaningful, thrill-packed life—and I have!—you've got to be passionate about your dreams. You've got to find out what you truly love to do, then passionately invest your life in the pursuit of that dream. When you live your life with passion, every minute of every day is full of wonder and significance. You can't help but succeed!

I love what bestselling author Jentezen Franklin said when he was a guest on my Orlando radio show: "When you discover your passion in life and pursue it relentlessly, you become like a heat-seeking missile." Think about what a heat-seeking missile does. It searches for a source of heat, locks on to it, then chases it with single-minded focus. If the heat source moves left, the missile goes left. If the heat source soars skyward or dives earthward, the missile follows unerringly. When you are passionate about your dreams, you become just like that missile. That's the power of passion—the power to launch you unerringly toward your goals and dreams.

Where does this power come from? What is it about this thing called *passion* that enables us to work harder, last longer, and achieve more? Why isn't it enough to simply set goals, then work methodically and dispassionately to achieve them?

The fact is, we were given an intellect with which to think logically, plan rationally, set reasonable goals, and advance step-by-step toward those goals. But we were also given emotions that propel us, motivate us, energize us, and enable us to accomplish more than intellect alone can do. If we have a passion for one big dream, that passion will keep us from being distracted and pulled off course. Passion keeps us focused on the tasks we need to complete in order to reach our goals. The power of passion keeps us moving forward instead of spinning our wheels and settling for sameness. Passion focuses our minds on our dreams instead of on momentary interruptions and passing fads. The emotional power of passion keeps us on track for success.

Never be content to live in the gray areas of life. Get fired up! Get motivated! Live passionately!

Passion: The Key to Focus and the Key to Success

Inventor Thomas Alva Edison (1847–1931) produced more than a thousand inventions that still affect our lives today—from the lightbulb to the electric power grid that powers our world. Edison routinely worked from sixteen to twenty hours a day, and he was never happier than when he was working. Why? Because he was passionate about his ideas and inventions.

I've read a number of biographies on Thomas Edison, and one facet of his personality that is mentioned again and again as the source of his success is his passion for the work of invention. Notice the words and phrases I have emphasized by use of italics in each of these quotations. Edison biographer Martin Woodside wrote, "Work was his *passion*."[4] Another Edison biographer, Carole Cramer, observed, "He poured into research and development more money than his enterprises yielded—his ambition for wealth was repeatedly subverted by *his passion for invention*."[5] Blaine McCormick wrote, "Edison succeeded because he worked hard and delivered on his promises . . . His early successes taught him that *talent and passion alone mattered*."[6] And Robert E. Conot concluded, "It was as inevitable for Mr. Edison to invent as for fish to swim. It was his nature, or it may be described as *an all-devouring passion*, which nothing can satiate." That passion, Conot wrote, was the result of a union between "the restless spirit of American enterprise and the scientific genius of the present age."[7]

The great American novelist Theodore Dreiser interviewed Edison when the inventor was in his early fifties, and the interview was published in *Success* magazine in February 1898. Dreiser asked, "What do you think is the first requisite for success in your field, or any other?"

The inventor replied, "The ability to apply your physical and mental energies to one problem incessantly without growing weary."

"Do you have regular hours, Mr. Edison?" Dreiser asked.

Edison hinted that, when he was a younger man, he worked much longer hours. "I do not work hard now," he said. "I come to the laboratory about eight o'clock every day and go home to tea at six, and then I study or work on some problem until eleven, which is my hour for bed."

"Fourteen or fifteen hours a day can scarcely be called loafing," said Dreiser.

"Well," Edison responded, "for fifteen years I have worked on an average of twenty hours a day."

"What makes you work?" Dreiser asked. "What impels you to this constant, tireless struggle?"

Edison replied with a simple expression of his passion for his work. "I like it," he said. "I don't know any other reason. Anything I have begun is always on my mind, and I am not easy while away from it, until it is finished." That is passion talking, pure and simple.

Dreiser was still dumbfounded by Edison's seemingly Spartan way of life—especially the long hours he devoted to working in his laboratory. "You lay down rather severe rules for one who wishes to succeed in life," he said.

"Not at all," Edison replied. "You do something all day long, don't you? Everyone does. If you get up at seven o'clock and go to bed at eleven, you have put in sixteen good hours, and it is certain with most men, that they have been doing something all the time. They have been either walking, or reading, or writing, or thinking. The only trouble is that they do it about a great many things and I do it about one. If they took the time in question and applied it in one direction, to one object, they would succeed. Success is sure to follow such application. The trouble lies in the fact that people do not have an object—one thing to which they stick, letting all else go."[8]

My friend Gregory Morris, in his book *In Pursuit of Leadership*, commented on the Edison-Dreiser conversation, saying, "In that brief exchange, Edison revealed one essential ingredient for personal, professional, or spiritual success: *Focus!* All too often we do not accomplish all that we could or should because we lack crystalline focus."[9] Exactly so! Edison succeeded because of his intense focus on each of his inventions—and his intense focus was a direct result of his passion for invention. As Edison himself said so simply yet profoundly, "I like it."

Once, after Edison had put in an extremely long session at his Menlo Park laboratory, his wife said, "Tom, you've been working too hard. You need a vacation."

"But where would I go?" he said. "What would I do?"

"Just think about one place you'd rather be than any other place on earth. Then go there."

"All right," the inventor replied, "tomorrow morning, I will."

True to his word, the very next morning, Edison went back to his laboratory and put in another long day in the only place on earth he truly wanted to be![10] Edison was focused on his passion, and his passion drove his success. When your work is your passion, you can't wait to start working—and you never want to stop. That's why passion is the key to focus—and the key to success.

Garth Brooks is one of the most successful entertainers of all time. Before his fortieth birthday, he had sold more records than Frank Sinatra, Elvis Presley, Barbra Streisand, and Elton John in their entire careers. He's the bestselling artist of the Nielsen Soundscan era (roughly sixty-eight million albums sold), and the all-time second-bestselling artist in the United States (second only to the Beatles). In 2001, he gave an interview to *Parade* magazine that I think expresses the true source of his success: "The house lights go down, and you smell that vanilla smoke that makes all the stage lights show. All of a sudden, you hear the crowd, and suddenly your body takes a different posture—your stomach is in, your shoulders are back and . . . Boom! . . . Those nights seem to last ten seconds in your head, but you're out there two or three hours, and nobody has sat down all night, and nothing—nothing—is wrong! That's the feeling! That's the euphoria!"[11] And yes, that's the passion.

With five Olympic gold medals in her trophy case, Bonnie Blair is one of the most decorated women athletes in Olympic history. When I was writing *How to Be Like Women Athletes of Influence*, I devoted an entire chapter to Bonnie Blair. I interviewed her husband, speed skater Dave Cruikshank, over the phone, and he told me that the key to Bonnie's success was a *passion to win*. "Bonnie has the ability to drop everything around her and focus on the task at hand," he explained. "Once she was on the line, nothing would rattle her. When you saw that burning intensity in her eyes, you knew she was ready to conquer. She was so intense that nothing else mattered."

One of the truly great role models of passionate living is the late, great basketball coach Jimmy Valvano—known simply to fans and friends as Jimmy V. It was a privilege to know Jimmy and to interview him a few times on my radio show. I also shared the lectern with him at a couple of speaking engagements. He is remembered primarily as the coach of the North Carolina State Wolfpack in the 1980s, and he amassed a career record of 346–212. After retiring from coaching, he worked in the broadcast booth at ABC and ESPN, where he was often paired with veteran commentator Dick Vitale. In June 1992, Jimmy's doctors diagnosed him with an aggressive form of bone cancer.

On March 4, 1993, Jimmy was honored with the Arthur Ashe Courage and Humanitarian Award at the inaugural ESPY Awards event. In his acceptance speech, Jimmy said, "To me, there are three things we all should do every day . . . Number one is laugh. You should laugh every day. Number two is think. You should spend some time in thought. Number three is, you should have your emotions moved to tears. Could be happiness or joy. But think about it. If you laugh, you think, and you cry, that's a full day. That's a heck of a day. You do that seven days a week, you're going to have something special."[12]

Laughing, thinking, emotion—that's the passion of Jimmy V. That's the passion that powers all intensely focused people to achieve their dreams. In his book on the life of coach Jimmy Valvano, author and motivational writer Justin Spizman wrote about the success ingredient called *passion*:

> Once you figure out the blueprint for your dream, it is vital to put your heart into it. No dream has ever become a reality without a strong belief system.
>
> Passion for your dream is like gas for your car. It makes it go. It powers it. Without it, your dream would be stranded. . . .
>
> While a dream needs thought and passion to become a reality, without action behind the meticulous planning and a strong belief in your dream, you will have nothing. You can talk about it forever and the whole world can be

excited about your passion for your dream, but without action, your dream will be nothing more than a noble thought on paper.[13]

The great twentieth-century artist Pablo Picasso was once asked where his creative abilities came from. He replied, "Where do I get this power of creating and forming? I don't know. I have only one thought: work. I paint just as I breathe. When I work I relax: doing nothing or entertaining visitors makes me tired. It's still often three in the morning before I switch off my light."[14] This kind of artistic passion is undoubtedly common to all great artists. As the Italian Renaissance artist Michelangelo once said, "Lord, grant that I may always desire more than I can accomplish."[15]

Is that the prayer of your soul? Do you truly and passionately desire to achieve something that seems beyond the reach of your abilities? Then you have the first and most important thing you need in order to focus on your dreams and achieve them. You have *passion*.

Harness the Passion!

I have a copy of *Investor's Business Daily* (*IBD*) delivered to the end of my driveway every morning. There is one feature in that publication that is must-reading for me—the "Leaders & Success" section. In that section, *IBD* digs into the lives and thoughts of great leaders to reveal the wellsprings of their success. One writer who has contributed many of those pieces for *IBD* is Michael Mink. I have gotten to know Michael, and he has been my writing partner on a couple of books.

Over his career, Michael has written at least five hundred articles for *IBD*, and all of that research, interviewing, and writing he has done over the years has given him a depth of insight into the principles of authentic leadership and success. I once asked him, "Michael, based on all the study and writing you have done about great people in business, politics, the military, sports, and science, is there *one* common trait that you have observed in *all* high-achieving people?"

"Absolutely," he said without hesitation. "Every one of those people had an intense, even obsessive passion for what they did. Passion is the common denominator."

Carl Yastrzemski, the great Red Sox left fielder and first baseman, was an eighteen-time All-Star in his twenty-three-season career. He once described his passion for the game this way: "I think about baseball when I wake up in the morning. I think about it all day, and I dream about it at night. The only time I don't think about it is when I'm playing it."[16]

The power of passion helps to keep you from veering off onto detours, rabbit trails, and dead-end streets. The person who is passionate about one great goal doesn't get distracted by five or ten lesser goals. A great passion keeps you single-mindedly focused on your most important dreams and goals. It helps to keep your energies channeled into the one thing you want more than anything else. Here are some ways you can harness the power of passion to stay focused on achieving your dreams and goals:

1. Focus on That One Thing You Are Truly Passionate About

Peter G. Peterson is the cofounder and senior chairman of the Blackstone Group, an asset management and financial services company. A graduate of the University of Chicago Graduate School of Business, Peterson studied under the Nobel Prize–winning economist Milton Friedman. Peterson recalled that

Friedman "worshipped free markets and was also a powerful advocate of Adam Smith's concept of comparative advantage: Focus on those things you do better than others. That has been enormously helpful in defining our business strategies."

Peterson recalled that when he and Steve Schwarzman founded the Blackstone Group in 1985, many advisers urged them to specialize in acquiring companies through hostile leveraged buyout transactions. But Peterson and Schwarzman refused to go that route. "We felt that our advantage was that we were on friendly terms with many American CEOs and boards," he recalled. "So we took the contrarian position. We would only do strictly friendly investments. As a result, so-called corporate partnerships have become a major foundation—and a very profitable contribution—to our business."[17]

When you know what you do best, when you know what your true passion is, then you know where to focus your energies. You are able to sift through advice from others and sense what advice is good for you and what does not fit. Your passion enables you to focus on what you do best—and a well-targeted focus greatly increases your odds of success.

When Larry Page was a graduate student at Stanford, he wasn't sure what he wanted to do with his life. "I had about ten different ideas of things I wanted to do," he recalls, "and one of them was to look at the link structure of the [World Wide Web]. My advisor, Terry Winograd, picked that one out and said, 'Well, that one seems like a really good idea.'"

And was it a good idea? Well, Page took that idea and used it as the basis for a new concept in Internet search engines. In 1998, Larry Page cofounded (with his friend Sergey Brin) a company called Google. Perhaps you've heard of it. In fact, if you're like most people, you use the Google search engine dozens of times each day. You type in the name of something you're looking for, click the "Search" button, and your results pop up in roughly 12/100ths of a second.

In 2009, Larry Page was listed as the eleventh-richest person in America on the *Forbes* list of billionaires. How much is Larry Page's annual salary? One dollar a year. The bulk of his wealth comes from Google stock. Yes, focusing on the link structure of the World Wide Web was indeed a very good idea.[18]

2. Seek Out Mentors Who Will Encourage You in Your Passion

Andrea Guerra is CEO of Luxottica, the world's largest maker of eyewear, including sunglasses and prescription frames. He said that when he was a young man, just starting out in the business world with the Marriott hotel chain, his boss told him, "In your first years of business life, you shouldn't go chasing after fancy titles, but try to find people who can teach you something."[19] In other words, *seek out mentors*.

At the age of nineteen, Pete Sampras startled the world by becoming the youngest men's champion at the 1990 U.S. Open. It takes more than talent to set the tennis world on its ear the way Sampras did. It takes an understanding of the physical, mental, and emotional dynamics of the game—an understanding that usually requires years of intense training and experience. How did Sampras achieve greatness at such an early age?

Sampras grew up in Rancho Palos Verdes, California, and discovered the game of tennis while he was in elementary school. In a profile of Sampras in *Investor's Business Daily*, writer Michael Mink observed that, for young Sampras, the game of tennis "was his passion right off." When he was in high school, Sampras decided he wanted to be mentored by the best. So at age seventeen, he contacted Czechoslovakian tennis star Ivan Lendl, who was once the number one professional tennis player in the world.

"I stayed at his big, beautiful home in Connecticut," Sampras recalls. "Without saying anything, [Lendl] showed me what it takes to be a champion, how organized he was, how focused he was. That certainly was a good experience for me." The seventeen-year-old Sampras was especially impacted by witnessing Lendl's rigorous work ethic, which included daily thirty-mile bike rides to build his endurance.

Sampras was also mentored by his coach, Tim Gullikson, and by another number one tennis star, Jim Courier. "You take little pieces of the puzzle from everyone," Sampras observes. He was able to go farther, climb higher, and achieve greatness faster than any other player because he was passionate about the game—so passionate that he sought out the best mentors available. These mentors taught him shortcuts that propelled him to his dreams.[20] If you want to go further and get there faster, seek out mentors who can teach you how to leverage your passion into hard work and achievement.

3. Focus on Your Passion, Not on Pleasing Others

Herbert Swope (1882–1958) was a newspaper reporter and editor. He won the first Pulitzer Prize ever awarded for journalistic reporting. He once said, "I cannot give the formula for success, but I can give you the formula of failure—which is to try to please everybody."[21] That's great advice. If you want to succeed in any endeavor, then focus on your passion, not on pleasing other people.

Bob Iger, president and CEO of the Walt Disney Company, received—and offers—the same advice. He recalls, "My father wrote in my sixth-grade yearbook, quoting *Hamlet*—Polonius to his son, Laertes: 'To thine own self be true.' I was twelve years old, but it had a powerful impression on me then, and I've often thought of it since."[22] That is great success advice: Be true to your dreams, be true to your goals, be true to your values and your character. Don't get caught in the trap of trying to meet everyone else's expectations. Don't waste your life being a people pleaser. Be true to your own passion, focus on that passion with single-minded intensity—and one day you, too, may rule over a Magic Kingdom.

4. It Doesn't Matter Where You Come From— Just Go Wherever Your Passion Takes You

Mike Miller now plays guard and forward for the Miami Heat, but he was drafted by the Orlando Magic (fifth pick overall) in 2000. During his first season with the Magic, Mike won the 2001 NBA Rookie of the Year Award and was the only first-year player in the NBA to appear in all eighty-two regular-season games. He was once asked to name the biggest obstacle he had to overcome in order to play in the NBA.

"I think where I grew up," he said. "I grew up in South Dakota, and there weren't a lot of NBA basketball players coming out of there. So to get out and get seen was probably the hardest thing."

As a boy, Mike Miller had a passion for basketball. His father was the school principal, so he could borrow the keys to the gym anytime he wanted—and that was usually where you would find young Mike Miller. If he couldn't get into the gym, he would play on an outdoor court—even if the court was knee-deep in snow.

While it's true that the plains of South Dakota have produced very few NBA stars, Mike Miller believes that with a passion for the game, you can start anywhere and you can reach any height. "You get out what you put in," he says. "I think that is the whole key to basketball: how much work you put in is how successful you are going to be at the end . . . There are only so many people [in the NBA] and it is for a reason. There are a lot of good basketball players that don't ever make it. So you have to make the right decisions and work hard."[23]

And Mike Miller made the right decisions, starting when he was a boy in South Dakota, borrowing the gym keys from his dad, spending hours and hours alone with a basketball, and pursuing his passion with single-minded intensity. It truly doesn't matter where you come from. You can go anywhere in this world if you follow your passion.

5. Be a Doer, Not a Dabbler

John Haggai puts it this way: "When you're doing what you like to do, your mind is occupied with one thing. 'This one thing I do,' said [the apostle] Paul (Philippians 3:13). Dwight L. Moody added that most people today would have to change this and say, 'These fifty things I dabble in.'"[24] A passionate, focused person is a doer, not a dabbler. Doers succeed and achieve their dreams while dabblers are still waiting to get started.

Neal Gabler, in his book *Walt Disney: The Triumph of the American Imagination*, observed, "Walt Disney seldom dabbled. Everyone who knew him remarked on his intensity; when something intrigued him, he focused himself entirely as if it were the only thing that mattered."[25]

Let Your Passion Drive You

One individual who truly exemplified passion was Johnny Unitas, the legendary quarterback of the Baltimore Colts. Widely regarded as one of the greatest quarterbacks in the history of the National Football League, Unitas was the NFL's most valuable player in 1959, 1964, and 1967. From 1956 to 1960, he set a record of throwing at least one touchdown pass in forty-seven consecutive games—a record that still stands today. Johnny Unitas once expressed his philosophy of football and life this way: "If you want something badly enough, and I mean badly enough, chances are that you'll wind up getting it."

Through most of his early years, however, Johnny Unitas was told that he wasn't cut out to play football. When he applied for a football scholarship at Notre Dame, the coach told him that, at only six feet tall and 145 pounds, he wasn't big enough to play college football. He was also turned down at the University of Pittsburgh. Finally, he got a chance to play football at the University of Louisville, where he experienced some success. After college, he was drafted in the ninth round by the Pittsburgh Steelers, but he was cut before the season began. With a wife and a child to support, Unitas took a construction job in Pittsburgh and played semipro football with the Bloomfield Rams, earning $6 per game.

"I was disappointed, but not discouraged," Unitas later recalled. "I had enough of a taste of the big game to know I could play if I had the chance, no matter what anybody else thought."

His passion for football drove him to put in long hours of practice on his own time. "I'd get to the park about nine in the morning," he said, "do calisthenics, run four or five laps and then practice throwing to some high school kids if they were around. If I was by myself, I'd hang an old tire between the light standards and throw at it. I'd begin at 10 yards and then gradually move back to 30. I'd throw on the run, while moving back after imaginary fakes."

In 1956, when one of his Bloomfield Rams teammates was offered a chance to try out for the Baltimore Colts, Unitas borrowed gasoline money from friends and went with him. Unitas made an impression on Colts head coach Weeb Ewbank, and soon became the Colts' starting quarterback. And the rest, as they say, is history.

Johnny Unitas never claimed to have a lot of natural gifts and abilities as a football player. His greatness came purely as a result of his passion for the game. Where did he learn to approach life with such a tenacious passion? He gives all the credit to his mother and the example she set for him when he was a little boy.

He remembers being impressed by the way his mother held the family together after the death of Johnny's father. Johnny's mother was left with four children, ages ten and younger. "She kept my father's little coal truck business going for a while," Unitas recalled. "She also worked from nine to one at night, scrubbing floors in office buildings. She was always improving her jobs to make things better for us. She left the scrubwoman's job to work in a bakery, and then she sold insurance. At night, she went to school and studied bookkeeping and got the highest mark on the civil-service exam . . . She never got discouraged, and she taught us to think the same way. She taught us more about football by example of what it takes to get ahead than any of my coaches."[26]

That is quite a tribute! Johnny Unitas's mother had a passion for her family—a passion to provide a good life and a good living for her four fatherless children. That passion motivated her to work hard for long hours. It drove her to continually improve herself, so that she could earn more and be a better provider for her children. But more important than the money she brought home was the example she set. She was a living example of a profound success principle: focus on your *passion* in life, and see how far it takes you.

3

Focus
on
Tomorrow

While visiting Las Vegas for a speaking appearance, I asked my driver, Neil, about some of the memorable people he had chauffeured.

"Oh, I've driven Elton John, Michael Jordan, Shaquille O'Neal, Ben Affleck, Rodney Dangerfield—"

"Really?" I said. "What can you tell me about Rodney Dangerfield?"

"Well, Mr. Dangerfield was in Las Vegas for a personal appearance, and I drove him to the hotel where he was to do a show. He got out of the car and I asked him, 'Mr. Dangerfield, do you want me to stay here or go in with you?' He said, 'What do *you* want to do?' I said, 'Well, what do *you* want me to do?' We went back and forth like that a couple of times, and finally he said, 'Stay right there and think what you're going to do with your life.'"

I laughed. "Neil," I said, "have you done that? Have you thought about what you're going to do with your life?"

He said, "Every day."

Rodney Dangerfield was known for his bulging-eyed, collar-tugging, I-don't-get-no-respect comedy shtick, but my driver got to see another side of Rodney Dangerfield. More than just a comedian, he was a man who dispensed good advice for living: We all need to sit down and focus on what we're going to do with our lives. We all need to focus on tomorrow.

People of *extreme focus* are constantly dreaming of tomorrow—then setting goals to make those dreams come true. Our tomorrows are a direct result of the thoughts we think and the actions we take today. Our future goals shape our daily "Things to Do" list. By focusing on what we wish to achieve *tomorrow*, we identify the steps we must focus on *today*.

Goals Are Dreams with Deadlines

I once spoke at a huge sales convention in Orlando. I asked my host, "Who were the most memorable speakers you've ever had at these conventions?" Without hesitation, he replied, "Norman Schwarzkopf and Norman Vincent Peale." My first thought was that I should change my name to Norman!

My host continued, "I'll never forget when Dr. Peale came to speak. He was ninety-two years old at the time, and he gave a rousing speech that had everybody on their feet. Afterward, I drove Dr. Peale to his hotel and said, 'What time should I pick you up to take you to the airport?' He said, 'Six AM.' I knew his flight wasn't until ten, so I told him, 'You don't need to be so early.' He said, 'Oh, I like to get there early. I use the time to write and plan. At the moment, I'm outlining my goals for the next ten years.'"

Isn't that amazing? At age ninety-two, Dr. Norman Vincent Peale was making plans and setting goals for the next decade of his life. As it turned out, he lived to be almost ninety-six years old—and I don't doubt that he completed many of the goals on his ten-year plan before he left us. He was continually focused on tomorrow.

Hal Urban, author of *Life's Greatest Lessons: 20 Things That Matter*, says that many people are confused about what a *goal* actually is. "Goals are dreams with deadlines," he says. "Ask a hundred people what their goals are, and these are the three answers you'll get most frequently: to be happy, to be rich, to be famous. Those aren't goals; they're wishes. A wish is a vague dream that we hope happens *to* us. There is a vast difference between that and a goal. A goal is a clear picture that becomes an achievement because we *make* it happen. It requires hard work, self-discipline, and good use of time."[1]

A few years ago, I was invited to speak to a student audience at a prep school in Texas. Over lunch, I had twenty-five minutes to talk to the seniors who were the captains of the sports teams— eighteen sharp young people, every one a leader, and most of them headed to Ivy League schools after graduation. I said, "Tell me about yourselves. Tell me your name, where you're going to college, what you plan to major in, and what you plan to be doing with your life ten years from now."

They all, in turn, gave me their names, colleges, majors, and plans for ten years down the road—and it was that last item that I found the most revealing. Of those eighteen young leaders, fifteen gave vague answers to the question of what they saw themselves doing a decade from now: "I want to be happy." "I want to be rich." "I want to be successful." "I want to be married." Only three had specific, concrete goals: "I plan to be a research oncologist, seeking a cure for cancer." "I plan to have a novel on the *New York Times* bestseller list." "I plan to be in Washington, DC, working to affect policy as a public advocacy attorney."

It was clear to me which of those eighteen young people had the best shot at achieving great objectives in life. We spent some time that day talking about the difference between "making wishes" and setting clear, well-defined goals.

James Cash Penney founded his J. C. Penney stores on the foundation of the Golden Rule: treat the customer as you would want to be treated. He was also a strongly goal-oriented businessman. He once said, "Give me a stock clerk with a goal and I'll give you a man who will make history. Give me a man with no goals and I'll give you a stock clerk."

Penney's aphorism was truly prophetic. One of his stock clerks was a goal-oriented young man named Sam Walton. The young Sam Walton spent eighteen months, from 1940 to 1941, working for J. C. Penney, earning about $75 a week plus commissions. During that time, he was personally mentored by J. C. Penny himself.

When Sam Walton left Mr. Penney's employ, he took everything he had learned about retailing and goal setting, added a few innovative ideas of his own, and founded the mega-successful Walmart empire. There, Sam Walton proceeded to mentor other young success-minded men and women in the principles he had learned from James Cash Penney.[2]

Walton believed in setting extreme goals, focusing intently on those goals, and fulfilling them ahead of schedule. In 1976, when Walmart reported $340.3 million in sales for the year, Walton publicly announced a goal of *tripling* his sales within five years. "Write it on the wall now if you want to," he told a *Financial World* reporter. "By January 31, 1981, we'll be a billion-dollar company." He achieved his goal one year ahead of schedule.[3]

My friend Brian Tracy has written extensively about the importance of goal setting. "The ability to set goals and make plans for their accomplishment," he says, "is the 'master skill' of success. It is the single most important skill that you can learn and perfect. Goal-setting will do more to help you achieve the things you want in life than will anything else you've been exposed to . . . The payoff for setting goals and making plans is being able to choose the kind of life you want to live. So why do so few people set goals? According to the best research, less than 3 percent of Americans have written goals, and less than 1 percent review and rewrite their goals on a daily basis."[4]

Brian goes on to list four basic reasons why people avoid setting goals—four self-imposed obstacles to achieving the success we all desire in life:

REASON NO. 1: Some people are simply not serious about success. They want to be successful, they imagine being successful, they wish they were successful—but they haven't taken the serious steps that are needed to achieve their dreams. Brian adds an observation that I have often noticed myself: whenever you talk to a person who has achieved something great in life, this person will often make a statement along the lines of, "My success came when I finally got serious about my goals." Most people are content to drift through life, idly dreaming and wishing for success, but never truly getting serious about their dreams. Until we are willing to take serious steps to make our dreams come true, nothing will come of all that dreaming.

REASON NO. 2: Some people fail to understand the function and importance of goal setting. People who achieve success at an early age often come from families that repeatedly emphasized the importance of setting goals in life. Those who grew up in an environment where goal setting and achievement were continually emphasized have an advantage over those who had to learn goal setting in the "School of Hard Knocks."

REASON NO. 3: Many people fail to set goals because they fear rejection and criticism. This is the case for people who, at some key point in childhood, had their dreams crushed by a parent, teacher, or other adult authority figure. Children like to dream of limitless possibilities. They dream of becoming a professional athlete or the president of the United States or the first man or woman on Mars. But as soon as they voice that dream aloud, along comes an adult who feels a moral obligation to knock that child's dreams down to size.

So some children learn not to express their dreams aloud. They learn not to dream on a grand scale. Talking about your goals only gets you criticized—so the best plan is to keep your dreams to yourself, or don't dream at all. What a tragedy that so many dreams that might have changed this world for the better were strangled in infancy. If you are a dreamer who learned to keep your dreams to yourself, it's time to shut out those voices of criticism. It's time to stop listening to those who want to cut your dreams down to size. It's time to unleash your dreams and start turning them into reality.

REASON NO. 4: Many people are simply afraid of failure. "The fear of failure," says Brian Tracy, "is probably the greatest single obstacle to success in adult life."[5] Success requires risk, and risk entails the possibility of failure. So we must be willing to accept the *risk* of failure—and yes, the *experience* of failure from time to time—if we are going to experience the thrill of success. Failure is a great teacher, and it is often only by learning the lessons of failure that we gain the mastery and skills for achieving our dreams.

How to Set Goals

It's time to set aside our self-imposed obstacles. It's time to get serious about our dreams, to realize the importance of goal setting, and to stop listening to our fear of criticism and our fear of failure. Now let's focus your energies on the dreams that matter most. Here's a plan to help you to stop procrastinating and start goal setting:

1. Do It Now

Don't say, "Someday, when I get some spare time, I really ought to set some goals." Start right now. If you can't take time right this instant, then make a pact with yourself that you will not let your head hit the pillow until you have spent some serious time setting serious goals. Don't put your dreams off for even one more day. Goal setting is the key to your success.

2. Brainstorm

Take ten minutes or so to dream. Let your mind roam free. What would you like to accomplish in life? What would you like to experience? What would you like your life to look like? If you are not happy in your career right now, what sort of career would you like to have? What sort of artistic accomplishments would you like to achieve? What would you like your financial picture to look like in five or ten years? What educational goals would you like to achieve? What physical goals would you like to achieve, in terms of your health, weight, strength, stamina, and appearance? What kind of service would you like to donate to your community and the world around you?

All of these questions are thought-starters for your brainstorming session. Perhaps you can think of other kinds of goals you would like to strive for. One of the best ways to brainstorm is to visualize how you would like your life to look in a few years: What would you like your family to look like? What kind of house would you like to live in? What kind of work environment would you like to have? What kind of leisure activities would you like to engage in?

Perhaps the most important question of all is this: When you have completed your life's work, and your friends and family gather to memorialize you and celebrate the life you've lived, what one accomplishment would you like to be known for? The answer to that one question will define not only your dreams and goals but your passion in life.

Above all, make sure that the dreams and goals you brainstorm are truly *yours*, not a set of expectations that other people have set for you. The goal of brainstorming is *not* to please other people. Instead, focus on imagining a rewarding and satisfying life that you can live *on your own terms*.

It's important to consider the feelings, dreams, and goals of your life partner, but as you do, remember to remain true to your own values, character, and dreams of a better life. Discuss your goals with your family members, especially those goals that will impact their lives. Enlist them in helping you to meet your goals. You may be surprised at how willing your family members are to make sacrifices to help you find success and achieve your dreams.

As you brainstorm, write down the dreams and ideas that occur to you. Dash them off in the form of keywords or short phrases—don't write an essay! You may want to jot them down on Post-it Notes so that you can easily rearrange and prioritize them later as you organize your goals. If you carry out this brainstorming session in the way that I've described, you will see your dreams and goals begin to take visible shape.

3. Clarify and Define Your Goals

Once you have brainstormed your goals, it's time to clarify them and organize them into a set of clearly defined objectives.

Here are some suggested ways to sharpen the focus of your brainstormed goals:

First, make sure you have stated your goals in a positive form. "Avoid bankruptcy" is a negative goal, not a positive goal. If you tend to state your goals in a negative way, practice translating them into positive goals: "Accumulate $500,000 in investments."

Second, set goals that are as precise and measurable as you can make them. If possible, include deadlines and amounts: "Write a thousand words of my novel before noon of each weekday." "Lose a pound a week, for a total of fifty-two pounds by January 1 of next year."

Third, break down big goals into a series of smaller, achievable steps, and assign a deadline to each step. Let's say you want to build a sailboat. Instead of setting one big goal, "Build sailboat by June 1," set a series of smaller step-by-step goals: "Acquire sailboat materials by January 1, trace pattern and cut plywood by February 1, assemble hull and seal seams by March 1, finish out stowage and cockpit by April 1, install mast and complete painting by May 1, hoist sails and rigging by June 1—then christen and launch!"

Or, if you have a goal of becoming debt-free and building net worth within three years, you could break that goal into a series of attainable steps: "Step 1, set up a budget. Step 2, eliminate $4 coffee, movies, and concerts, and most other luxuries. Step 3, refinance mortgage to lower interest rate and payment. Step 4, devote 10 percent of income to debt reduction, over and above minimum payments. Step 5, once the debt is zeroed out, devote 10 percent of income to building investments." Set target dates for each step.

It's a lot easier to tackle small, attainable steps than it is to tackle a huge, intimidating challenge. Breaking large goals into small steps is a great way to conquer procrastination.

Fourth, prioritize steps and goals. Sometimes it's hard to know which step to take first—and this leads to indecision and paralysis. Instead of being overwhelmed by a long list of bewildering goals, create a checklist of prioritized steps—then follow each step in turn, checking off each one as you go. This will give you a sense of accomplishment as you steadily proceed toward the realization of your dreams.

Fifth, keep your goals realistic and achievable. You set yourself up for failure if you set unreasonable and overly ambitious goals. Your goal should challenge and motivate you, not intimidate and discourage you.

4. Set Goals in Stages

I have my goals staggered in stages of ten years, five years, one year, monthly, and of course, I have a daily "Things to Do" checklist. It's important to differentiate between short-term, medium-range, and long-term goals. In general, most of your short-term goals will tend to support your medium-range goals, and your medium-range goals will advance you toward your long-range dreams.

If you have difficulty getting started in the morning, it may be the result of not knowing where to begin. If, at the end of each workday, you take five minutes to create tomorrow's "Things to Do" list, that problem will disappear. Every morning, instead of fretting and procrastinating, you'll be able to dig right in to your most important priorities—and you'll be amazed at how energizing it feels to check each item off your list in turn. Small accomplishments produce big achievements that take you all the way to your grandest dreams.

I recently interviewed singer and author Sandi Patty on my radio show. In her new book *The Edge of the Divine*, she talks about the progress she's making in controlling her weight. The issue of weight control has been a struggle for Sandi throughout her life—but today she's eating right, exercising, and feeling great about her life. She says, "Here's the key. I have to make a plan the night before. I have to have my plan in place for the next morning. If I don't have a plan, it's not going to happen on its own. The key to everything is that I must have my breakfast planned, my workout schedule planned—everything must be planned out the night before, *in writing*. If not, the day will just take me over." Sandi Patty has learned the power of setting goals in stages.

In November 2010, I lined up with forty-five thousand other runners from around the world for the forty-first running of the New York City Marathon. Before the race, I was reading the *New York Times* and saw on the front page of the sports section a story about a ninety-year-old man who was running in the marathon. My first thought was, *Wow! That's got to be a record!* But the next paragraph said that, no, it wasn't a record. A ninety-four-year-old had finished the race a few years earlier. Well, that got me thinking: *Twenty-five years from today, I could be standing at the starting line, getting ready to break the age record!* So I now have a new long-range goal. A quarter century from now, I'm going for it!

What goals have you set for the next twenty-five years? What goals have you set for the next ten years? Five years? One year? Next month? Tomorrow?

5. Write Down Your Goals and Post Them Where You Will See Them Every Day

Don't keep your goals in your head—write them down. As Brian Tracy says, "A goal that is not in writing is not a goal at all. It is merely a wish, and it has no energy behind it."[6] Post your goals on the fridge, by your bathroom mirror, on the dashboard of your car, or next to your computer—wherever you are likely to see them and be reminded on a daily basis.

6. Review and Recalibrate Your Goals on a Regular Basis

Keep your goals in a computer file so that you can review them and revise them from time to time. You may find that you have underestimated or overestimated the time it takes to reach your short- and medium-range goals. It's okay to adjust your goals in order to make them as realistic and attainable as possible. You want your goals to be ambitious, even audacious—but not wildly unrealistic.

I have many goals for writing projects, but I continually have to readjust my written goals. Every project I plan is subject to circumstances beyond my control. Before I can begin a new book, I have to answer a number of questions: Is there a publisher who wants to publish this book? If so, when do they want to release it? Can I line up the right writing partner? How about that writing partner's schedule? Is he or she even available? So I'm continually recalibrating my goals. I have fifty books I want to write over the next few years, but nothing happens until a number of circumstances align and it becomes clear that the time is right.

So be flexible as you pursue your dreams. Life isn't static. Times and events may impact your goals. Be prepared to make adjustments as circumstances change. Make it a point to review your plans and goals on a regular basis—say, every six months— to make sure that your goals are appropriate to the way you envision your life.

7. Keep Faith with Your Goals

Commit yourself to a plan of action—then carry out that plan on a daily basis. Maintain a daily, even hourly focus on your goals. When you achieve an important step toward your dream, celebrate it! This will remind you of all the accomplishments and celebrations to come.

My wife, Ruth, works at Franklin-Covey, teaching time management, organizational skills, and how to use the Franklin Planner. She encourages people to make "Things to Do" lists in order to experience the joy of checking items off the list. Every time you check off an item, your body releases a little druglike substance called an endorphin. It's like a shot of drugs—a natural high.

While finishing this book, I've been starting work on my next book, which is about the leadership style of Coach Bear Bryant. I have a long list of Alabama football players who were coached by Bear Bryant, and I've been trying to get an interview with each one. Whenever I complete a call, I check it off my list—and I really do get a rush of joy and satisfaction at having moved this project a little farther down the tracks. The last player on my list has been the hardest to get ahold of—but I reached him: the great Joe Willie Namath. After I got through talking to him, I put the biggest check mark of all next to his name. I got a double dose of endorphins on that one!

If you keep faith with your goals, you will be rewarded with a life of meaning and satisfaction—plus an endorphin rush now and then. Most important, you *will* achieve your dreams.

Focus on Tomorrow by Preparing Today

On January 15, 2009, U.S. Airways Flight 1549 struck a flock of Canadian geese during its climb from LaGuardia Airport in New York City. The bird strike disabled both engines of the Airbus A320, causing a complete loss of engine power. At the controls, Captain Chesley "Sully" Sullenberger stunned the world when he safely landed the crippled airplane on the surface of the Hudson River, saving the lives of all 155 people aboard. Had another pilot been at the controls that day, the story might have ended differently.

Captain Sullenberger was uniquely prepared to glide an unpowered Airbus to a splash landing. As the Associated Press observed (and note the words "prepared" and "preparing" in this article):

Pilot's Life Had Prepared Him for "Miracle" Flight

Chesley Sullenberger spent practically his whole life preparing for the five-minute crucible that was U.S. Airways Flight 1549.

He got his pilot's license at 14, was named best aviator in his class at the Air Force Academy, flew fighter jets, investigated air disasters, mastered glider flying and even studied the psychology of how cockpit crews behave in a crisis . . .

"This is someone who has not just spent his life flying airplanes, but has actually dug very deeply into what makes these things work, and I think he proved it," said Robert Bea, a civil engineer who has known Sullenberger for a year.[7]

In an interview on PBS *NewsHour*, Captain Sullenberger told interviewer Jeffrey Brown, "Many people who have found themselves in such an extraordinary circumstance . . . really do feel like their entire lives [have] been a preparation for that moment. And I think that's especially true in my case, because I remember vividly as a child knowing that I needed to be prepared for whatever might come . . . It's been said that a smart person learns from his or her own experiences, but a wise person learns also from the experiences of others . . . In fact, in flying jet fighters, if you don't learn from other people's experiences, and you learn only from your own, you might not survive."[8]

Not only was Captain Sullenberger prepared for this emergency, but the city of New York was uniquely prepared to respond—one positive result of the tragic events of 9/11. Less than five minutes after splashdown, the floating Airbus was surrounded by ferry boats, tugboats, and helicopters, all taking highly trained first responders out to rescue the passengers. All of those emergency personnel had drilled and prepared for such an event. Focused preparation was the key to turning a potential disaster into a heroic success.

One of the most important ways we can focus on tomorrow is by preparing ourselves today. Unfortunately, we live in an instant-gratification culture, and many people today lack the patience to adequately *prepare for success*—and that is why they fail. Being fully prepared enables us to approach our goals with confidence and an intense focus. If you take time to make sure that nothing is left undone, nothing is left to chance, then you can face any challenge with the confidence that comes from knowing you are fully prepared.

In order to prepare for tomorrow, we must use our time wisely today. Preparation isn't always glamorous or fun, but you won't succeed if you aren't willing to invest time and effort in preparing for success. As tennis champion Arthur Ashe once said, "One important key to success is self-confidence. An important key to self-confidence is preparation."[9]

The late UCLA basketball coach John Wooden was a good friend to me, and I had the privilege of writing two books about his life, his character, and his success principles. He was famous for his oft-quoted sayings known as "Woodenisms." One of his best-known sayings was this: "Failing to prepare is preparing to fail." If you want to focus on your goals and achieve your dreams, you must spend time in planning, practicing, and preparing for your moment of crisis or opportunity. Here, then, are some steps you can take to help you to prepare for tomorrow.

Step 1: Practice Anticipating the Future

Baseball Hall of Famer Reggie Jackson often referred to winning as "the science of preparation," adding that "preparation can be defined in three words: leave nothing undone. No detail is too small."[10] I would suggest that those three words—leave nothing undone—can be condensed to a single word: *anticipation*. Successful people are those who have learned to *anticipate the future* and prepare for it by leaving nothing undone.

Eddie Lampert, chairman and CEO of ESL Investments explained how he learned to anticipate the future. He said that as a boy, he and his father would toss a football in the yard. His dad would say, "Go out ten steps. Turn to your right." So Eddie would follow his father's instructions, go out, turn, and the ball would fly into his arms and hit him in the chest just as he turned—a perfect reception.

When Eddie asked why he needed to learn to run routes this way, his father explained, "If I waited for you to turn [before I throw the ball], you and the defensive player would have an equal chance to get the ball." This way, Eddie would have the advantage—because he could anticipate the future and the defender could not.

Anticipation, Eddie Lampert concludes, is the key to success in business. "You can't wait for an opportunity to become obvious. You have to think, 'Here's what other people and companies have done under certain circumstances. Now, under these new circumstances, how is this management likely to behave?' The plays my father designed for me helped me learn to think ahead. Lots of days I asked him, 'Why can't we just invite kids over and play a game?' In order to do something well, he explained, you have to keep practicing and preparing."[11]

Step 2: Commit Yourself to Following Your Game Plan

Good planning is indispensable to achieving our goals. French writer and aviator Antoine de Saint-Exupéry put it this way: "A goal without a plan is just a wish."[12] In his book *Quiet Strength*, Super Bowl–winning coach Tony Dungy recalls that when he was a defensive back with the Pittsburgh Steelers, his coach, Chuck Noll, used to say, "Leaving the game plan is a sign of panic, and panic is not in our game plan."[13] Those are wise words. One key to focusing on tomorrow and preparing for the future is to commit yourself to sticking to your game plan.

Case in point: In November 2003, the fighting Irish of Notre Dame hosted the Middies of Navy. In past years, the Irish had won thirty-nine consecutive victories over Navy—but this year, Navy tasted blood. The injury-plagued Irish limped into their own stadium with a lackluster 3–6 record, facing 6–4 Navy. The Middies were convinced that this was their chance to finally defeat their detested rival.

One of the biggest holes in the Notre Dame lineup was the placekicker position. Starting placekicker Nick Setta had been injured several games earlier, and his replacement was D. J. Fitzpatrick, a junior walk-on. In the first half of the game, Fitzpatrick missed two field-goal attempts, fifty and forty-two yards, respectively.

Finally, in the closing seconds of the game, the score was tied, 24–24. Notre Dame moved the ball within field-goal range. Notre Dame coach Ty Willingham had no choice. He had to put the game in the placekicker's hands and trust him to boot the ball through the uprights, even though Fitzpatrick had already missed two previous field-goal attempts. So D. J. Fitzpatrick went out on the field to attempt the kick.

But just as the ball was about to be snapped, Navy called a time-out. This, of course, is standard operating procedure, intended to "ice" the kicker—to interfere with his focus and concentration, to stir up butterflies in his stomach and get him off his stride. After the time-out, Fitzpatrick got ready to attempt to kick—and Navy called *another* time-out.

For a third time, Fitzpatrick got ready to make the kick. The center snapped the ball, the Navy defenders rushed in to block the kick, Fitzpatrick booted the ball—and he heard a loud *thump*. A Navy safety had gotten a hand on the ball as it was kicked, deflecting it slightly. Fitzpatrick watched the ball wobble askew—but the trajectory was good enough. The ball went the distance and stayed between the uprights. "Those were two or three of the longest seconds of my life," Fitzpatrick later said. "I guess that little extra adrenaline helped. I just thanked God it went over."

Navy's attempt to break Fitzpatrick's concentration had failed—and coach Willingham explained that it was because D. J. Fitzpatrick was well prepared, knew the game plan, and stuck to it. "We've put him through similar freeze situations in practice," Willingham said, "where we line up, wait, come back, wait, come back. I felt good about him making the kick."[14]

No matter what your endeavor, when the pressure is on and you're tempted to abandon your game plan, don't panic. The key to success is to prepare yourself for every situation, develop a game plan for every contingency, and then, when the heat is on, carry out that plan.

Step 3: Don't Cling to a Plan That's Not Working

This may sound like I'm contradicting the advice I just gave you to follow your game plan. But no, the advice I just gave you is that you should not abandon your game plan *out of panic.* However, if circumstances have changed and your original plan clearly has no chance of succeeding, then it's foolish to stick with a plan that doesn't fit the new reality. Never abandon a good plan out of panic, but never stick with an obsolete plan out of mule-headed stubbornness.

General Dwight D. Eisenhower, the chief mastermind of the Allied victory in Europe during World War II, once said, "In preparing for battle, I have always found that plans are useless, but planning is indispensable."[15] In other words, events "on the ground" have a way of ruining our best-laid plans, forcing us to alter and adapt our plans to changing conditions. Even so, we would be foolish to go into battle with no plan at all! So make your plans—then be flexible and shrewd enough to adjust those plans as conditions change.

Planning and preparation are necessary for success, but changing circumstances force you to adjust. Thoughtful planning tries to anticipate everything, even unforeseeable events. Your planning and preparation should always include at least a Plan B— and it's not a bad idea to have Plans C through Z on hand as well!

Lee Roy Jordan was a legendary linebacker for the University of Alabama and the Dallas Cowboys. He played for Bear Bryant, then played his entire NFL career for Tom Landry. I once asked him what these two coaching giants had in common. "Oh, that's easy," he said. "Meticulous planning and thorough preparation. They were on top of every detail so we had the best chance to win the game that week."

Step 4: Condition Yourself to Think Positively

Most people see problems and interruptions as obstacles. Winners see them as opportunities to prove what they can do. Champions eat problems for breakfast.

Let's say you have a speech to give. You have prepared yourself well for that speech. You know the outline of your talk by heart, you have great stories to tell and several great applause lines strategically placed throughout. You have an outstanding PowerPoint presentation to illustrate your talk. Your host has thoughtfully placed a glass of water on the lectern for your convenience.

The appointed time comes, and you sit in the room as the audience files in. Your host gets up to introduce you—and accidentally bumps into the lectern. The water spills all over your notes—and your laptop computer. Your laptop screen goes dark—and so does the PowerPoint projector.

Now it's just you and the audience—no notes, no graphics. What are you going to do now? Is this a disaster—or an opportunity? Are you going to freeze up—or knock 'em dead? If you have prepared yourself to go into that situation with a positive attitude, no matter what happens, no matter what technical difficulties arise, you will be able to take a deep breath, smile, and launch into your presentation. Imagine what an impression you'll make when the audience sees you coolly and calmly turn a seeming disaster into an absolute triumph.

And imagine how your confidence will soar when you pull it off!

We all know that a positive mental outlook has a direct result on our performance. So maintaining a positive mind-set is an important part of preparing for tomorrow. If you see problems and interruptions as potential land mines that can blow up your performance, then you set yourself up for failure. But if you see problems as opportunities to show what you can *really* do, then you position yourself for success.

Whenever unforeseen events arise, meet them with a smile and a positive attitude. If you feel a case of "butterflies in the stomach," if you sense your breathing and heart rate racing, then pause, take a deep breath, say a prayer, think a positive thought, and tell yourself, "I can do this!" No one around you will know what's going on inside you—but as you take deep breaths, you feel the flow of calming, relaxing oxygen into your body. Keep your posture straight and confident. Move around, smile, make eye contact with the people around you, and think positive thoughts. You've trained and practiced and prepared for this moment. You are ready. You can do it.

Step 5: Prepare for Tomorrow by Being Organized Today

Howard Schnellenberger is currently the head football coach at Florida Atlantic University. He is famed for recruiting Joe Namath to Bear Bryant's Alabama Crimson Tide in 1961, and he also served as offensive coordinator for the Miami Dolphins, serving under coach Don Shula during the Dolphins perfect season in 1972.

I asked Howard to explain to me the secret of Don Shula's extraordinary coaching success. "Don Shula is the most organized and disciplined person I've ever met," Howard said. "Every date on his monthly planner was blocked out a month in advance. He could look at his planner and tell you exactly what he'd be doing at least thirty days out. Those dogged organizational skills allowed Shula to remain at a high performance level on a consistent basis. Coach Shula was disciplined and dedicated. I've worked under some of the greatest coaches in the game—Shula, Bear Bryant, George Allen, Blanton Collier—and the common denominator among these coaches was that they were extremely disciplined and totally dedicated to their profession. Inordinately so."

My writing partner, Jim Denney, once interviewed Bob Griese, who quarterbacked Shula's undefeated Miami Dolphins in 1972. I asked Jim if Bob had shared with him any insights into Coach

Shula's leadership style. Jim said:

> Absolutely. Don Shula replaced George Wilson as Dolphins head coach, and Bob said that the difference between Wilson and Shula was night and day. Bob called Wilson "a likable guy, the kind who would go out after practice and have a beer with players." Bob liked George Wilson but knew that his style of coaching would never get the Dolphins to the Super Bowl. Under Wilson, the Dolphins were the worst team in the league, finishing the 1969 season with a 3–10–1 record.
>
> When Don Shula came aboard as coach, everything changed. When someone asked Shula to describe his coaching style, he said, "I'm as subtle as a punch in the face." And Shula was famed for his grueling, punishing practices. But Shula wasn't just tough. He was methodical and organized. He imposed a systematic discipline on the Dolphins they had never had before. He focused heavily on precision execution and technique. He told Bob Griese that they would soon start winning games, and that was what Bob wanted to hear. Because of the intense discipline Don Shula imposed on the Dolphins, they quickly became the least-penalized team in professional football. Bob said, "I was ready to follow this guy into battle—just say the word."
>
> And just look at the difference Don Shula made. In 1969, the Dolphins were dead last in the league. Shula came aboard in 1970—that was a year of restructuring. Then in 1971, the Dolphins won the AFC [American Football Conference] championship, but lost Super Bowl VI to the Dallas Cowboys. In 1972, the Dolphins had their undefeated season and won Super Bowl VII. In 1973, they came back

and won Super Bowl VIII. In that short space of time, they went from the bottom of the barrel to the top of the heap, becoming the first team to reach the Super Bowl in three consecutive years. How did they do it? Bob Griese says it's because of the way Coach Shula prepared his team, imposing organization and discipline on his players. I think that speaks volumes.

Indeed it does. One of the most important ways to prepare for tomorrow is by getting organized today.

Step 6: Don't Overcomplicate Your Planning and Preparation

The purpose of preparing yourself today for the challenges of tomorrow is to enable you to focus and be your best under pressure. If you overcomplicate your preparation, you will actually put more pressure on yourself by giving yourself too many details to remember. Having to remember complicated plans and details interferes with the concentration you need for peak performance.

Baseball Hall of Famer Robin Yount enjoyed a successful twenty-year career as a center fielder and shortstop with the Milwaukee Brewers, 1974 to 1993. "I believe in reducing everything to its simplest state," he once said. "In baseball, I spend my time figuring out what I want to do at the plate before I come out of the dugout. When I get into the box, I want to concentrate on one thing: see the ball, hit the ball. I don't want anything else in there. You can't be up there thinking, *I've got to get a hit.* Being prepared frees your mind from all outside thoughts. If I'm blessed in any way, it's with concentration. I can blot things out and tunnel my focus. To me, concentration is the one skill that ties together every sport—golf, baseball, racing."[16]

Step 7: Visualize a Brighter Tomorrow!

Rubén González is an Argentine Olympian who competed in the luge from 1984 to 2010. A luge, as you may know, is a sled in which the sledder lies faceup and travels feetfirst down a hardpacked, high-walled track of ice. The sledder steers and controls the speed of the luge through a combination of body motions (exerting pressure with legs and shoulders, plus shifting body mass). González holds the distinction of being the first athlete to compete in four different Winter Olympic Games in four different decades.

Now retired from the sport, Rubén González looks back on his Olympic career and says, "Being focused on your dream is critical to making it become a reality. Back in 1984, when I made a decision to take up the sport of luge and make a run at the Olympics, I took an eight by ten photo of a luge racer and hung it up across from my bed. The first thing I saw every morning was 'The Luge Man.' He reminded me to work out, eat right, and surround myself with winners. The last thing I saw every night before I turned off the lights was 'The Luge Man.' All night long I would dream about the luge and about the Olympics."

That's wise advice. Our sense of sight is one of the most powerful of all our senses. So as we seek to focus on tomorrow, let's engage that powerful sense of vision and use it to motivate us on a daily basis to work toward our dreams. Posting images and motivational slogans where you see them every day will help keep you motivated and focused on your dreams. As Rubén González concludes, "Your ability to single-mindedly focus on your top priorities will determine how much you accomplish."[17]

González also says he was inspired by the story of the famed hotelier Conrad Hilton. During the Roaring Twenties, Hilton was making money hand over fist, but when the crash of 1929 tipped the nation into the Great Depression, the hotel industry collapsed. Hilton always paid his employees before he paid himself, and at times he would have to borrow change from one of his bellboys in order to eat.

One day, Conrad Hilton came across a magazine article featuring the fabulous Waldorf Hotel in Westminster, London. The magazine photos depicted the Waldorf in its heyday, when it boasted six kitchens, five hundred waiters, and two thousand rooms. The Waldorf was such a grand hotel that it actually had a private railroad station in the basement and a hospital with a full-time staff of doctors and nurses. Hilton clipped the article from the magazine and placed it under his glass desktop, so that it would always be in front of him, reminding him of his grand dream of owning the greatest hotel in the world.

In the depths of the Depression, Hilton later recalled, it was "a presumptuous, an outrageous time to dream." But he worked hard and gradually rebuilt his fortune—and in October 1949, Conrad Hilton achieved his dream. He acquired the Waldorf Hotel in London, which is now known as the Waldorf Hilton.

So don't just set goals and make plans. Visualize a brighter tomorrow! Make your dreams tangible and visible with a photo on the wall, on your computer desktop, or in your wallet. Keep your goals and dreams out where you can see them. Visualize them today—and experience the reality of your dreams tomorrow.

Know Where You're Going

American biologist David Starr Jordan (1851–1931) once said, "The world stands aside to let anyone pass who knows where he is going."[18] It's true. Focus on tomorrow, know exactly where you want to go, and chances are, you'll get there.

Ever since he was a boy growing up in British Columbia, Rick Hansen has been focused on tomorrow. He was a fanatic about sports, an intense competitor with natural abilities that enabled him to win All-Star awards in five high school sports. He dreamed of representing Canada in the Olympic Games.

When Rick was fifteen years old, he and a friend decided to hitchhike home after a summer fishing trip. A driver offered them a lift in the bed of his pickup—but when the truck skidded off the winding road, both boys went flying out. Rick's friend escaped with cuts and bruises, but Rick suffered a spinal cord injury. He was never able to walk again.

But was that the end of Rick Hansen's dreams? No way! As Rick himself would later say, a shattered spine is not a shattered spirit. Though paralyzed from the waist down, he made up his mind to dream new dreams and set new goals. After a lengthy rehabilitation, Rick found a new way to get involved with his lifelong passion for sports. He became the first student with a disability to graduate from the University of British Columbia with a degree in physical education. While at UBC, he became involved in wheelchair sports—and it was there that he met Canadian runner Terry Fox.

At that time, Fox had recently had his right leg amputated after being diagnosed with bone cancer. Rick invited Terry to stay in shape by playing wheelchair basketball, which Terry did, winning three national championships. Terry would later go on to be fitted with an artificial leg, and he embarked on a cross-Canada run to raise awareness and benefit cancer research. Though Terry's cancer forced him to end his cross-continent run and ultimately took his life, his courageous spirit inspired Rick Hansen to pursue his own journey.

On March 21, 1985, Rick Hansen set out in his wheelchair on what he called the "Man in Motion World Tour." He started at Oakridge Mall in Vancouver, British Columbia, and he continued his trek for more than two years, wheeling his way across thirty-four countries on four continents. At first, the public paid little attention to what Rick Hansen was trying to accomplish. But as he passed through city after city and country after country, reporters began telling Rick's story. Soon, crowds lined the roads on which Rick and his wheelchair traveled.

Finally, on May 22, 1987, after logging more than forty thousand km (twenty-five thousand miles) around the world and across Canada, he arrived in Vancouver's BC Place Stadium to the roar of thousands of cheering fans. Across Canada and around the globe, Rick Hansen was hailed as a hero.

Even after that amazing accomplishment, Rick Hansen continued to dream new dreams. Fired up by his trademark maxim, "Anything is possible!," Rick has gone on to win nineteen international wheelchair marathons, including six Paralympic medals. He was also named Athlete of the Century by British Columbia Wheelchair Sports Association. Today, as president of the Rick Hansen Foundation, he continues to generate millions every year for spinal cord injury research.

Though paralyzed as a teenager, Rick Hansen refused to let a shattered spine limit his dreams. "Wheeling around the world may seem to be an unrealistic goal . . . but the greater challenge was to successfully communicate the message, the meaning behind the goal."[19]

What are *your* dreams? What obstacles do you face in achieving those dreams? Rick Hansen didn't let a paralyzing injury stop him or even slow him down. He remained focused on his dreams, focused on tomorrow. His example challenges and inspires you and me. Your bright tomorrow awaits you. Don't let anything keep you from your dreams.

4

Focus
on
Today

Dru Scott Decker, author of *Finding More Time in Your Life* (2001), tells the story of her close friend Margaret, a woman who discovered at the all-too-young age of forty-two that she had one week to live. Margaret had gone to her doctor after suffering a bout of intense headaches. The doctors found a brain tumor. In fact, the cancer was so advanced that she was beyond treatment.

When Dru learned of Margaret's diagnosis, she was devastated. "I had just seen her four weeks earlier, and she looked as vital and happy as ever. Margaret had two wonderful sons, a great marriage, a satisfying career, and everything to live for. The sudden appearance of this tumor seemed so senseless and cruel."

Soon after Margaret received the diagnosis, Dru talked to her by phone. Though Margaret's speech was slowed by the pain medication, her spirit was strong. "For some reason," Margaret said, "during the past six months, I've been thinking about how I spend my time. I had always viewed myself as primarily a career woman, but lately I've begun to realize that my family is most important to me. I've been spending more time with my husband and my boys. Dru, it's so much easier to go through this now because I've been spending my time doing what really counts."

Dru concluded, "As I thought back over my memories of Margaret, I realized that if I had just learned I had a week to live, I couldn't make that statement. I hadn't been spending my time on the things that mattered most. If not for Margaret's words that day, I might never have taken the time to discover what really counts in my own life and to invest my time in the things that are most important in life. Margaret taught me to seize this irreplaceable moment and invest it wisely."[1]

"You don't really pay for things with money," writes Charles Spezzano in *What to Do Between Birth and Death*. "You pay for them with time. 'In five years, I'll have put enough away to buy that vacation house we want. Then I'll slow down.' That means the house will cost you five years—one-twelfth of your adult life. Translate the dollar value of the house, car, or anything else into time, and then see if it's still worth it."[2]

Time is not money. Time is *life*, and we each only receive a finite number of years, days, and seconds in which to reach our dreams. Have you ever said, "I'm just killing time"? Think of it this way: whenever you "kill time," you are really killing a piece of your life. The time you have is precious. Don't kill a single moment of it. If you want to achieve your dreams, focus on *today*—on this precious, irreplaceable moment called *now*.

Our Days Are Numbered

Great coaches know the value of the present moment. They know that future victories and championships are shaped by the actions that we take right now. That is why the late UCLA basketball coach John Wooden often told his players, "Make each day your masterpiece."[3] And that is why the great Alabama football coach Paul "Bear" Bryant kept a framed plaque on his desk that read:

What Have I Traded?

This is the beginning of a new day.
God has given me this today to use as I will.
I can waste it or I can use it for good.

What I do today is very important because
I'm exchanging a day of my life for it.
When tomorrow comes, this day will be gone forever,
leaving something in its place I have traded for it.

I want it to be gain, not loss; good, not evil;
success, not failure, in order that I shall not
forget the price I paid for it.[4]

David Roper suggests that an apt metaphor of our lives is found on a tombstone. It's that little hyphen between the date of birth and date of death. That really puts our lives into perspective, doesn't it? Roper also notes that while children measure their ages in small increments—"I'm not six, I'm six and a half!"—it would be foolish for a grown-up to insist, "I'm sixty and a half!" Time passes much too quickly for us to observe such fine increments at our age.

"It's good to ponder the brevity of life now and then," David Roper concludes. "Life is too short to treat it carelessly. In Psalm 90, after describing the shortness of life, Moses prayed, 'Teach us to number our days, that we may gain a heart of wisdom.'"[5] How do we "number our days"? We number our days by *focusing on today* and making sure that we spend each day on the things that matter most.

You may ask, "But what if I'm too old to pursue my dreams? I'm beginning to feel that life has passed me by." Well, you can't have yesterday back. But you still have today. You have this moment. And if you use it well and invest it wisely, it will be enough.

Don't waste your life waiting for "someday, when I have more time" or "someday, when everything is just right." As philosopher José Ortega y Gasset wisely observed, "We cannot put off living until we are ready. The most salient characteristic of life is its urgency, 'here and now' without any possible postponement. Life is fired at us point-blank."[6]

I was general manager of the Orlando Magic when we drafted a true superstar to our team, a seven-feet-one-inch center named Shaquille O'Neal. When I first met him, I could tell that Shaq was a young man who knew where he was going and what he wanted out of life. Years later, I discovered that Shaq learned the importance of *today* from one of his earliest (and favorite) coaches—his mother Lucille.

"My mother had a different way," he once said. "She was strong, like my father, but she was gentle, too." Lucille's advice to her son: "There is no opportunity like now. This is the time when you can show people."

When Shaq was in high school, he was a good player, but not the dominant Big Man he later became. "I didn't feel like I could stand out among those other players [on the team]," he recalled.

"I tried to brush her off and tell her I couldn't do that right now, maybe later."

But Lucille told her son, "You never know if there will be a 'later.' There are no guarantees in life, and 'later' doesn't always come to everyone."

Those words made a big impression on young Shaq. He realized he had to start building his dreams *now*, not later. "You work hard *now*," he said. "You don't wait. If you're lazy or you sit back and you don't want to excel, you'll get nothing. If you work hard enough, you'll be given what you deserve." That realization, Shaq says, was the turning point in his life—and the launching pad for his successful career.[7]

Apple Computers cofounder Steve Jobs agrees. "Your time is limited," he once said, "so don't waste it living someone else's life. Don't be trapped by dogma, which is living with the results of other people's thinking. Don't let the noise of others' opinions drown out your own inner voice. And most important, have the courage to follow your heart and intuition. They somehow already know what you truly want to become. Everything else is secondary."[8]

We often wonder why some people seem to accomplish so much more than the rest of us. It's almost as if they are able to pack more time into a day than the normal twenty-four-hour allotment. But as motivational speaker Denis Waitley reminds us, "Time is an equal opportunity employer. Each human being has exactly the same number of hours and minutes every day. Rich people can't buy more hours. Scientists can't invent new minutes. And you can't save time to spend it on another day. Even so, time is amazingly fair and forgiving. No matter how much time you've wasted in the past, you still have an entire tomorrow."[9]

Better than that, you still have the rest of today! So what are you going to do with this moment, this "now," which is yours to invest in any way you choose?

Tips for Focusing Productively on Today

You and you alone are responsible for the way you spend this day. There's no one else to blame. If someone else sets the agenda for your day, it's because you've given that person permission to do so. You own this day. Take charge of it. Use it well.

If you want to reach your dreams, it's essential that you learn to prioritize, organize, and manage your time each and every day. As management consultant Peter Drucker once observed, "Time is the scarcest resource, and unless it is managed, nothing else can be managed."[10] Let me suggest a few ways that you can get the maximum return on your investment in *today*.

1. Organize and Prioritize Your Goals for Today

You can't invest your day wisely unless you decide, first of all, to *prioritize your time*. There are many things we do every day that consume vast portions of time, but that do not move us closer to our dreams. We spend about a third of each day sleeping—and that is time well spent! We need sleep in order to be alert and energized throughout the working day. We should also set aside time for exercise and good nutrition.

But do we need to spend as much time as we do checking that BlackBerry, or updating our Facebook page, or watching *Dancing with the Stars* on TV? I suggest that all of us could probably do a better job of prioritizing the blocks of time we spend each day. How might our lives change if we actually set aside serious time on a priority basis for our long-term dreams and goals?

The best way I know to prioritize time is to make a "Things to Do" list, and to write down our tasks and goals in descending order of priority. Then, as we go through our day, start with Priority 1 first, complete it, then move on to Priority 2, then Priority 3, and so forth. Don't let phone calls, e-mails, or text messages pull you off task. Don't yield to distractions. Attack your "Things to Do" list in an aggressive, disciplined way, and by the end of the day, you'll be amazed at how much you've accomplished.

2. Cut Big, Intimidating Tasks Down to Size

Sometimes we stymie ourselves by setting a goal or challenge for ourselves that is so daunting that we don't know where to begin. My writing partner, Jim Denney, has written fiction as well as nonfiction, and he explains his approach this way:

> If you set a goal for yourself of writing the Great American Novel, you'll probably be too intimidated to write the first line. The idea of writing the Great American Novel is so big and scary that most people wouldn't know where to start. But if you break that huge goal down into a series of subgoals and tasks, what once seemed impossible now becomes doable.
>
> Instead of trying to take a giant leap, turn your "Things to Do" list into a series of simple steps:
>
> 1. Outline the plot.
> 2. Write character sketches.
> 3. Research setting.
> 4. Begin Chapter 1.
>
> And so forth. Every day, set a reasonable productivity goal—say, one thousand or two thousand words a day. Some people write quickly, some slowly. Set a goal that is high enough to challenge you, but not so extreme that you end each day discouraged. That's how books get written—in steps, not leaps.

READER/CUSTOMER CARE SURVEY

HEFG

We care about your opinions! Please take a moment to fill out our online Reader Survey at **http://survey.hcibooks.com.**
As a **"THANK YOU"** you will receive a **VALUABLE INSTANT COUPON** towards future book purchases
as well as a **SPECIAL GIFT** available only online! Or, you may mail this card back to us.

(PLEASE PRINT IN ALL CAPS)

First Name _____ MI. _____ Last Name _____

Address _____ City _____

State _____ Zip _____ Email _____

1. Gender
- [ ] Female [ ] Male

2. Age
- [ ] 8 or younger
- [ ] 9-12 [ ] 13-16
- [ ] 17-20 [ ] 21-30
- [ ] 31+

3. Did you receive this book as a gift?
- [ ] Yes [ ] No

4. Annual Household Income
- [ ] under $25,000
- [ ] $25,000 - $34,999
- [ ] $35,000 - $49,999
- [ ] $50,000 - $74,999
- [ ] over $75,000

5. What are the ages of the children living in your house?
- [ ] 0 - 14 [ ] 15+

6. Marital Status
- [ ] Single
- [ ] Married
- [ ] Divorced
- [ ] Widowed

7. How did you find out about the book?
(please choose one)
- [ ] Recommendation
- [ ] Store Display
- [ ] Online
- [ ] Catalog/Mailing
- [ ] Interview/Review

8. Where do you usually buy books?
(please choose one)
- [ ] Bookstore
- [ ] Online
- [ ] Book Club/Mail Order
- [ ] Price Club (Sam's Club, Costco's, etc.)
- [ ] Retail Store (Target, Wal-Mart, etc.)

9. What subject do you enjoy reading about the most?
(please choose one)
- [ ] Parenting/Family
- [ ] Relationships
- [ ] Recovery/Addictions
- [ ] Health/Nutrition
- [ ] Christianity
- [ ] Spirituality/Inspiration
- [ ] Business Self-help
- [ ] Women's Issues
- [ ] Sports

10. What attracts you most to a book?
(please choose one)
- [ ] Title
- [ ] Cover Design
- [ ] Author
- [ ] Content

TAPE IN MIDDLE; DO NOT STAPLE

BUSINESS REPLY MAIL

FIRST-CLASS MAIL PERMIT NO 45 DEERFIELD BEACH, FL

POSTAGE WILL BE PAID BY ADDRESSEE

Health Communications, Inc.
3201 SW 15th Street
Deerfield Beach FL 33442-9875

FOLD HERE

Comments

Fact is, that's how most goals are achieved—by breaking big goals into smaller steps, by making steady progress day by day, by keeping faith with our goals and our "Things to Do" list on a consistent basis. Baby steps, not great leaps—that's how to achieve your dreams.

3. Group Together Related Actions for Maximum Effectiveness and Efficiency

As much as possible, eliminate wasted motion. Why make three separate trips if you can make one three-stop trip instead, saving time, gasoline, and the environment? And while you travel, listen to an audio book and enrich your mind at the same time!

I like to build my body and my mind at the same time. I pump my stationary bike in the morning and read five newspapers while exercising my heart and lungs. When I'm out jogging, I carry my speaking notes on 3 × 5 cards so that I can memorize the main points of my speeches.

My singing-songwriting daughter Karyn has caught this same mania from me. I noticed a posting on her Facebook page, not long after she landed a recording contract. She wrote, "I just had another 'I'm-becoming-my-father' moment. So I'm in the recording studio tonight, and my producer has to take a phone call. While I wait for him to return, I get down on the floor in the vocal booth (headphones on and all) and start doing sit-ups. Then it hit me: *I used to make fun of my dad for doing stuff like that!*"

4. Set Deadlines—and Keep Them

Deadlines motivate us to work faster and smarter. When you know that you have a limited amount of time to reach a goal, you have a better idea how much time to spend on each step toward that goal. Deadlines impose discipline. Most of the high-achieving people I know enjoy competing against themselves and meeting their deadlines.

If you place a deadline on yourself, make sure it's realistic. Don't set your deadline too far off, or you might be tempted to stretch out the tasks to fill the time. And don't set it too short, or you'll place yourself under too much pressure. Also, take into account other factors that may impact your ability to meet your deadline—family responsibilities, travel plans, and so forth. Include a little cushion in your schedule to allow for unforeseen contingencies.

And if something happens that totally upsets your plans, don't let it upset you. Setbacks happen. Be flexible. Adjust to changing circumstances, set a new deadline, then keep moving forward. Don't be too hard on yourself. You're going to make it.

5. Determine the Most Important Thing That Needs to Be Done and Do It Now

Lou Holtz, retired head football coach at Notre Dame University, has a list of 107 dreams he wants to accomplish in his lifetime. Last I heard, he had achieved 101 of them. For example, he once had dinner at the White House, so he checked that off his list. He's appeared on *The Tonight Show*, so he checked that off. He's even jumped out of an airplane at ten thousand feet and parachuted to earth. He was relieved to check that one off and insists that once was enough.

Another dream on Coach Holtz's list was to go white-water rafting. He said he saw some people white-water rafting on TV, and it looked like fun. So he got his family together, hired a professional guide, and went to Hell's Canyon on the Snake River, at the Oregon-Idaho border.

He got into the raft with his guide, and about ten minutes into the trip, his guide shouted, "Coach, get ready, we're going through Big Chain."

"What's Big Chain?" Holtz asked.

"It's a class five rapids. The most dangerous rapids you can go through."

"Give me an example of a class six rapids."

"Niagara Falls."

So Coach Holtz hooked his thumb into the rope along the gunwale and held on for dear life as the raft hit the Big Chain. It wasn't long before the raft bounced up, tossing Coach Holtz through the air and into the icy, tumbling water.

He struggled to get back to the surface for a breath of air—only to bump his head on the underside of the raft. He swam through the churning water, trying to get clear of the raft, then pushed himself up to the surface again—and again he bumped his head on the bottom of the raft.

Now, there were several things at that moment that Coach Lou Holtz might have been concerned about. He might have been concerned about whether or not Notre Dame was going to win a national championship that year. Or he might have been concerned about the fact that, when he got thrown out of the raft, his thumb was broken in four places. But neither of those concerns was on his mind at that moment.

Coach Holtz later recalled, "The second time I came up underneath the raft, I realized that winning the national championship wasn't that important. There was only one thought on my mind—it was the word WIN, or 'What's Important Now.' And if anything was important now, it was to get out from underneath the raft. With this realization I finally got my head above water and kept it there."[11]

Coach Holtz's WIN theory is a great tool for making wise decisions under pressure. It's a great tool for determining what you need to do next as you pursue your goals and dreams. Just ask yourself, "What's Important Now?" and the answer will probably become obvious. I once heard Lou Holtz give a talk in which he explained his WIN theory this way: "Look at what's happened to you in the past. Look at where you want to go in the future. That tells you what's important now. That's the WIN theory: figure out the most important thing you need to do right now—then do it. *And do it now."*

6. Don't Let Other People Steal Your Time

Many people fail to achieve their dreams because they are constantly getting yanked off course by other people. Sometimes, people use guilt or manipulation to get you to serve *their* goals and priorities. Always remember that you have a right to set your own agenda. Your day belongs to you, not to anyone else.

Yes, you owe your employer an honest day's work for an honest day's wage. But once you are "off the clock," you are your own boss. Don't let other people boss you around. If someone asks you to set aside your priorities to help them with theirs, you have a choice to make. If you *want* to help that person, you can certainly *choose* to do so. But remember that it is your choice and *you have a right to say no.*

Many people seem unaware that they have this choice. If someone places a demand on their time, they feel obligated to say yes. Or they feel they need to have a good excuse for saying no. Please understand: you don't owe anyone an excuse! You have a right to say no, period. You don't have to make up a lie. You don't have to justify yourself. You have a right to invest your time in any way you choose without explaining yourself to anyone.

So cultivate the time-management skill of saying no. Don't let yourself be used and manipulated by others. You have a dream to catch.

7. Use the Power of the Grab 15 Principle

This is a profoundly important tool for plugging the leaks of priceless, irreplaceable time that so easily slip through our fingers.

The Grab 15 Principle was originated by Dru Scott Decker, and it is the key to "procrastination-proofing" your life. The concept is simple yet incredibly powerful. Here's how it works:

First, focus on one task that you have wanted to accomplish, but have been unable to find the time to complete. Everybody has a project like that—a goal you've been putting off until "someday, when I get more time." It may be that foreign language you wanted to learn, that new exercise program you wanted to start, the Internet business you wanted to launch, that screenplay you wanted to write. Stop waiting until "someday." Focus on today!

Second, make a commitment to "Grab 15" every day. In other words, devote fifteen minutes of every day to that goal without fail. Make a promise to yourself that you won't let your head hit the pillow until you have spent a minimum of fifteen minutes working on that project.

Sounds simple, right? But if you put the Grab 15 Principle to the test, you'll find out that it is incredibly powerful. It may just change your life. As Dru Scott Decker explains, even if you take one day a week off from your "Grab 15" commitment, those fifteen-minute chunks of time multiplied by six days of the week add up to ninety minutes. Multiply that by fifty-two weeks, and you have almost effortlessly added seventy-eight hours of time to your life in a single year. Those are hours that would've just fallen through the cracks—yet you have added the equivalent of almost two forty-hour workweeks to your life in one year. What would you pay if someone could magically give you two extra weeks per year to work toward your most important goals?

And consider this: You will probably find that, once you get rolling, you will find it hard to stop at fifteen minutes! You'll easily keep working at your goal for twenty minutes, thirty minutes, a full hour or more. You'll get caught up in the enthusiasm and excitement of working toward your goals, and you'll blow past the fifteen-minute mark without even noticing. That will add even more time to your life and accelerate you along the path to your dreams.

There's another benefit to the Grab 15 Principle that may be the most powerful aspect of all: this principle boosts your productivity and creativity because it keeps you thinking about your project every day. If you only worked at your goal on a sporadic basis, you would waste precious time reacquainting yourself with the project. Now, instead of thinking, "Hmmm, where was I?" you will be thinking about your project all the time. Ideas and insights will occur to you while you're eating breakfast, while you're exercising, while you're in the shower, and just before you drift off to sleep. Those fifteen-minute blocks of time will keep your mind focused on your dream throughout the day, every day.

So take the advice of Dru Scott Decker and "Grab 15" each day. Focus on today—and I'll meet you at your dreams tomorrow.

In the Moment—and in the Zone

Phil Jackson, in his book *Sacred Hoops: Spiritual Lessons of a Hardwood Warrior*, writes, "In basketball—as in life—true joy comes from being fully present in each and every moment, not just when things are going your way. Of course, it's no accident that things are more likely to go your way when you stop worrying about whether you're going to win or lose and focus your full attention on what's happening *right this moment.*"[12]

Sometimes being present in the moment is literally a matter of life and death. In her book *Band of Sisters: American Women at War in Iraq*, Kirsten Holmstedt tells about two helicopter pilots, Army Captain Robin Brown and Chief Warrant Officer Jeff Sumner, who were flying their Kiowa Warrior chopper near Fallujah,

Iraq, during the Iraq war. They were flying at a low altitude—a mere one hundred feet—when an explosion shook their aircraft. The Kiowa lost engine power. Captain Brown knew that she had to make a series of split-second, flawless decisions—or die.

"As the aircraft dropped to the ground," Holmstedt wrote, "Brown focused on the positive. This might work out. She considered all the steps as they were happening. It felt like the action was occurring in slow motion and very deliberately. While she thought through each step, she felt calm and detached."

Calm and detached? In a life-and-death emergency? How is that possible? It's possible because Captain Brown was totally focused and totally in the moment. Brown called out instructions to Sumner. Working together, they kept the rotors in auto-rotation to slow the aircraft's descent. Brown knew they couldn't make a landing, but perhaps they could achieve a "controlled crash." The wounded helicopter fell heavily but safely, its skids plowing into the Iraqi sands, its whirling rotors tilted madly.

Homestead writes, "It felt to Brown as if fifteen seconds had passed from the time they were struck to when they hit the ground. It was more like half that time. In combat, senses come alive and perception of time slows down. Like a car accident, everything seemed to happen in slow motion."[13]

The fallen helicopter was a mass of smoking wreckage. The rotors continued to flog the air overhead. Brown and Sumner looked around, amazed to be alive—banged up, but alive. They could scarcely believe they had survived a crash from treetop level. They had practiced emergency landings before—but from a *thousand* feet, not a hundred. In practice, they'd had plenty of time to think and respond—but in an actual emergency, there was simply no time to think. There is only time to focus and react in the moment.

In that emergency, Brown and Sumner underwent what is

known as an "in the zone" experience. For people who are in the moment and "in the zone," time slows down. Focus and concentration are intensified. Awareness is magnified. People are able to respond in a seemingly superhuman way, and they enter that magical, mystical realm where "impossible" dreams come true. Some people call the "in the zone" experience by a different name: "flow." A person experiencing "flow" feels positive and optimistic, and all of his or her energies are aligned with the task or goal at hand. Many people report feelings of intense joy during an "in the zone" or "flow" experience.

I have experienced a sense of being "in the zone" four times during my sports career. The first time I felt it was while playing in a high school basketball game. During the game, I felt a mystical sense of being totally in tune with my teammates, with the ball, with the hoop, with the flow of the game. Every outside shot I put up went in. The instant the ball left my hands, I absolutely knew it was good. I saw everything happening around me in slow motion, so I was able to react unerringly to everything my opponents did to try to stop me. In those days, there is no name for what I experienced—the phrase "in the zone" had not been invented yet. I had never heard anyone speak of such an experience before. All I knew was that something strange and wonderful had taken place during that game. The next game we played, it was gone.

I went to Tower Hill School, a prep school in Wilmington, Delaware, where my dad was a teacher and coach. Our baseball team went to play against Philadelphia's Germantown Academy—and once again, I had an "in the zone" experience. Just as in the basketball game, I had that sense of everything happening in slow motion. When I was at bat, I felt I had plenty of time to watch each pitch as it approached the plate. I was literally able to see the stitches on the ball—and that mystical "in the zone" experience resulted in two home runs and a line-drive single.

I'll never know if I could have extended that "in the zone" level of performance for another day because the following day we played Haverford School. Their team was coached by my uncle. He had heard how well I had played against Germantown, so he had his pitcher walk me four times in a row.

My third experience of being "in the zone" came during my college baseball career at Wake Forest University. We were playing at Georgia Southern University in Statesboro. Again I had that weird sensation of time slowing down, of everything happening in slow motion. That day, I went four for five and got a home run on a fake bunt and swing.

The fourth and final time in my athletic career that I experienced "flow" was during my first year in pro baseball in Miami. We were in Tampa in 1962, playing against the Reds' farm club in the Florida State League. Once again, time slowed down and I got four hits. It was almost spooky, seeing a fastball come crawling in and practically stand still over the plate. It was like hitting a ball off a batting tee.

When I look back over those four "in the zone" experiences in my athletic career, I remember that in each case, I had gone into those games with an intense sense of focus and concentration. I was "in the moment" to a degree that was far beyond the norm. I was able to enter an "in the zone" experience four times in my playing career. Perhaps if I had understood the power of extreme focus, I might have been able to enter that "zone" on a more consistent basis—and who knows what kind of playing career I might have had.

But the story doesn't end there. While this book was being written, I had a fifth "in the zone" experience! What's more, I'm convinced that the process of writing this book actually made this latest "in the zone" moment possible. Here's what happened: I received an invitation to speak on behalf of Deutsche Bank at the company's convention on the Mediterranean coast of southern Spain. There were 150 delegates from thirty nations attending, and the company paid me well to be a part of that event. But there was one condition attached: after speaking on Saturday, I had to stay until Sunday and play in their golf tournament. Ooh, I resisted that! I've got to be the only person in Orlando who doesn't play golf. I used to golf a few years back, but I gave it up because it caused me more angst than anything I've ever done.

When I tried to beg off from the golf tournament in Spain, my hosts informed me that it was a package deal—I was being paid for the speech *and* for a round of golf. So I reluctantly agreed.

I decided that, since I was writing a book on extreme focus, I should put the principles of extreme focus to the test. I took several chapters of this book with me on the plane and reread them. Then I closed my eyes and visualized myself on the golf course. Some thirty thousand feet above the Atlantic Ocean, I played an entire practice round of golf—entirely in my head.

Arriving in Spain, I delivered my speech on Saturday, then on Sunday morning, a group of us headed off for the golf course. There were a dozen of us from all over the world, including this reluctant duffer from Orlando. From the first tee, I felt surprisingly relaxed and confident. I was actually having fun! I couldn't wait to get to the next tee.

My putting has always been horrible, and this day was no exception—but I had a great game off the tee, and I was ripping balls out of the weeds and driving them through the trees and having a grand old time. It was a mystical experience—the ball actually seemed to be the size of a cantaloupe sitting on the tee. Unbelievable!

When we reached the ninth hole, they told me we wouldn't have time to play the back nine—and I was actually disappointed! I said, "Are you sure? I'm ready to go nine more!" Here I had been dreading this outing—and now I didn't want it to end! My hosts said that we'd have just enough time for lunch, then they had to get me to the airport.

On the bus ride back, they computed all the scores and handicaps, then they announced, "Pat! You won the tournament!" I was astonished. "What?"

"You won! You told us you never played golf!"

I reached into my bag and pulled out the six golf balls I had sneaked through security. The reason I brought so many was that I had come prepared to lose a few balls—but I hadn't lost a single one. So I autographed all six and handed them out to my partners. They gave me a little medal, which declared that I was the champ. And I felt like a champion, because I had experienced a memorable day "in the zone."

Swen Nater played center for Coach John Wooden's UCLA Bruins and helped UCLA win two NCAA titles. He went on to play pro basketball for the San Antonio Spurs, the New York Nets, the Milwaukee Bucks, and the Los Angeles Lakers. He helped lead the Lakers to the NBA finals in 1984, after which he retired from the game.

During Swen's days with the Lakers, the team went to Cleveland to play the Cavaliers. It was a long bus ride from the hotel out to the arena—about forty-five minutes. Swen decided to use that time to test a theory. "A week before," he said, "I had read something about the value of visualization and how doing something in your mind over and over again can actually help you do it in real life." So he sat in the back of the bus and practiced visualizing a specific scenario in his mind.

"I chose a rebounding scenario," he recalled, "where one of my teammates was shooting a free throw and I was lined up on the side of the key, ready to rebound. The offense and rebounders are given the second position from the basket. The other team has the inside position. So for me to get a rebound in that situation is nearly impossible."

Swen pictured a play in which a defender tried to block him away from the board, so he spun off the defender and rolled into the middle of the key. Then, as the ball was bouncing straight out over the key, he coiled into a squat position like a spring, then leaped high into the air and tipped the ball toward the basket. Swen even visualized the *swoosh* of the net as the ball dropped through.

The first few times he tried to visualize this scenario, the mental image was blurry and his movements lacked grace and quickness. But he kept rewinding the scene and replaying it over and over again in his mind. Each time he visualized it, the scene became clearer, almost as if he was seeing it with his physical eyes. As he replayed the visualization, he actually felt a contraction in his muscles, as if his body was playing along with his mind.

The bus arrived at the arena, and the Lakers took the court against the Cavaliers. At one point in the game, Swen checked in for Kareem Abdul-Jabbar—and he found himself in exactly the scenario he had been visualizing for forty-five minutes on the bus. His teammate, James Worthy, was fouled and went to the line. Swen was on the left side of the key as Worthy prepared to shoot the free throw. At the exact moment that Worthy released the shot, Swen made his move—exactly as he had visualized. Worthy missed the shot and the ball bounced straight out. Swen spun off the defender, rolled into the key, coiled like a spring, launched himself at the ball, and tipped it—

Right into the basket!

It all seemed to happen in slow motion. "I thought I was in the Twilight Zone or something," Swen recalled. "Did that really happen?"[14]

Yes, it happened. It happened to Swen Nater on a basketball

court in Cleveland. It happened to Pat Williams on a golf course in Spain. It can happen to you. The "zone" is not just for athletes. The "zone" is for everyone.

Time Slows Down

Stockton, California, sports reporter Bob Highfill examined the phenomenon of the "zone" experience in local athletes. He found one Stockton resident, Dave Bolles, who bowled three consecutive perfect games—thirty-six strikes in a row—to win a PBA Tour event. Even though he was weakened at the time by a bout of food poisoning, he managed to screen out distractions and bowl at a superhuman level. "All I had was a target line in my head," Bolles said. "Everything I had worked on just clicked. I got myself into such a good state of mind . . . [the pins] just kept falling."

Volleyballer Nicole Davis played for the University of Southern California (USC) and for the U.S. Women's National Volleyball Team (winning the silver at the 2008 Beijing Olympics). She said, "When I feel like I'm in the zone, everything happens in slow motion. It's automatic. There isn't a lot of thought involved."

Basketball standout Adam Jacobsen said, "It's when you really have peace of mind, so you're almost not thinking about anything. If you try to get into the zone, you're thinking too much. It's a trusting place. You just play."

And four-time Olympic high jumper Amy Acuff said that physical and mental preparation, including training and diet, were essential to getting into "the zone." She added, "The key is not overthinking things or being too analytical. It's kind of like letting the artistic side of your brain come out." When the "artistic" side of your brain unleashes your physical performance, Bob Highfill concludes, "great things can happen."[15]

One of the great examples of an "in the zone" performance took place in Game One of the 1992 NBA Finals, the Chicago Bulls versus the Portland Trail Blazers. The player who was "zoned," of course, was Michael Jordan. NBC sportscaster Marv Albert recalled that he and his broadcast partners, Mike Fratello and Magic Johnson, interviewed Jordan before the game—and Jordan predicted that he would hit a lot of three-point shots.

The game began, and just as Jordan had predicted, he came out shooting threes. In the first half alone, he drained six three-point field goals and scored thirty-five points, setting two NBA Finals records. After that sixth three-point shot, Jordan jogged right in front of the announcers' table with his hands raised and a grin on his face. He shrugged as if to say, "I can't explain it either!" And that game has been known as "The Shrug Game" ever since.[16]

The "zone" experience is certainly not confined to athletes. Artists, musicians, dancers, public speakers, and writers often speak of experiencing a state of "flow" while they are creating or performing. In *The Michelangelo Method*, Kenneth Schuman and Ronald Paxton describe how Michelangelo created the paintings on the Sistine Chapel ceiling while undergoing an "in the zone" experience:

> For four years, Michelangelo worked cramped upon the elaborate scaffolding he had erected . . . Most of the time, Michelangelo stood high above the ground, his back arched in a painful curve, his vision strained, toxic paint dripping in his eyes . . .
>
> Michelangelo was no glutton for punishment. He preferred the controlled working environment of his beloved sculpture studio. But he understood responsibility. He understood that when there is something you want to

do, you should throw yourself into it and do it right . . . Michelangelo determined not to just go through the motions but to create a masterpiece . . .

Some call it flow. Some call it being in the zone. Others don't have a name for it, but they know it when they feel it. Whatever you call it, it's that feeling you get when you're creating something amazing. And doesn't it feel good? And wouldn't it be nice to always feel like that when you're working on your masterpiece?[17]

Michael J. Cassutt is a television producer and screenwriter who has worked with such shows as *Beverly Hills 90210*, *The New Twilight Zone*, *The New Outer Limits*, and *Eerie, Indiana*. He once recalled an "in the zone" experience he had in the 1980s while working as a screenwriter for a CBS television drama:

We were scrambling late at night to add a holiday element to an episode that had to start filming in the morning. In the middle of the scramble, I sat down with the script and a pencil (of all things) and—with no prior thought or discussion, sitting on the couch in an office filled with producers, assistants and actors, just closing my eyes and picturing a conversation, I wrote a scene about a homeless teen recalling the best Christmas he'd ever experienced. It took all of fifteen minutes. I handed in the pages to be typed into the script. Half an hour later the typist returned, tears streaming down her face, demanding to know how I'd done that.

I didn't know. I had just been In the Zone.[18]

The power of the "in the zone" experience is available to us all, regardless of our field of endeavor. The key to getting into "the zone" is to live in the moment, to focus intently on the *now*, on this *present moment* of time.

Experiencing the Zone

Hungarian psychologist Mihály Csíkszentmihályi has conducted pioneering investigations into the "zone" or "flow" experience. Csíkszentmihályi formerly chaired the psychology department at the University of Chicago, and is now at Claremont Graduate University. He suggests that there are a number of factors that seem to accompany an "in the zone" experience, including:

1. The individual has a clearly defined goal that is challenging yet attainable and that will demand that he or she delivers a peak performance in order to achieve that goal.
2. That person focuses on that goal with a high degree of concentration.
3. The individual loses self-consciousness, does not think about himself or herself, and has no self-doubts. Awareness merges with action, so that instead of thinking, "I must try to hit this ball" or "I must try to deliver this speech," the individual simply acts without trying.
4. The person becomes so focused that his or her subjective sense of time becomes altered. Time seems to slow down.
5. The person experiences a sense of complete mastery and control over the situation, and the action seems effortless.
6. The individual has no sense of bodily needs and is not aware of feelings of pain, exhaustion, bladder pressure, or hunger.
7. The person becomes so absorbed in focusing on the activity or goal that he or she is completely immune to distractions from the outside world. Concentration has become complete.

In his book *Beyond Boredom and Anxiety: Experiencing Flow in Work and Play*, Csíkszentmihályi cited a study of chess players who had undergone an "in the zone" experience. The game of chess, he said, is "well adapted to induce the flow experience." Because of the rules and organization of the game, a player can shut out the distractions of the outside world and concentrate in a focused way on the artificial world of the game. Players commonly experience a suspension of the awareness of time. Someone asks, "Do you want to play chess?" So they set up the pieces and begin playing—and before they know it, the two players have spent several hours absorbed in the game. The study of the "in the zone" experience among chess players has produced these interesting findings:

> When asked whether they have to make an effort to concentrate on the game, 91 percent of the players gave an unequivocal "no." . . . [Players reported that] "concentration is like breathing: you never think about it. The roof could fall in and, if it missed you, you would be unaware of it." . . . One player said that she has difficulties in concentrating "only in the very beginning or when it is clear to me that either my opponent or myself is in trouble, and when I get tired. Or if I have personal worries. Distractions are people talking, their various nervous habits, or my own thoughts. I have to ask others to stop making noise, and for my own thoughts it requires determination and I struggle to 'dig in.'" This statement illustrates the precarious permeability of the flow state. Intrusions are always possible from within or without. But when the flow situation is optimal . . . the activity becomes all-absorbing.
>
> Asked whether they think about other things while they are playing a good game, 74 percent said that they

do not: "I generally do not think of other things while playing, but I'm wholly concentrating on the game." Some mention that as soon as their mind wanders, they lose.[19]

Most people think of "the zone" as a mysterious experience that strikes like lightning—and vanishes just as quickly, the result of unpredictable factors such as a surge of adrenaline or a rush of endorphins. I disagree. I believe it is possible to create the conditions that make it possible to enter "the zone" on a recurring basis.

I don't want to overpromise and say that anyone can enter a state of "flow" at will, like flipping on a light switch. You can't force your way into the "zone." You can't predict when it will happen. But through the power of extreme focus, you can create the inward and outward conditions that make "flow" more likely to take place. We create the perfect conditions for an "in the zone" experience whenever we are intensely focused on a well-defined goal, when we lose ourselves in the moment, when we are so well-prepared that we feel a sense of mastery and confidence, and when we can shut out distractions within and without. Here, then, are some practical insights that will help you enter the "flow" of peak performance:

1. Prepare Yourself Mentally

Something magical happens when we are playing at our optimum ability. Nothing exists except the game. Some people call it playing in "the zone." It doesn't happen all the time, but when it does, we feel as if we are in complete control and that we can sense what is going to happen before it does.

Concentration helps us focus and, in effect, turn off our minds. Thinking too much can actually hamper our performance . . . Concentrating helps to turn off the mental chatter that can distract us. It can also help to eliminate extra babble—when we are focused we are not thinking about what phone call to return or whether or not we'll have time to pick up our dry cleaning. We are completely involved in our game or our workout. We will discover the time passing without our even noticing.[20]

Physical training also contributes to mental preparation. By repeatedly practicing and rehearsing your physical skills, you build up so-called muscle memory (which is actually located in specific areas of the brain) that enables you to perform those skills effortlessly and unthinkingly at just the right time, even under pressure. When you are physically well prepared to take on any challenge, you feel a boost in your confidence, which enables you to concentrate—and perform at the peak of your abilities.

2. Prepare Yourself Physically

Tim Gallwey calls the physical realm "the outer game." The outer game includes the care of our bodies and the way we physically engage with the world around us. Before you begin a performance or attempt any great challenge, make sure you are well practiced and well coached in the skills you need. Get plenty of exercise, nutrition, and rest. Familiarize yourself with the "arena" in which you will compete and the opponents you will compete against.

Sometimes, aspects of your outer game can affect your inner game. Poor nutrition, lack of sleep, and physical exhaustion are all "outer game" factors that can interfere with your ability to focus and maintain a positive mental attitude. But when your inner game and outer game are working together harmoniously, you create the conditions for entering "the zone" and staying there.

3. Relax

Whether you are about to run a marathon, give a speech before an audience, or sit down at your computer to work on your novel, it's important to be relaxed and loose. A certain amount of nervous energy is normal and desirable, because that energy helps to power your performance. But *too much* nervous energy can paralyze you, physically and mentally.

Relax by taking four or five deep breaths from your diaphragm to flood your body with oxygen and settle yourself down. Visualize yourself giving a brilliant performance, the best performance of your life—and visualize it all happening effortlessly, with a sense of joy and enthusiasm. In your thoughts, imagine that a sense of power is flooding your nerves and muscles, the cells of your body and brain. You are tingling with power, ready to take on the world. Your mind and body, your inner and outer game, are now seamlessly joined and ready to perform.

4. When Things Don't Go Your Way, Think "Feedback," Not "Setback"

If you make an error or fall short of your goal, don't scold yourself. Instead, coach yourself to *believe in you*. Don't think of mistakes or failures as "setbacks." Instead, think of them as "feedback," as opportunities to learn and grow. Come back from these "feedback" experiences with a renewed sense of confidence and mastery. Always fill your mind with positive and affirming thoughts.

5. Spend Time Around Winners and Positive Thinkers

Seek out friends, teammates, coaches, and mentors who will encourage you and empower you. If you spend time with champions, you'll quickly soak up the mind-set, habits, and actions of a champion.

6. Feed on Positive Thoughts

Australia's Kieren Perkins achieved his dream of greatness as a distance swimmer, breaking a dozen world records and winning Olympic gold in 1992 and 1996, plus the silver in 2000. Perkins believes that positive thoughts are an essential part of living in the moment during competition. "I start months before the event," he says. "I just sit there and visualize the race in my mind. I dive into the pool. I'm swimming strongly. I'm out in front. The crowd [is] roaring, I can hear them. No one can catch me. I even see myself . . . with the gold medal placed around my neck."[21]

During the 1996 Summer Olympic Games in Atlanta, a bad qualifying heat in the 1,500-meter freestyle shook his confidence. He struggled with doubts during the twenty-four-hour wait leading to the final race. His worried mind wouldn't stay in the moment—he kept picturing himself losing. He couldn't stay focused on today.

Perkins realized that his negative thoughts might sink his Olympic dreams—so he decided to flood his mind with positive, affirming thoughts by reading a motivational book. He read constantly during every waking minute, right up until it was time to suit up and get into the pool. On the day of the race, when Kieren Perkins emerged from the pool, he had won the gold medal.

Reading a motivational book was just the edge he needed to clear the negative cross-talk from his brain and keep his mind focused on the present moment. "It's hard to explain," he told reporters after the race, "but when you are focused, you almost have no thought. Sitting behind the blocks I was 100 percent focused and I didn't have a single thing in my mind. I knew what I had to do, and it was just a matter of letting my instincts take over."[22]

Earlier, I related four times I have been "in the zone" as a young athlete. Today my playing days are far behind me, a warm but distant memory—yet I still find myself entering "the zone" on a regular basis. Why? Two reasons.

First, I run marathons. As I write these words, I have just completed the 2010 New York City Marathon. The marathon weekend came at a busy and inconvenient time in my life. I had a speaking engagement in Washington, DC, on Saturday, attended a dinner later that night, then took a four-hour train trip to New York. I had hoped to grab some rest on the train, but I was too keyed up to sleep. The train arrived in New York at 2 AM—but before I could go to my hotel, I had to stop by the marathon expo to pick up my running number. Then I headed for the hotel and finally got to bed at around 3 AM—but I didn't sleep well. My alarm went off at 6:15 AM, and I dragged myself out of bed, got dressed, and took a cab to the Staten Island Ferry.

As I headed across the water to get ready for the start, I thought, *There are forty-five thousand runners here today—and I'll bet none of them had the hectic time I've had getting here. What's going to happen to me out here? I might be asleep on my feet before I hit the second mile!*

I started the race feeling like death warmed over—but just a couple of miles into it, I seemed to come alive. Where moments before I was feeling sleep-deprived, I now felt energized and fully in the moment. My training took over, and my body became a running machine. My surroundings, which had been a blur, came into focus, and I noticed details with amazing clarity. I was aware of each of my fellow runners, the cheering crowd lining the street, the buildings that towered around me, the smells in the air, the sensation of the pavement beneath my feet.

Most of all, I felt the *joy* of being there, of running that marathon, of being fully alive. And that sense of joy carried me all the way to the finish line. It was the best marathon I've ever run. Only after it was over did I stop and realize, *Hey! I was in the zone! I started this day as a zombie, and I finished with my best day ever on the trail!*

I have a theory about that day. I approach most marathons with my schedule cleared, with time to rest up before I run. That means I have time to *think*—and time to get nervous. This time, I had such a busy schedule, I had no time to think. I had to just go out there, feeling depleted and off-balance—and my physical training and my unconscious mind took over and locked me into that zone of peak performance.

The second reason I still find myself entering "the zone" on a regular basis is that I am a professional public speaker. In an average year, I deliver about 150 speeches to corporate meetings, sales conferences, conventions, youth rallies, and so forth. And I have learned that these principles truly do apply in every setting, from the sports arena to the public speaking arena. Before I get up to speak to an audience, I apply all of these principles: I prepare myself physically, I prepare myself mentally, I relax, I feed on positive thoughts.

And then, when I go out before that audience and begin talking, I can feel it. When I give a talk, I never read from a script. Instead, I have a conversation with the audience. The general outline of my talk is planned—but I select the words and form the sentences extemporaneously, in the moment. I sometimes go off-script and tell a story I hadn't planned to tell. I often interact with individuals in the audience.

As I speak, I can sense a mystical connection with the audience. We are communicating and connecting with each other. I read the emotions in their eyes, their body language, the nodding of their heads, their laughter and applause. I'm not talking "at" them; we are *communicating* back and forth, the audience and me. And all the while, my brain is processing at lightning-fast speed—and it feels magical, effortless, joyous, fun!

Why? Because I'm "in the zone," my friend. Because I'm experiencing "flow." And you can do it, too—no matter what your goal, your endeavor, your dream. Focus on *today*, focus on *now*—for this moment holds the key to all your dreams.

5

Focus
on
Self-Discipline

om Smith, a former athletic trainer for the Orlando
Magic, told me this story over lunch one day:

One morning, in the middle of the summer, I came to
work and looked in the weight room. Over in the corner I
saw an athlete working out—and I did a double-take when
I realized that it was the Lakers' legendary shooting guard,
Kobe Bryant. I thought, Wow! What is Kobe doing in the
Magic facility at this time of year? So I went over to him
and said, "Kobe, what brings you here in the off-season?"

He told me he'd brought his family out for a weeklong

vacation at Disney World. I asked him about his workout schedule, and here's what he told me: He came to our facility at 6:00 AM and worked out hard until 9:00 AM. Then he showered, drove thirty miles back to the hotel, picked up his family, and got to Disney World by 11:00 AM. That meant he had to be up by 5:00 AM to get to our place by 6:00! He kept up this schedule every day, Monday through Friday, throughout his vacation. If anyone wants to know why Kobe Bryant is the best player in the game today, there's your answer. It's called "self-discipline."

Author Brian Tracy defines self-discipline as "the ability to make yourself do what you should do when you should do it, whether you feel like it or not."[1] Self-discipline is an indispensable component of focus—and one of the keys to your success. An undisciplined person is doomed to fail. You could be handed enormous wealth, influence, and a brilliant career on a silver platter, but if you lack self-discipline, you would squander those advantages in no time.

You could have all the other components of *extreme focus*—intense passion, lofty goals, and meticulous preparation—but without self-discipline, you're going nowhere fast. Your goals are the road map—but self-discipline fuels you on your journey.

Our success depends on our ability to be self-disciplined in every aspect of life: physical exercise and conditioning, good nutrition, spending and investing, reading and continued intellectual growth, stress management, and more. A person who is self-disciplined is positioned not only to achieve extreme levels of success, but also to maintain that success over the long haul.

One Mile to Reach His Dream

"The man who can drive himself further once the effort gets painful is the man who will win," said Roger Bannister.[2]

Today, Sir Roger Gilbert Bannister is the retired master of Pembroke College at Oxford and a distinguished neurologist. But on May 6, 1954, Bannister gained worldwide fame for achieving a feat that was once considered humanly impossible: he became the first human being to run a mile in less than four minutes.

Prior to breaking the four-minute barrier, Bannister was an Olympic runner. He qualified for the 1952 Olympics, but entered the Helsinki games feeling unhappy with his performance. In the 1,500-meter event (sometimes called the "metric mile"), Bannister finished fourth—a strong showing, but out of the medals. He left Helsinki feeling it was time to give up competitive running and focus on a career in medicine.

When he told his coach he was giving up running, the coach replied, "Roger, I think you are the man who can break four minutes in the mile. I wish you'd give it one last try."

The four-minute mile! Bannister didn't know how to respond to that. It seemed impossible—yet his coach believed he could do it. Bannister spent a sleepless night pondering the possibility. By morning, his mind was made up. He would attempt to break the four-minute mile.

Bannister devoted himself to an intense nutritional and work-out regimen. He focused on interval training, which involved periods of grueling, high-intensity (near-maximum exertion) workouts alternating with intervals of jogging for specified distances. These interval workouts increased Bannister's endurance to go the distance and increased his ability to summon bursts of energy and speed as needed near the end of the course.

In 1953, he made two attempts at the record, each time bettering his time closer and closer to four minutes. In early 1954,

Bannister ran the mile three times, clocking at 4:02.4, 4:02.6, and 4:02.6, respectively. These were stunning times, but still short of the record of 4:01.3 set by Gunder Hägg of Sweden in 1945—and well short of four minutes. At the same time, Bannister was aware that other runners—notably Wes Santee of the United States and John Landy of Australia—were also attempting to break the four-minute barrier. Bannister felt the pressure and knew he had to work harder.

He increased his training regimen, maintaining a seemingly inhuman level of self-discipline. On May 6, 1954, he entered a track meet between the British Amateur Athletic Association and Oxford University held at Iffley Road Track in Oxford. Conditions on race day were unfavorable, with winds up to twenty-five miles an hour. Bannister considered dropping out of the race in order to conserve his strength for another track meet under better conditions. But shortly before the race was to begin, the winds died down, and Bannister decided to go on with the race. Before a crowd of three thousand people, and with the race broadcast live by BBC Radio, Roger Bannister took his place at the starting line beside two other runners.

The gun sounded and the runners took off. The track was damp and not conducive to breaking world records. Yet, by the end of the third lap, Roger's time was just a half second over three minutes flat. If he still had any kick left at the end of the fourth lap, he could do it!

But would he? As Bannister later recounted to Olympic gold medalist Bob Richards, he was in agony throughout that fourth and final lap. "I don't believe I've ever been so tired," Bannister recalled. "My step began to falter and I felt dead and all of a sudden my head was throbbing and my lungs were bursting and I thought to myself, 'Well, maybe I'd better slacken the pace and just come in to win.'" For a few seconds, Bannister's self-discipline faltered and his pace slackened. Then—

"I can't understand it," he recalled, "and I can't communicate it to you, but all of a sudden something welled up within me and it said, 'Roger, if you run until you collapse on that track you're going to make this four-minute mile . . . For five months you've trained. *You can do it.'"*

Bannister fought his way through the pain, quickened his stride, and actually began to *sprint* the final quarter mile. As he came through the final curve, he looked down the stretch and his heart nearly failed him. "I just felt like there was an eternity between the end of that curve and that tape, fifty yards away," he said. "But I just closed my eyes and gritted my teeth and forced myself to hold stride, and I went pounding on down that stretch."

Running with his eyes closed, opening them only for an occasional glimpse, he poured his heart and soul into those final strides. He opened his eyes wide as he broke the tape and collapsed into the arms of his coach.

The race was over—but what was the time?

Announcer Norris McWhirter teased the crowd, dragging out the announcement to the limits of human endurance: "Ladies and gentlemen, here is the result of Event Nine, the one mile: First, number 41, R. G. Bannister, Amateur Athletic Association and formerly of Exeter and Merton Colleges, Oxford, with a time which is a new meeting and track record, and which—subject to ratification—will be a new English Native, British National, All-Comers, European, British Empire and World Record. The time was 3 minutes 59.4 seconds—"[3]

The crowd went wild!

A few months after the historic race, Bannister became the first-ever recipient of the *Sports Illustrated* Sportsman of the Year Award. Though this would not be his last race, he retired from athletics a short time later to pursue a medical career. He was knighted by Queen Elizabeth II in 1975—not for breaking the four-minute mile, but for his work as the first chairman of the Sports Council of Great Britain.

Bannister only had to run one mile to reach his dreams, but it took every ounce of energy, endurance, and self-discipline he possessed to go that distance. In achieving that goal, he proved his own adage: when the effort became painful, he drove himself further—and he reached his dreams.

The Stuff Dreams Are Made Of

I recently spoke to an audience at Florida State University, where my longtime friend Mike Martin is the head baseball coach. Mike has coached many Florida State University (FSU) players who have gone on to successful careers in Major League Baseball (MLB). We had some time to chat, so I asked Mike about one of his protégés, Buster Posey, who is a catcher and first baseman for the San Francisco Giants. "Mike," I said, "that young man has gotten off to a phenomenal start in his career. How do you account for that?"

"Simple," Mike said. "It's a matter of discipline. Of all the players who have passed through my program, I have never met one who had the intense self-discipline of Buster Posey."

Buster was drafted by the Giants fifth overall in the 2008 Major League Baseball Draft after his junior year at Florida State University. He was moved up from the Fresno Grizzlies AAA farm club on May 29, 2010. By July, Posey had become the team's everyday catcher and the best defensive player in the game. In the month of July, Posey batted a league-high .459, knocking seven homers and twenty-three RBIs. Posey's phenomenal performance prompted Jeff Fletcher of MLB Fanhouse to write, "Buster Posey has become a big bat much quicker than anyone could have reasonably expected."[4]

In his first season in the majors, Posey became the sparkplug for the team and was a major factor in getting the Giants to the 2010 World Series against the Texas Rangers. He hit his first postseason home run in game four, and the Giants went on to win the World Series, four games to one. Buster Posey hit .305 for the season, with 18 homers and 67 RBIs, and was voted National League Rookie of the Year.

The young phenom describes his philosophy of self-discipline this way: "I feel like if you're committed to do something, why not do it 100 percent? Let's say, for example, I'm playing ball but I decide to slack in school. I feel like that's going to carry over to baseball, that mentality. So I've always tried to put my nose down and just give everything I've got in whatever it is I'm doing."[5]

At age fifteen, Romanian gymnast Nadia Comaneci conquered the world, winning three gold medals at the 1976 Summer Olympics in Montreal. Four years later, she came back and won two more gold medals at the 1980 summer games in Moscow. Almost single-handedly, Comaneci popularized the sport of gymnastics throughout the world and was named one of the Athletes of the Century by the Laureus World Sports Academy in 2000. She is often asked the secret to her success—and her answer is disarmingly simple: self-discipline.

"If I work on a certain move constantly," she says, "then finally, it doesn't seem so risky to me. The idea is that the move stays dangerous and it looks dangerous to my foes, but not to me. Hard work has made it easy. That is my secret. That is why I win."[6]

So discipline yourself to master your skill and your profession. Concentrate on making the most challenging thing you do look effortless. Whenever you see a gymnast, an athlete, a musician, or an actor perform an amazing feat of skill, remember that you are not just seeing talent at work. You are witnessing the result of countless hours of practicing and rehearsing until the well-nigh impossible seems utterly simple. Self-discipline, good habits, and hard work will take you to your dreams.

Sir Vidiadhar Surajprasad Naipaul—better known as novelist V. S. Naipaul—is one of the most successful writers in the world. He is a British Trinidadian of East Indian descent and the author of such works as *A Bend in the River, The Enigma of Arrival,* and *In a Free State.* He was knighted in 1990 for his literary accomplishments. In 2001, he received the Nobel Prize in Literature; and in 2008, *The Times* of London ranked him seventh on its list of "The 50 Greatest British Writers Since 1945."

Both V. S. Naipaul and his father, journalist Seepersad Naipaul, had dreams of writing novels. But the father never published a single novel and died before his son achieved international acclaim for his work. Seepersad gave his son a lot of good advice for becoming a successful writer, urging him to be a voracious reader, to develop his own style, and to carry a notebook to jot down his ideas and impressions.

Yet it was the son who attained the success that always eluded the father. V. S. Naipaul possessed one great strength that his father lacked: self-discipline. The younger Naipaul often arose before dawn and wrote in the early hours of the morning. For him, writing was a daily regimen, an unbreakable habit. His father, however, procrastinated and made excuses for not writing, seeming to fear rejection and failure more than he desired acceptance and success.

Father and son exchanged letters, and in those letters V. S. Naipaul urged his father to develop habits of self-discipline. "Your experience is wide and if you write merely one page a day, you will shortly find that you have a novel on your hands . . . You have enough material for a hundred stories. For heaven's sake start writing them . . . Stop making excuses. Once you start writing you will find ideas flooding upon you." Excellent advice—but the older man either couldn't or wouldn't take it. Seepersad Naipaul wrote a number of short stories and submitted them to magazines. When the stories came back with rejection notes, Seepersad became despondent and stopped writing for weeks. His son, V. S. Naipaul, also wrote short stories, submitted them, and received many rejections—but he refused to accept an editor's rejection as an excuse to stop writing. Instead, he saw each rejection as motivation to increase his self-discipline and work all the harder. As he wrote in a letter to his sister, "My story about Rosie was rejected, just one of a number of rejections. Still this is my apprenticeship, and one expects rejections."[7]

What a stark contrast! Here are two writers, not only from the same culture, but from the same family. Seepersad Naipaul was a professional journalist, so he clearly knew how to write. What was the one difference that separated the wannabe novelist father from his Nobel laureate son? Self-discipline.

Self-discipline is the stuff dreams are made of.

How to Discipline Yourself for Success

You may ask, "What do I do now? I'm not a naturally disciplined person. I can be lazy at times. I have a lot of bad habits. I don't even know where to begin to become a self-disciplined person." Well, let me suggest some practical ways to discipline yourself for success:

1. Commit Yourself to a Lifelong, Year-Round Lifestyle Change

We tend to make temporary commitments in hopes of producing permanent changes. We say, "I'll go on Weight Watchers or

Jenny Craig for six months so I can get into my skinny clothes again." But what we need is not a "weight-loss program" but a whole new approach to health, exercise, and diet that we can live with for the rest of our lives.

In professional football, it's not uncommon for players to come into training camp overweight and out of shape after an off-season of lounging around. Many players continue eating pasta, pizza, and fried chicken, yet they never go near the weight room and never burn off those calories. As a result, many players are doing lifelong damage to their arteries, heart, and other body systems. To counteract this problem, some teams have begun offering off-season conditioning programs to keep players lean and mean all year round. As Mike Shanahan, head coach of the Washington Redskins says, "If you want to be good at anything, you've got to work at it all year."[8]

The legendary players all know the importance of year-round discipline. As NFL cornerback Kevin Smith once said of 49ers running back Jerry Rice (now retired), "What a lot of guys don't understand about Jerry is that with him, football's a twelve-month thing. He's a natural, but he still works. That's what separates the good from the great."[9]

2. Self-Discipline Isn't Easy, but the Gain Is Well Worth the Pain

Robin Roberts is a television personality and coanchor of ABC's *Good Morning America*. She attended Southeastern Louisiana University and finished her college career as the school's third all-time leading scorer in basketball while graduating cum laude with a degree in communications. She recalls, "My freshman year in college I remember doing a drill during basketball practice. We had to stay down in a crouched defensive position and slide our feet all the way around the court. I was in the middle of the pack. It was painful to stay down all the way around the court, but Coach Puckett told me to stay down and so I did. We're all huffing and puffing. She gets right up in my face and says, 'Hon, hon, you're going places in life because you listen. You're disciplined. You're the only one who stayed down.' That meant so much that she acknowledged me like that. It was a simple thing of just following the rules."[10]

3. Seek Out Mentors Who Exemplify Self-Discipline

When singer-actress Lena Horne died in May 2010 at the age of ninety-two, jazz historian Will Friedwald wrote a fond obituary for the *Wall Street Journal*. Singer Tony Bennett had toured with Lena Horne during the early 1970s, so Friedwald related some of Bennett's recollections of working with Miss Horne.

Despite suffering a number of painful personal losses during those years, Lena Horne shut out all the distractions and gave herself totally to her rehearsals, to her performances, and to her audiences. "She taught me discipline," Tony Bennett recalled. "Even at rehearsals, she'd be sweating to get it just right. I never saw that kind of intensity in anyone else."[11]

Tony Bennett is just one among many successful people who is grateful to have had a mentor, a role model, to demonstrate the power of self-discipline. As you are discovering what it takes to be successful in your chosen field, seek out mentors who can show you how to discipline yourself for success.

4. Be Disciplined in the Small Things

Every big picture is made up of small details. In order to be successful in the big things, you must be diligent in all of those details. Are you careful to listen well and follow directions? Do you proofread all of your written work—your résumé, your reports, your PowerPoint presentations, and even your e-mails?

Are you attentive to the fine details in the way you dress, your manners, the way you speak and conduct yourself? Are you thorough in your attention to detail in the work you do and the image you project? All of these details add up to excellence—and success.

As Gen. Colin Powell once observed, "If you are going to achieve excellence in big things, you develop the habit in little matters. Excellence is not an exception, it is a prevailing attitude."[12]

5. Discipline Yourself to Keep Your Commitments

Al Kaline is a Baseball Hall of Famer who played his entire career, 1953–74, with the Detroit Tigers. He still works in the Tigers front office today, and is fondly known as "Mr. Tiger." During his boyhood in Baltimore, Al's family was poor. But his parents could see that he possessed a ball-playing ability beyond his years. To build on those skills, they entered him as a player in several different amateur and semipro leagues.

On Sundays, young Al would play two or three games. Between games, his dad or one of his uncles would pile him into the car to rush him to the next game while he changed uniforms in the backseat. It wasn't easy playing all those back-to-back games in different leagues when he was growing up. "I suffered a lot as a kid playing in all those games," Kaline recalls. "When everybody was going on their vacations, going swimming with all the other kids, here I was Sundays playing doubleheaders and all because I knew I wanted to be a ballplayer . . . There were a couple of times when I told my dad I wasn't gonna play Sunday, I was going to go down to the beach with my girl or with a bunch of the guys to go swimming. And he says, 'Now look, like I told you in the beginning when you agreed to play for these people, they're going to be counting on you, so if you're not gonna play, tell 'em to tear your contract.' So I would go play, but it was these things he did to me that showed me the right way and pushed me in the right way."[13]

By the time Kaline turned eighteen, he had caught the eye of Major League Baseball scouts, including the Detroit Tigers. Though he was young, he had more baseball experience under his belt than most players five years his senior. The Tigers never even put him into the minor leagues. Instead, the team paid Kaline a $30,000 signing bonus (a whopping sum of money in 1953) to start his career in the big leagues. He turned half of his bonus over to his father to retire the mortgage on the house and to pay for an operation to save his mother's eyesight.[14]

Kaline's dad taught him to discipline himself and to keep his commitments. The values he learned at an early age served him well throughout his career. Kaline—"Mr. Tiger"—is still living his baseball dreams to this day.

6. "Good Enough" Is Never Good Enough

Discipline yourself to always strive for excellence. Never settle for "average." Business writer Lou Vickery put it this way: "Nothing average ever stood as a monument to progress. When progress is looking for a partner, it doesn't turn to those who believe they are only average. It turns instead to those who are forever searching and striving to become the best they possibly can."[15]

My daughter Karyn and I ran in the Chicago Marathon in October 2007. That marathon made headlines because of a record-breaking heat wave. Temperatures topped 88°F, sending more than 350 runners to the hospital. As Karyn and I ran, we saw runners dropping like flies all along the route, victims of heat prostration. Emergency helicopters thundered overhead, and the wail of ambulances was almost continuous. Coming from Florida,

Karyn and I thought it was a lovely day for running. We had worked out in the 95°F summer heat and 100 percent humidity of Orlando, so we were fine.

But for most of the runners, temperatures in the high eighties were truly dangerous. Aid stations ran out of water. Runners dropped out with cramps or nausea. Some fainted. The course looked like a war zone, with casualties strewn on either side.

When Karyn and I were near the sixteen-mile mark, the Chicago Fire Department put up roadblocks. The marshals of the marathon waved people off, saying the marathon was terminated. They pointed to the left and shouted, "Go this way! Go this way! Head straight to the finish line!"

I called out to one of the marshals, "Do we still get a medal?"

"Yes," he said, "you still get a medal."

So we took the shortcut. As we crossed the finish line, I felt a sense of great joy. We had cut two hours and ten miles of our run—and I still got a medal for participating. We returned to the hotel with two extra hours to rest and freshen up before dinner.

For me, the highlight of a marathon weekend is always the dinner after the race. Karyn and I had reservations at Miller's in Chicago (the favorite spot of the late Bill Veeck). It was an excellent meal—but as we ate, I felt something was missing. Though I enjoyed relaxing and sharing wonderful father-daughter time with Karyn, something nagged at me, something was wrong.

Then it hit me: I wasn't tired enough!

Normally, on the evening of a marathon, I could feel every bone and joint and muscle barking at me. I would feel pleasantly exhausted—and the meal felt like a fitting reward for having pushed myself to the limits of my endurance. I would always wear my medal proudly at dinner—but on that night, I left the medal at the hotel. Why? Because I knew I hadn't earned it. My body missed those final ten miles. I even felt a little guilty, almost as if

I had cheated, though I hadn't done anything wrong. Marathon runners are allowed to wear their medals for a twenty-four-hour period called "show-and-tell." When you complete a marathon, you have bragging rights, and you wear your medal so that people can gape and know what you've accomplished. But on this occasion, I had simply tucked my medal away in my suitcase. I knew deep inside that getting a medal for running a "good enough" race wasn't good enough.

We should never be satisfied with "good enough." Anytime we give less than our all, we should feel a nagging sense that something isn't right. Those who are truly focused on a lifestyle of self-discipline should never feel right about getting paid in full for doing half a job. We should only accept a reward for doing the job right and doing it completely. "Good enough" is never good enough.

7. Be Disciplined in Your Work Ethic

Paul "Bear" Bryant coached the University of Alabama Crimson Tide football team from 1958 to 1982. During his twenty-five seasons at Alabama, he coached his teams to thirteen conference championships and six national championships. He retired in 1982 with the record for most wins of any head coach in collegiate football history. Bear Bryant had a ten-point "Winning Formula" that he taught to his players. Two of those ten points were about the importance of maintaining a disciplined work ethic:

Work hard. There is no substitute for hard work. None. If you work hard, the folks around you are going to work harder. If you drag into work late, what kind of impression is that going to leave on your fellow workers? If you leave early, what kind of impression is that going to leave?

Don't tolerate lazy people. They are losers. People who

come to work and watch clocks and pass off responsibilities will only drag you and your organization down. I despise clock watchers. They don't want to be part of a winning situation. They won't roll up their sleeves when you need them to. If you have lazy people, get rid of them. Remember, it is easy to develop the bad habits of lazy people.[16]

When I interviewed Joe Namath for my forthcoming book on Coach Bryant, he told me, "The man knew how life worked. His message was, 'Life is hard. You've got to do hard things whether you like it or not.' He stressed that it takes effort to be successful. As young athletes, we thought we knew it all, but still we took his word for it. I have two daughters, ages nineteen and twenty-four, and I can relate a whole lot better now as to what Coach Bryant was telling us."

Retired NBA star and former senator Bill Bradley learned the importance of a disciplined work ethic at an early age. At fourteen, he attended a weeklong basketball camp that was run by "Easy Ed" McCauley, who was a star forward for the St. Louis Hawks. In addition to basketball technique, McCauley and his staff taught their players the fundamentals of a good attitude and a strong work ethic. "If you are not practicing," McCauley told them, "just remember—someone, somewhere, is practicing, and when you two meet, given roughly equal ability, he will win."

Those words stuck with young Bill Bradley. "I decided I never wanted to lose simply because I hadn't made the effort, and I intensified an already intense routine." He set a grueling practice schedule for himself that he maintained throughout his teen years and into his professional career. He ran long distances to improve his speed and stamina. He wore weights on his shoes and practiced his jump shot to improve his vertical leap. He practiced dribbling with blinders on so he could learn to dribble without watching the ball. He practiced ball-handling around folding chairs to master his crossover dribble, and he shot over stacked chairs to simulate play against a seven-foot center.

Bill Bradley even sacrificed his love life for the game. "When a fifteen-year-old female classmate telephoned one night to flirt," he recalled, "I somewhat doltishly protested that my real girlfriend was basketball." Now, *that* is self-discipline!

The habits and self-discipline Bradley acquired as a teenager have served him well throughout his adult life and career. "In the U.S. Senate, along the campaign trail, or on any number of projects I became involved with after Princeton," he said, "it was the same story. I was determined that no one would outwork me. Basketball had lit that fire, and it burned in many directions. As I grew older and met my basketball heroes, and even defeated some of them, I realized that my way of doing things was not at all unique. Most of the pros had developed their skills by paying their dues in practice time. The biggest myth in basketball is that of the 'natural player.' Remember that Michael Jordan was cut from his high school team."[17]

If you want to discipline yourself for success, then work for it. Surround yourself with hard workers, and set an example of a strong work ethic. As Major League Baseball Hall of Famer Don Sutton once said, "Luck is the byproduct of busting your fanny."[18] There's no substitute for hard work when it comes to reaching for your dreams.

The Cello Player and the Basketball Player

As parents, we need to teach self-discipline to our children every day. My kids are all grown and out of the house now, but when they were young, we used to drill into them a four-part definition of self-discipline that was formulated by Bobby

Knight, the former head basketball coach at Indiana University. "Self-discipline," Knight said, "is doing what needs to be done; doing it when it needs to be done; doing it the best it can be done; and doing it that way every time you do it." My nineteen children could all recite that statement forward and backward, because they had heard it hundreds of times.

When Bobby Knight coached at Indiana, he would bring successful people from all walks of life to talk to his players about the discipline and attitude needed for success. On one occasion, Coach Knight brought in a cellist. That's right, a classical musician, a cello player. When his players heard that they were going to get a motivational lecture from a cellist, they wondered if Coach Knight had lost his mind. But after hearing the cellist speak, the players all agreed with their coach: this man was one of the smartest invitations Coach Knight had ever made.

The musician's name: János Starker. The Budapest-born performer has earned fame around the world as "the king of the cellists." Born in 1924, he has taught at the Indiana University Jacobs School of Music since 1958, and he teaches there to this day, holding the title of Distinguished Professor.

János Starker told the players that he had been playing cello since age six. He didn't choose a life in music; his mother chose it for him—but very early in life, he realized that a life in music was all he wanted. He wanted to listen to music, make music, and think about music all day long. He told the players that it came to him at an early age that "anyone who can go through a day without wanting to be with music or hear music or make music is not supposed to be a musician."

Furthermore, he said, "I believe that to be valid for every single profession. If you can go through a day without wanting it or thinking it or living with professionalism in the profession that you are in, you are not supposed to be in it." That, of course, is exactly what it means to practice *extreme focus* to achieve your dreams.

As he grew older, János Starker shut everything out of his thoughts except his concentration on his music. Everything he listened to, thought about, read about, or devoted his attention to was music. When he went onstage to perform his music, nothing else existed—not the audience, not the concert hall, not the stage—just the pure sound and emotion of the music itself.

"Discipline means concentration," János Starker told Coach Knight's players, "and concentration means discipline. Discipline means that you have a routine that you follow with total conviction of priority . . . The practice is just as important as the moment when you are in front of everybody."

He asked what the parallels were between music and basketball. The musician spends a lifetime developing skills in order to find the proper note. The basketball player trains for a lifetime in order to find the basket. The musician must practice thousands of hours to acquire the skills and build the strength to play the challenging music, because the fingering and bowing of the instrument demand considerable dexterity and muscle power from the musician. "We are hitting strings with the fingers," he said, "sometimes at the speed of two thousand notes per minute."

Self-discipline is essential to both the cello player and the basketball player, because the time inevitably comes when the coach is not there to give instructions. The player must have every skill and habit imprinted in his brain and body. During a performance or a game, there is no time to stop and think about what to do next. The player must respond reflexively and fluidly in order for the performance to be successful. And that demands self-discipline.

"When I watch you guys," János Starker concluded, "sometimes I notice that artistry and grace are involved, and the fluency of motions that we are doing in music. How to improve it and to make it consistent is what we are all trying to do in every field. That's . . . the discipline that is required."[19]

Whether in music or in basketball, whether you are writing a novel or righting social wrongs, whether you dream of owning your own little antique store or a global corporation, whether you want to make a billion dollars or serve the poor, *you must discipline yourself for success*. You must devote yourself to an *extreme focus* on your goals and dreams. Everyone has dreams. Those who are self-disciplined make their dreams come true.

6

Focus on **Things** You Can **Control**

My daughter Karyn won the Miss University of Florida competition in the spring of 2001, and that summer she finished as first runner-up in the Miss Florida pageant. After the pageant, she was offered a recording contract opportunity. Karyn pursued the dream, but in time, when the doors to a singing career remained shut, she eventually found herself working in a real estate office, answering phones.

One day, she read this anonymous quotation at the bottom of an e-mail she received from a friend: "No one can go back and make a brand-new beginning, but anyone can start right now to make a brand-new ending."

That little quote was like the sky opening up for Karyn. She instantly realized that she had the power to take control of her own life. She went back to the University of Florida and got her degree in radio and communications, then moved to Nashville to pursue her dream of singing, songwriting, and inspirational writing.

In 2009, Karyn signed a publishing deal with Brentwood Benson/Universal Music Publishing—a huge affirmation of her talent as a songwriter. Then in 2010, she signed a contract with Nashville's Mission House Music Label Group. Her first single, "Rejoice" was released in the summer of that year and her first full-length studio album is set for release in early 2011. You can find her music at http://www.karynwilliams.com, along with the inspiring book that Karyn and I wrote together, *The Takeaway*. I'm so glad that Karyn didn't give up on her dreams. I'm proud of her for writing a brand-new ending to her story.

As we pursue our extreme dreams and goals, there are some things we *can* control and other things over which we have *no* control. Unfortunately, many people are easily lured off course. Instead of controlling what they *can* control, they fret and obsess over factors and conditions that are totally *beyond* their control. Successful people control what they can and let go of the rest.

Legendary UCLA basketball coach John Wooden recalled that his father, Joshua Wooden, gave him some very good advice when he was a young man—though John didn't understand the advice until he was older. His father told him, "Johnny, remember this and remember it well: Never try to be better than somebody else, but never cease trying to be the best *you* can be. You have control over that. Not the other."[1] In other words, you control your own effort, but you can't control what other people do.

Tennis champion James Blake received a similar word of life-changing advice from his father. At age thirteen, Blake was diagnosed with severe scoliosis, a deformative curvature of the spine. He had to wear a confining and painful back brace during every waking hour, except while on the tennis court. Inspired by his hero, Arthur Ashe, James Blake kept reaching for his tennis dreams. In 2001, he achieved an important milestone by being named Rookie of the Year. He seemed destined for greatness. Then, in 2004, disaster struck. While playing a practice match in Italy, Blake ran to return a drop shot when his foot caught on the playing surface. He tripped and flew headfirst into a steel net post, colliding with a loud, sickening sound. He fell to the ground stunned, unable to catch his breath. He had fractured his neck.

Later, he became thankful for that broken neck. Because of his injury, he flew back to the States for treatment (he had planned to spend the next few months in Europe). Soon after his arrival in Connecticut, he learned that his fifty-seven-year-old father, Tom Blake, was dying of stomach cancer.

Before Tom Blake died, he gave James this advice: "You can't control your level of talent, but you can control your level of effort." After recovering from his accident, James Blake returned to the game with a new level of focus and intensity, and he became a more dominant player than ever before. Most important of all, he remembered his father's advice: no matter what happens in your life, regardless of the factors beyond your control, *you can always control your effort.*[2]

Focus on the Things You Can Control

I began my sports management career at the tender age of twenty-four as the general manager of a minor league baseball team in Spartanburg, South Carolina. I was eager for success and obsessed with controlling every detail of the operation. I worried about the weather, fearing that a few rained-out games could hurt our bottom line. I worried about how the team was playing, fearing that our fans might desert us if we went into a slump.

I was the original "control freak"—and I was "freaking out" over every detail, including the factors that *no one* could possibly control. The team owner, Mr. R. E. Littlejohn, saw that I was giving myself an ulcer. So he took me aside and gave me some of the best advice I've ever received.

"You need to take it easy, Pat," he said. "Learn to control those things you can control—and let everything else go. Ask yourself this question: 'What can I control?'"

I thought it over. "Well," I said, "I can control how the ballpark looks. I can make sure the restrooms are clean. I can control how our employees treat the fans. I can control the promotional events and the quality of the food at the concessions."

"What about the weather?" Mr. Littlejohn asked. "With all your worrying, Pat, you can't turn off the rain or turn on the sunshine. And you can't control whether the team wins or loses. You can't even control whether the parent organization calls your best pitcher up to the next level. All of those factors are out of your control. Pat, you need to focus your attention on the things you can control, and let go of everything else."

I knew Mr. Littlejohn was right. Time spent obsessing over the things I couldn't control was time taken *away* from the things I *could* control. Once I learned to focus on the things I controlled, I began to make real progress toward my dreams and goals.

When Walt Disney opened his Disneyland theme park in 1955, he hired outside companies to handle some aspects of the operation, such as park security and crowd control. When he saw how these outside companies mistreated his guests, Walt Disney fired those companies and placed the entire Disneyland operation under the direct control of the Walt Disney Company. Later, while he was building his new Walt Disney World park in Florida, he said:

> The one thing I learned from Disneyland was to control the environment. Without that, we get blamed for things that someone else does. When . . . [our guests] come here they're coming because of an integrity that we've established over the years, and they drive for hundreds of miles and the little hotels on the fringe would jump their rates three times. I've seen it happen, and I just can't take it because, I mean, it reflects on us. I just feel a responsibility to the public when I go into this thing that we must control that, and when they come into this so-called world, that we will take the blame for what goes on.[3]

Walt learned the hard way that his success depended on his ability to control everything that he could control. When he placed every aspect of the Disneyland experience under his company's direct control, he was able to offer his guests the kind of top quality experience that the Disney name is famous for.

Pat Riley, former head coach and now the president of the Miami Heat, once told a reporter for *Sports Illustrated*, "I think to have long-term success as a coach or any other position of leadership, you have to be obsessed in some way. Am I a control freak? No. Do I believe in organization? You bet. In discipline? In being on time and making sure everything at the hotel is ready and right? Definitely. I don't control players; I try to control the environment around the players so they can flourish."[4]

When you focus on controlling what you can control, and you let go of the rest, you experience real personal empowerment—a sense that you are truly in control of your own life and destiny. The legendary Boston Celtics point guard Bob Cousy expressed it this way: "I have my own world, a lighted patch ninety feet by fifty feet. I control

the ball. I control my team . . . In that lighted patch, I control life."[5]
The most successful people in every field of endeavor will tell you that it's a mistake to try to control every aspect of every situation. Race car driver Mario Andretti put it this way: "If everything is under control, you're going too slow."[6] Our success demands that we learn to accept a degree of uncertainty in our lives. If we stay focused on our dreams, if we prepare well and maintain our self-discipline, odds are that we can control everything we need to in order to achieve success.

Control What You Can—but Don't Be a "Control Freak"

People who are obsessed with controlling every situation and relationship in life are called "control freaks." And that, of course, is not a compliment. Control freaks are people who simply can't stop themselves. They have to be in control all the time. They live in perpetual fear: "If I don't control the world, the world will control me." It's healthy to want to control your own life and your own destiny. But it's dysfunctional and destructive to want to control all the people and situations around you. Whether in the home or in a business environment, control freaks are unpleasant people to be around. They damage relationships and drive people crazy. Most important of all, control freaks undermine their own success and kill their own dreams.

If you want to focus on your dreams and make those dreams come true, it's essential that you control what you can control—but don't become a control freak! It's wise to always remember the Serenity Prayer, which was composed years ago by theologian Reinhold Niebuhr:

God, grant me the serenity
To accept the things I cannot change;
The courage to change the things I can;
And the wisdom to know the difference.

If you tend to obsess over details and factors over which you have no control, I would encourage you to meditate on this prayer at least once a day—and maybe several times a day. Whenever you start to worry or obsess over some issue or problem, recite that prayer, then ask yourself this question: "Is this an issue I have control over? Is this a factor I can change?" If the answer is yes, then take a few moments and formulate a plan for controlling that situation and solving that problem.

But if the answer is no, then it's time to stop stressing over that issue. It's time to mentally move on and focus your attention on the issues, factors, and problems that you can change. Those matters need your concentrated attention. It's time to get to work on meeting those goals and deadlines that actually move you closer to your dreams.

Here, then, are some of the factors that you can and should control as you work toward achieving your dreams:

1. Control the Risk Factors That Affect Your Health

Obviously, you can't control whether you will always be healthy or not. You can take good care of yourself, maintain good health and hygiene habits, and still find yourself knocked flat by a chronic illness, an injury, or a seasonal flu. We all get sick from time to time.

But through diet, exercise, weight management, regular check-ups, and avoiding certain bad habits (such as smoking), you can control the risk factors that could increase your odds for heart disease, cancer, diabetes, and other debilitating illnesses. Most of us have more control over our health than we realize, and we need to take responsibility for the choices we make that can either improve or degrade our health and well-being. When you take responsibility for your own healthy choices, you empower yourself to become a stronger, more energetic, more effective human being.

Your personal energy level is a huge factor in your ability to work toward your goals and dreams. Make good choices, live a healthy lifestyle, and enjoy your future!

2. You Can't Control the Questions, but You Can Control the Answers

When you go into a job interview or a media interview, you have no control over the questions that are put to you. But you have total control over the answers you give. It's important to remember that when you are interviewing for a job or being interviewed by a reporter, anything you say can be used against you, so you must be careful to control what you say and how you say it. You can't afford to appear defensive, hostile, or evasive.

Achieving our goals often depends on our ability to give an effective interview. We need to be articulate and appear relaxed and confident. Whenever you are being interviewed, you are selling yourself and your dream. Here are some tips for controlling the answers whenever you face questioning you cannot control:

- *Know what you want to say.* Approach every interview with three strong points you want to convey. Tailor your answer to fit the question you are asked, but limit your answer to those three points. Your message will be succinct, persuasive, and memorable, and you will make an impression as a thoughtful person with a focused message.
- *Never stonewall the media.* Always face the cameras and

give reporters a statement—even if you wish you didn't have to. If you hide under your desk, reporters will hound you and corner you. Give them something interesting to report, and they'll take it and leave you alone.

• *When you are wrong, admit it.* People respond well and are quick to forgive whenever we admit mistakes and take responsibility. But the public is quick to punish those who shift the blame and avoid responsibility. When it's time to confess an error, be bold! Say, "I blew it. No one else is to blame. I take full responsibility." People will love you for your candor. Whatever you do, never make one of those impersonal pseudoapologies devoid of any personal pronouns: "Mistakes were made." Ugh! That kind of nonapology apology reeks of cowardice! Instead, take the advice of Washington insider Lanny Davis who said, "Tell it early, tell it all, tell it yourself."

• *Practice good speaking habits.* One of the best ways to control your future is to improve your public speaking skills. I recommend a technique called "video feedback." Simply practice your speech in front of a video camcorder or have someone record you when you give a speech. Watch the playback, and you will probably discover habits and mannerisms you can improve.

• *Tell stories.* Maintain a mental repertoire of interesting stories that portray your goals in a positive way. Stories are memorable, and they enliven your message. If you ever want to make your audience sit up straight and listen, just say, "Let me tell you a story . . ."

• *Communicate with energy.* Use your voice to project authority, confidence, and competence. Use gestures and movement to emphasize your key points and express enthusiasm. Maintain good eye contact to make a connection with your interviewer and your audience. A downcast or shifting gaze makes you look ill-at-ease and lacking in confidence. Nervous mannerisms undermine the content of your message. So communicate with confidence and energy, and you'll appear poised and persuasive.

Pete Carroll is head coach of the NFL's Seattle Seahawks. He has previously coached the Jets, Patriots, and the University of Southern California Trojans football teams. In his book *Win Forever*, Pete Carroll described some excellent advice he got from the late college basketball coach Jimmy Valvano before he interviewed for the coaching job at USC:

> Coach Valvano told me that my goal should be to walk out of the interview with "no negatives." Every comment, phrase, or story must be positive, and I had to be prepared to talk only about things that put me in the best light. No matter what the topic, it was my job to turn every answer into a response that highlighted my strong points. Like his point guard, who controlled the court, or my middle linebacker, who controlled our defense, I had to control the interview. He taught me that if they asked a question that I couldn't answer, then I shouldn't answer it but instead find a way to turn the question to something I could talk about comfortably, positively, and honestly. He explained the importance of being disciplined in that setting and avoiding any and all negative thoughts. If I spoke with positivity and confidence, it would be evident that I believed in myself, and that belief is what the interviewer would be looking for. Coach Valvano's advice, like so much else in life, came

down to practice: The bottom line was that if I was to control the interview, I would have to be prepared on so many levels that I could speak about a variety of subjects with conviction and strength no matter which way the conversation went.[7]

You don't control the questions, but you can control your answers. Job interviewers and reporters are always looking for negatives; make sure you supply nothing but positives. That is how to be persuasive and effective whenever you are interviewed.

3. Take Control of Your Schedule

Most people don't work nearly as hard as they think they do. Most of us could actually achieve vastly more than we imagine if we just focused on controlling our schedule and managing our time. So much valuable time is frittered away on aimless reading of e-mails and Internet surfing, meaningless chitchat and office gossip, overly long coffee breaks and lunch breaks, and day-dreaming. We spend too much time majoring on minors and not enough time focusing on high-priority tasks and goals. Managing your time is essential to managing your success. (For a more thorough discussion of time management ideas, see Chapter 4.)

4. Control the Performance of Your Organization

If you are a leader, you must manage the performance of your organization in order to achieve your dreams and goals. In any business environment, there are always factors that are beyond your control. You don't control the global economy, the rate of inflation, the regulatory environment that government imposes on you, and so forth, but all of those external factors put together probably add up to no more than 10 percent of the factors that determine your success. The other 90 percent is (or should be) under your control. If you don't control those factors, someone or something else will.

Orlando businessman Jim Hewitt is a good friend and one of the first people to envision an NBA franchise in Orlando. He worked tirelessly with me and a few other dedicated people to make the Orlando Magic a reality. A few years ago, I asked him to list for me the keys to running a successful business. "Well, Bubba," he said (Jimmy calls everybody Bubba), "I'll tell you . . ." And he proceeded to lay out a formula for success that is all about controlling what you can control:

First, you can't control the marketplace, but you can control how you respond to it. Before you open a new business, you need to do your research and make sure that the marketplace is ripe for your product or service. Then you've got to design a business that is a good fit for your marketplace.

Second, you control the timing and the location of your business. You don't want to open a lemonade stand in Orlando in the middle of January. If you start a new business at the wrong time of year, you'll fail. You control where and when you open your business, so open it at a time and place that's to your advantage.

Third, you control the start-up capital. And you'd better build in some cushion, because you can't control or even predict future market conditions and downturns. You must have sufficient capital to carry you through the lean times during the start-up.

Fourth, you can't control the cash flow—but there's a lot you can do to grow your cash flow through aggressive marketing and promotion. If you can show a strong, positive cash flow in the first five years, odds are you'll make it. Fifth, you must control the staffing of your organization. A lot of employers complain that good help is hard to find these days. Well, good help has always been hard to find. You just have to do your homework. If you screen enough applicants, provide a good work environment, and offer generous incentives, you'll attract quality people who will work hard to make your company a success.

Sixth, you've got to acknowledge that some aspects of our lives are beyond our control. There will always be unexpected, uncontrollable circumstances, such as an illness, an accident, a global recession, a natural disaster, or some other unforeseen circumstance. When things spin out of my control, I have to turn everything over to the One who is always in control. I trust in the Lord and put Him first and make Him the chairman of the board of my company. The only way to know peace when your life is out of control is to know that He is always in control.

That's good advice. You, as a business leader, are responsible to control all of the factors in your business that lead to success or failure. You are responsible to control expenses, to hold your employees accountable for their performance and their budgets, to maintain clear and well-defined business processes, to regularly monitor your company's financial condition (make sure you understand every detail of your balance sheet and P&L statement, including revenue, expenses, employee costs, liquidity ratios, asset management, and borrowing), and to keep your employees motivated and fired up about achieving the company's goals. Even if it seems like the marketplace and the regulatory environment are totally out of control, there is still so much that you *do* control, and those controllable factors are the key to your success.

5. Control Your Fears

Success demands courage and bold risks, yet we all have fears. Courage, however, is the willingness to act boldly in spite of our fears. Courage is a defiant refusal to be controlled by our fears. As John Wayne once said, "Courage is being scared to death but saddling up anyway."[8]

Bill Walsh, the mastermind of the West Coast Offense during his years as head coach of the San Francisco 49ers, put it this way:

> When a wildebeest or zebra is finally entrapped by the lion, it submits to the inevitable. Its head drops, its eyes glaze over, and it stands motionless and accepts its fate. The posture of defeat is also demonstrated by man—chin down, head dropped, shoulders slumped, arms hung limply. This posture is often visible as players leave the field in the later stages of the game when things are going against them. I often brought this to our players' attention using the example from nature, and we became very sensitive to it. I would remind them never to allow this to occur. I would assert, "Even in the most impossible situations, stand tall, keep our heads up, shoulders back, keep moving, running, looking up, demonstrating our pride, dignity, and defiance."[9]

In other words, adopt a posture of defeat, and you will be defeated. Adopt a posture of courage and confidence (whether you feel it or not), and soon you will feel confident—and you are much more likely to prevail. Carry yourself like a hero, and you are well on your way to controlling your fears.

6. Control Your Anger

I'm not saying you should never feel the emotion of anger. For one thing, we can't control how we feel. We can only control how we *respond* to those feelings. Sometimes, you can't help feeling angry. But you can always control how you respond to that anger. For another thing, sometimes a little well-modulated anger is a good thing. If you're a coach, for example, and the media has treated one of your players unfairly, a little flash of anger may help persuade the media and the public to treat that player more fairly in the future. Great leaders rise to the defense of the people they lead.

Having said that, we also have to acknowledge that uncontrolled rage, irrationality, profanity, and boorish insults only serve to make you look foolish, or worse, dangerously out of control. Never lose control of your emotions by attacking the media, attacking people in your organization, or attacking the public. In all of your public pronouncements, maintain your dignity and your self-control.

Coach John Wooden was once asked, "As a coach, did you ever lose your temper?"

"I always told my players to control their tempers," he replied, "and I couldn't very well expect them to if I wasn't setting a good example myself. I lost my temper once in a while. But I never lost control. I never threw anything. I never threw a chair."[10]

7. Control Your Attitude

Canadian naturalist and painter Robert Bateman put it this way: "I have a pin that I wear on my lapel every day. It has one word printed on it: ATTITUDE. That word is the key to success in any field, because you control it. You can't control the weather, or your kids, or the economy, but you can control your attitude. Life doesn't owe you anything. It's what you make it . . . You're the only one who's got the power to improve your attitude."[11]

The ability to control your attitude begins with controlling your thinking and controlling what you say to yourself. Former track and field athlete Carl Lewis won nine Olympic gold medals and one silver at four different Olympic summer games from 1984 to 1996. He once explained how he maintained a winning attitude by talking to himself before each race. "My thoughts before a big race are usually pretty simple," he said. "I tell myself: 'Get out of the blocks, run your race, stay relaxed. If you run your race, you'll win . . . Channel your energy. Focus.'"[12]

Argentine Olympic luger Rubén González reflects, "My worst luge crash ever was a result of negative self-talk." It happened while he was in St. Moritz, Switzerland, training for a World Cup race, one year before the 2002 Winter Olympics in Salt Lake City. Rubén went out in the afternoon to watch the highly favored Italians as they trained on the luge track. He thought that by watching how the Italians trained, he could learn from the best.

He positioned himself at curve thirteen, the fastest point of the track. The Italians would come hurtling down the track at eighty-five miles an hour. As they shot past, Rubén González would say to himself, "I can't believe I do that!" Every time another sled flew past, he'd repeat, "I can't believe I do that!" He watched the Italians practice for two hours, and "I can't believe . . ." became a kind of mantra—and a self-fulfilling prophecy of doom.

"Up to that day," González recalls, "I had not had any major problems at that track. I was just looking for a way to take my abilities to the next level." But the following morning on his first run, he was shooting down the track and approaching curve thirteen. That's when the thought flashed through his mind, *Rubén, you can't do that!*

He froze mentally—and forgot to use his legs and body weight to steer. The sled shot out of the track and crashed. Rubén

González suffered a broken foot and a broken hand. Even worse than the damage to his body, he totaled his custom-built sled worth tens of thousands of dollars.

"That was the lowest point of my luge career," he recalls. "At that point I didn't know if I would be able to go to the Olympics. I was hurt, I could not afford another sled, and it was all because of a couple of hours of negative self-talk."

He sank into a depression for a few days, but as he was flying home from Switzerland, he made up his mind to adopt a new attitude. He took out a sheet of paper and wrote down these words: "I am being tested. I will pass the test. I have an opportunity to make an incredible comeback and show what I'm made up of."

Then he began repeating a new mantra to himself: "There is always a way. I will find a way, because there is always a way." When he recovered from his injuries, he borrowed a sled from a friend in New Zealand; then he qualified and raced in the Salt Lake City Olympics.[13] We control our attitude. The way we talk to ourselves determines whether we have an "I can't . . ." attitude— or the attitude of a champion.

You can't control your health, but you can control your risk factors. You can't control the questions, but you can control the answers. You can (and must) take control of your schedule. If you are a leader, you must control the performance of your organization. And, of course, you must control your fears, your anger, and your attitude. If you practice control in each of these areas, you will be well on your way to achieving your dreams.

A Low Point Becomes a Turning Point

Franco Harris played almost his entire NFL career with the Pittsburgh Steelers (he played one last season with the Seattle

Seahawks) and was a four-time Super Bowl Champion (Super Bowls IX, X, XIII, XIV). He is famed for his role in a historic play known as "The Immaculate Reception."

In a 1972 play-off game against the Oakland Raiders, the Steelers trailed 7–6 on fourth down with only twenty-two seconds left to play. Steelers quarterback Terry Bradshaw took the snap and was quickly forced out of the pocket. He fired a pass to his intended receiver, Frenchy Fuqua, but the ball was batted away by Oakland defender Jack Tatum. Franco Harris scooped the ball out of the air just before it hit the ground—and he ran it into the end zone to win the game. Immaculate indeed!

But there's another story I want to tell you about Franco Harris—a story about controlling what you can control. And this story has nothing to do with football. After retiring from the NFL, Franco Harris founded a company that sells nutritional doughnuts. That's right, *nutritional* doughnuts. He uses a pastry dough that is fortified with vitamins, minerals, and protein, and he sells his product to hospitals and schools. It's a concept he had been thinking about since his days at Penn State, where he majored in business administration and food services.

It wasn't easy for Franco Harris to start a second career, and he went through many times of discouragement along the way. He easily could have traded on his fame as a football player, but he wanted to see if he could become a successful businessman based purely on the quality of this product and service. So he called his company Super Bakery, Inc. His name and likeness do not appear anywhere on his products.

One of the lowest points of his career as a businessman came one Saturday morning when he received a call from a store asking to stock his product. Because it was Saturday, all of his employees had the day off. So Franco Harris loaded cartons of his product in a truck and drove an hour away to make the delivery.

As he carried the boxes into the store, he noticed a man and woman whispering to each other. The man pointed at him, and Harris distinctly heard him whisper, "I tell you, that's Franco Harris!"

The woman replied, "It can't be! A football star wouldn't be delivering doughnuts!"

Those words stung Franco Harris to his core. Did people think he was a failure just because he ran his own business and sometimes made his own deliveries? Then it occurred to him: if he hadn't had such a successful career in football, no one would think anything of the boss taking time to make a Saturday delivery. In fact, people would consider it admirable that a business owner was willing to do the grunt work to keep his business going.

Even though it was a low point for Franco Harris, that incident became a turning point. He realized that he couldn't control what people thought of him. But he could control what he thought of himself. He decided not to base his self-appraisal on what other people said. He later reflected, "Don't think that starting at the bottom is something to look down at. To me, it's very exciting." Today, Franco Harris continues to operate his successful business, and he also finds time to speak to businessmen's groups on the subject of starting a second career.[14]

Franco Harris knows: whether you dream of football glory or you just want to make the world's healthiest doughnut, you have to control what you can control—and let go of everything else.

7

Focus
on
Courage
and
Confidence

n 1974, I joined the Philadelphia 76ers organization as
general manager. The following year, we negotiated to sign
a phenomenal forward, George McGinnis. Though we
owned his draft rights, the New York Knicks jumped in
and signed McGinnis illegally. Larry O'Brien, the newly named
commissioner of the NBA, met this challenge head-on, slapping
the Knicks with a $1 million fine and returning McGinnis's draft
rights to the 76ers. We signed McGinnis, and the incident became
a huge national story.

I got a call to go on Howard Cosell's ABC weekend show for
a live interview about the controversy. Howard, of course, was
already a broadcasting legend by that time, well known for his

blustery, confident, "tell it like it is" persona. He had already gained fame reporting on the career of Muhammad Ali and providing commentary for *Monday Night Football*. Howard once said of himself, "Arrogant, pompous, obnoxious, vain, cruel, verbose, a show-off. I have been called all of these. Of course, I am." I didn't know it then, but I was about to see a very different side of Howard Cosell.[1]

I took the train from Philly to the WABC studios in New York. A staffer ushered me to the set where I met Howard for the first time just a few minutes before we were to go on the air. Finally, the studio lights came on, Howard introduced me, and we did a five-minute live interview.

After the show, Howard came over to me and thanked me for being on the show. Then he asked, "How did I do? Did I ask the right questions? Did I cover the important angles of the story? Were you pleased with the show?" This went on for about two minutes.

I was amazed. Before this, I had known Howard Cosell only by his television image—the brash, hard-nosed, supremely confident sports reporter. Yet here he was, eager to know if a young basketball executive approved of his work as an interviewer. I got to see a side of Howard Cosell that the public never saw: a little insecure and unsure of himself, and very eager for feedback and affirmation.

The "arrogant, pompous show-off" personality he projected was a role he played on television. He made a point of displaying boldness and confidence to the world, and he rarely let anyone see the insecure side of Howard Cosell. That day, he taught me an important lesson: if you want to be successful in broadcasting or any other endeavor, you must focus on your courage and confidence, not your fears and insecurities.

When the TV camera turned in his direction and the red light lit up, Cosell was *on*. He focused on his boldness and confidence—and that was the secret of his success.

Good Advice from an Idol

Audentes fortuna juvat, wrote Virgil in the *Aeneid*. In English: "Fortune favors the bold." Courage and confidence are essential to success. So if you want to achieve your grandest dreams, you must maintain an *extreme focus* on your courage and confidence.

One of the most underrated forms of courage is the act of maintaining a bold and confident front even when we feel insecure within. Dr. Thomas Lane Butts is pastor emeritus of the First United Methodist Church in Monroeville, Alabama. A white Southern pastor with an intense passion for racial justice, he signed the petition to integrate city buses in Mobile, and marched with Dr. Martin Luther King Jr. in Selma. Dr. Butts has written one book called *Tigers in the Dark*—and the theme of the book, of course, is courage.

In that book, he tells of watching a circus performance on television a number of years ago. The show was performed live before an audience. At one point during the show, the tiger trainer appeared with his whip and proceeded to go into a cage full of fierce Bengal tigers. The door of the cage was locked and spotlights illuminated the cage. The TV camera zoomed in as the trainer began to put the tigers through their routine.

Then, in the middle of the performance, a power failure knocked out all the lights inside the circus tent. The crowd gasped. Everyone knew that the trainer was in trouble. He was locked in the cage in the dark, surrounded by tigers—and tigers have excellent night vision. He couldn't see them, but they could see him.

The lights were out for almost half a minute. The TV screen was dark, but the crack of the whip and the growl of the tigers was audible over the murmuring audience.

When the lights came back on, the trainer was unhurt—and he proceeded to finish the performance. Afterward, the television host asked the trainer how he felt, knowing that the tigers could have leaped upon him at any moment and he would have been helpless in the darkness.

The trainer replied, "I just kept cracking the whip and talking to them until the lights came back on. And they never knew that I could not see them as well as they could see me."[2] Those are the words of a man who is focused on his courage, not on his fears, not on the threat that surrounded him. His courage served him well—and probably saved his life.

It takes courage to pursue our dreams. It takes courage to persevere through obstacles and opposition to make our dreams come true. It takes courage to dare great things to achieve our goals. Many people have dreams, but only people of courage get to celebrate the *achievement* of their dreams.

Ralph Waldo Emerson observed that the most important lesson he learned early in life was, "Make a habit throughout your life of doing the things you fear; if you do the thing you fear, the death of fear is certain."[3] We can turn a courageous act into a *habit* of courageous acts. By making a daily habit of facing our fears and insecurities, then overcoming them, we strengthen our confidence and courage—and we begin to live a bold and confident way of life.

You have probably never heard of Reginald Fessenden, but your life has been affected thousands of times by his inventions. The Canadian-born inventor, who died in 1932, was the first person to broadcast words and music over the radio. In his later career, Fessenden received hundreds of patents for devices ranging from submarine sonar to broadcast television.

But in his early years, it was hard for Fessenden to gain acceptance for his theories and inventions. The wireless radio was invented by an Italian, Guglielmo Marconi, but even though Marconi invented the radio, his theory of how the radio worked was totally wrong. Most other radio engineers adopted Marconi's flawed theory, and this prevented Fessenden's "continuous wave" explanation of radio from being accepted for a decade. The technological progress of radio was hindered throughout those years. But Fessenden persevered against the opposition of the industry, and he was ultimately proven right. Later, the *New York Herald Tribune* wrote of Reginald Fessenden's courageous perseverance, "It sometimes happens, even in science, that one man can be right against the world."[4] Fessenden once said, "I was ridiculed by journalists, businessmen, and even other scientists for believing that voice could ever be transmitted without using wires." Once his theories were proven correct, he became a wealthy man thanks to his patents, and "all of those people who had laughed at my ideas were twisting the dials on their newly bought radios to hear the latest weather and news."[5]

Someone once said, "Audacity is a force-multiplier." In other words, the greatest rewards go to those who are willing to decide, to act boldly, to take a risk. Those words describe Alabama-born singer-songwriter Taylor Hicks, who won the fifth season competition on television's *American Idol (AI)* in May 2006. Before his *AI* appearance, he was a struggling musician who barely made ends meet by singing and playing his music at parties. After *AI*, his debut single, "Do I Make You Proud," soared into the Hot 100 charts nationwide. In 2008, he appeared in a Broadway revival of the hit musical *Grease*, drawing rave reviews. Taylor Hicks also released a motivational book for young people, *Heart Full of Soul*, in which he preaches a message of courage and self-confidence:

Believe in yourself. Believe it to your soul. Be confident. As Joe Namath once said, "When you have confidence, you can have a lot of fun. And when you have fun, you can do amazing things." . . .

It's amazing what you can achieve when you combine belief, hard work, dedication, and hustle. Belief may be the most important, because a show of self-belief causes others to believe in you. It forges allies.

It's not easy, I know, to tamp down doubt. For most of us, there are a million breaks that don't go our way before there's a big one that does. But think of my example, and know that if it can happen for me, it can happen for you.

But don't wait for it to happen. Success is not something that just happens of its own accord. Success is what you're going to make happen right now.[6]

That's good advice from a performer who struggled for success, took risks, believed in himself—and is now living his dreams.

"Focus. Focus. Focus."

In Chapter 5, I told a story about Robin Roberts, the coanchor of ABC's *Good Morning America*. But there was another Robin Roberts, a Baseball Hall of Fame pitcher who I remember well from my boyhood days as a Philadelphia Phillies fan. He pitched for the Phillies from 1948 through 1961 and closed out his career with the Orioles, Astros, and Cubs. He was inducted into the Hall of Fame in 1976.

I watched Robin Roberts pitch many times, and I remember him as a guy who was always cool under pressure. Nothing ever seemed to get to him. He once said, "I think much of the reason nerves never bothered me when I pitched . . . was that I was able to concentrate so well on the mound. I just stood out there in total isolation, focused on throwing the ball as well as I could. Nothing bothered me and I was oblivious to even the batter. When I was throwing well, I would only see the bat when it swung, my concentration was so centered on the catcher. As far as I was concerned the ball was going to the catcher, not the batter."[7] In other words, the source of his confidence was his *extreme focus*. Nothing could break his concentration, so nothing could shake his confidence.

Roberts recalled standing on the mound during games against the New York Giants and being heckled by Giants manager Leo Durocher. "Like a lot of managers in those days," he said, "[Durocher] coached third base . . . He would really get on the opposing pitchers, calling them bushers or worse to try to distract them . . . When I was pitching, I concentrated so hard that I did not ever hear him hollering at me."[8]

Every time the Phillies played the Giants, Leo Durocher tried his best to get on Robin Roberts's nerves, but to no effect. One day, Roberts came off the mound after retiring the Giants, and Durocher was waiting for him. "Kid," the Giants manager said, "I really bother you, don't I?" Of course, Durocher knew he had not even scratched Roberts's ironclad concentration.

After that, Durocher tried a different tactic on Roberts. Instead of shouting insults at him, Durocher showered him with praise. "Leo changed tactics," Roberts recalled, "and I was the greatest pitcher who ever lived. He continually tried to butter me up. Leo never gave up. If one tactic failed to work, he would just try another. But bench jockeying was never a problem for me because my concentration was such that I just did not hear it."[9]

Robin Roberts approached the game with such intense concentration that he was not even aware of the crowds at the games. He remembered one game in particular, where he opposed Don Newcombe and the Dodgers. It was a hard-fought contest, and the Phillies won. After the game, Roberts asked his wife Mary, "Was there a big crowd tonight?"

"It was jammed," she replied. "Over thirty thousand people in the stands."

Roberts concluded, "Not once, warming up for pitching the game, would I look at the crowd, nor did I ever hear them. That is how intense my concentration was."[10]

Insecurity, fear, anxiety, worry—these are all distractions. A mind that is focused on the task at hand clears away all the cobwebs of distraction that keep us from our goals. When you are able to focus your mind and body on the immediate challenge, you are free to perform at the peak of your abilities.

As we discussed in Chapter 3, one of the keys to focusing intently on your goals is *preparation*. The better prepared you are, the more confident you will feel. And the greater your confidence level, the greater your ability to concentrate on your goals and performance.

Confidence and concentration go hand in hand. They are mutually reinforcing factors. The more confident you are, the more focused you are. The more focused you are, the higher your confidence level.

One of Coach John Wooden's most famous players at UCLA, Bill Walton, recalled Wooden's practice sessions as "nonstop, electric, supercharged, intense, demanding." Wooden would pace the sidelines "like a caged tiger, barking instructions, positive reinforcement, and maxims: 'Be quick but don't hurry.' He constantly changed drills and scrimmages, exhorting us to 'move quickly, hurry up.' Games seemed like they happened in a slower gear . . . because everything we did in games happened faster in practice."[11] That's the goal of practice and preparation: to build confidence and concentration, so that we can experience victory in real-life situations.

The greatest basketball player of all time was Michael Jordan. He claimed that the ability to focus powered his courage, and his courage in turn increased his ability to focus. "I think fear sometimes comes from lack of focus or concentration," Jordan said. "If I had stood at the free-throw line and thought about ten million people watching me on the other side of the camera lens, I couldn't have made anything. So I mentally tried to put myself in a familiar place. I thought about all those times I shot free-throws in practice and went through the same motion, the same technique that I had used thousands of times. You forget about the outcome. You know you are doing the right things. So you relax and perform. After that you can't control anything anyway. It's out of your hands, so don't worry about it."[12]

When I was researching my book on Michael Jordan, *How to Be Like Mike*, I was determined to uncover the secret of his phenomenal success. I knew it was more than just a matter of talent. I contacted everyone who knew him, including NBC newsman Tim Russert, who had interviewed Jordan on TV a number of times. Just before Christmas 2000, I wrote to Tim at his Washington office, and he replied:

Dear Pat,
Focus. Focus. Focus. Then get it done. That's the Jordan way.
Have a nice holiday,
Tim Russert

Of all the insights people shared with me about Michael Jordan's phenomenal career, I think those few words by Tim Russert come closest to the mark.

"I'd Rather Take the Risk Than Be a Spectator"

Back in October 1996, I was in Washington, D.C., for the twenty-seventh running of the Marine Corps Marathon. Before the start of the race, I chatted with the lady next to me and found out that she was from Baltimore and was running her first marathon. Appropriately enough, she wore a T-shirt printed with the words, "When Was the Last Time You Did Something for the First Time?" What a great statement of a bold attitude!

The starting gun sounded, and we were off! As I ran, I noticed a gray-haired woman loping easily along. Curious, I sidled up to her and asked, "How are you doing?"

"Fine, just fine," she replied cheerily, not even breathing hard.

"I'm from Orlando," I said. "How about you?"

"College Park, Maryland," she said, "and I know what you're wondering, so I'll tell you. I'm eighty-two. This is my eighth marathon. I ran my first when I was seventy-three."

I marveled and wished her well. As I continued on past her, I could only imagine the conversation between this lady and her children and grandchildren before she ran her first marathon: *Grandma, are you crazy? You want to have a heart attack? What if you fall and break your hip? Why would you want to do something so foolish?*

But I knew why. It's the same reason I still run marathons at my age. I saw that look of joy on her face, that light in her eyes. She was running and she was fully alive and she was accomplishing something that her kids and grandkids would never understand.

Well, running that marathon was an inspiring experience, and I got to meet two women who lived boldly, who took risks, and who demonstrated their confidence and courage in taking on a tough challenge. But the day was not over.

That evening, I had dinner with former senator George McGovern of South Dakota. McGovern ran for president against Richard Nixon in 1972, losing in a landslide. He is also a decorated air veteran of World War II who flew many hair-raising missions over Europe in a B-24 bomber. On his thirty-fifth mission, which was scheduled to be his last, he flew through a hailstorm of flak that wounded the waist gunner, knocked out the airplane's hydraulics, and punched more than a hundred holes in the fuselage. McGovern had to invent a landing approach that was not in the training manual—but he brought his plane down safely. Clearly, this man knows about risk, fear, and courage.

Senator McGovern shared with me many stories about his political battles, his famous friends (such as John F. Kennedy and Hubert Humphrey), and his opponents—especially Richard Nixon. He also told me about a twenty-six-year-old go-getter he had hired as his campaign director for the state of Texas during his presidential race. That young man's name was Bill Clinton.

We also talked about the 1972 election. George McGovern suffered a 61 to 37 percent loss in the popular vote to Nixon (in the electoral college, it was even worse: 520 to 17). McGovern carried only Massachusetts and Washington, DC—he even lost his home state of South Dakota. I asked, "How did it feel to lose so badly?" He said:

> Well, I knew it was an uphill fight all the way. To start with, I had to defeat an unprecedented field of seventeen candidates to win the Democratic nomination. Then I had to go up against a popular sitting president. People who only remember Nixon because of Watergate forget that he had high approval ratings in 1972. It hurt losing in such a big landslide, of course, but I don't have any regrets. It was the chance of a lifetime, and I went for it. I like to quote Marv Levy, who coached the Buffalo Bills to four consecutive Super Bowls and lost all four. He told the reporters, "I'd rather get to this final level and lose than be sitting home watching." I look at it the same way. I'd rather take

that risk and live the adventure than be a spectator to world events.

George McGovern didn't reach the White House, but he did live a life of adventure. Isn't that how you want to live your life? I know I certainly do! "Leaders take risks," observes author John C. Maxwell. "That's not to say that they are reckless, because good leaders aren't. But they don't always take the safest route. Rarely can a person break ground and play it safe at the same time. Often, leaders must take others into the unknown, march them off the map. Look at wise leaders who take risks, and you will find that they: Gather information wisely. Risk from strength. Prepare thoroughly. Fail successfully. Display flexibility."[13]

Most people choose to live their life as comfortably and safely as possible, and there's nothing wrong with that. But the people who dream big dreams and make those dreams come true are the people who are willing to take bold, courageous risks. "Wherever you see a successful business," said management guru Peter Drucker, "someone once made a courageous decision."[14] Jack Welch, the former CEO of General Electric, agrees: "Risk is stepping outside your comfort zone to a place where you cannot predict with any degree of certainty the outcome of your actions. Risk is taking on something that holds an enormous chance of failure. Most importantly, risk is the only real key to outrageous success."[15]

It's true. No start-up company ever became a global corporation without putting capital, reputations, and personal fortunes on the line. No NFL team ever got to the Super Bowl by punting in every fourth-and-one situation. No wannabe performer ever became an American Idol without risking public humiliation at the hands of Simon Cowell. Without risk, there is no adventure. Without risk, a dream is just a dream.

Consider the story of Google cofounder and president Larry Page. A *Fortune* magazine profile of Page reported, "Larry Page has pushed his people to take risks that have led to hot new applications like Gmail and Google Maps. Lately he has been thinking far outside the walls of his company. Page sees a world of opportunity—in areas ranging from energy to safer cars . . . Not enough people, he worries, are willing to place the big bets that could make a difference in meeting humanity's biggest challenges."

Page himself said, "If you look at where many of our new features come from, it's from these riskier investments." Did a willingness to take big risks come easy? No. Larry Page had to overcome the fear of failure in order for Google to succeed.

"When we started Google," he said, "we thought, 'Oh, we might fail,' and we almost didn't do it. The reason we started is that Stanford said, 'You guys can come back and finish your Ph.Ds if you don't succeed.' Probably that one decision caused Google to be created. It's not clear we would have done it otherwise . . . You have this fear of failing and of doing something new, which is very natural. In order to do stuff that matters, you need to overcome that."[16]

So true! The fear of failure is common to us all. But if you believe in your dream, you must overcome your fear and be willing to risk failure. After all, the greater the risk, the greater the potential rewards! If you believe in yourself and your dream, then who better to bet on than yourself?

How to Increase Your Confidence and Courage

Filmmaker George Lucas, creator of the *Star Wars* and *Indiana Jones* epics, said, "You have to find something that you love enough to be able to take risks, jump over the hurdles and break through the brick walls that are always going to be placed in front of you. If you don't have that kind of feeling for what it is you are doing, you'll stop at the first giant hurdle."[17]

And Jim Lehrer, news anchor for *Newshour* on PBS, put it this way: "Take risks . . . Be willing to put your mind and your spirit, your time and your energy, your stomach and your emotions on the line. To search for a safe place, to search for an end to a rainbow, is to search for a place that you will hate once you find it. The soul must be nourished along with the bank account and the résumé. The best nourishment for any soul is to create your own risks."[18]

So take risks, my friend—not foolish gambles, but calculated and prudent risks. Follow your passions boldly. Set extreme, even scary goals. Prepare thoroughly. Plan for every conceivable eventuality. Then *go for it!* The saddest thing in the world would be to come to the end of life and say, "If only I'd attempted this, if only I'd tried that." Don't waste a moment of your life on timidity or fear—or regrets. Focus on your courage.

You may think, "But I'm not a naturally bold and courageous person. I worry about failure, about making mistakes, about making myself look foolish, about losing my investment, and ending up broke! I don't take risks. I play it safe."

Do you think you're any different from anyone else? Do you think Howard Cosell, Taylor Hicks, Michael Jordan, George McGovern, Jack Welch, George Lucas, Jim Lehrer, and Pat Williams never had to overcome self-doubt, worries, or fear? Do you think you're any different from those two courageous women I met while running the Marine Corps Marathon—one of whom took up marathoning in her seventies and was still running marathons in her eighties? And remember what Larry Page thought before founding Google: "Oh, we might fail." But in order to "do stuff that matters," he said, you must overcome your fears. Everybody's afraid. Those who rise above their fears become successful and achieve their dreams. Let me suggest some concrete steps *you* can take to become a more confident and courageous person, willing to take bold risks to make your dreams come true.

Step 1: Give Yourself Permission to Fail

It's okay to make mistakes. In fact, if you're going to attempt anything worthwhile, mistakes are practically inevitable. But mistakes don't have to be fatal. Fletcher Byrom, the former president of Koppers, a global chemical and materials company based in Pittsburgh, put it this way: "Whenever I make a decision, I start out by recognizing that there is a strong likelihood that I'm going to be wrong. To worry about it puts obstacles in the way of clear thinking."[19]

Bold, courageous people learn to forgive errors and fallibilities in themselves and others. Brilliant, talented, capable people make wrong decisions every day, and that's okay. That shows you are making decisions and taking action. If you get down on yourself every time you make an error in judgment, you'll paralyze yourself with fear. Go easy on yourself. Forgive your mistakes and keep moving forward.

In the same way, if you are a leader of a team or an organization, be forgiving of the mistakes of your people. If you punish them every time they make an error in judgment, then you can count on one thing: they will soon stop making decisions altogether. If they know that you will jump on them for showing bold initiative, they will quickly learn to play it safe—and you and your organization will be the poorer for it. But when you give your people the freedom to make mistakes, you empower them to dare to achieve great things. Their success will become your success.

Step 2: Don't Listen to Your Self-Doubts and Fears

We all have doubts and insecurities. Everyone, when facing a great challenge, has a voice inside that says, "This is too hard! You can't do it. You shouldn't even try." Believe me, you're not the only one who struggles with self-doubt.

If you were to list the most successful novelists of the past fifty years, you would have to put Stephen King, the master of horror, near the top of that list. Would it surprise you to know that Stephen King struggled with self-doubt long after he achieved fame and success? In his book *On Writing: A Memoir of the Craft*, he describes that struggle—and how he overcame it:

> With the door shut, downloading what's in my head directly to the page, I write as fast as I can and still remain comfortable. Writing fiction, especially a long work of fiction, can be a difficult, lonely job; it's like crossing the Atlantic Ocean in a bathtub. There's plenty of opportunity for self-doubt. If I write rapidly, putting down my story exactly as it comes into my mind, only looking back to check the names of my characters and the relevant parts of their back stories, I find that I can keep up with my original enthusiasm and at the same time outrun the self-doubt that's always waiting to settle in.[20]

Stephen King refuses to listen to his doubts. To keep a step ahead of his doubts, he simply jumps into the task at hand and writes as fast as he can, racing to complete his novel before the self-doubt can catch him. This same technique will work in any endeavor. Instead of trying to argue with your doubts, *act as if you have no doubts*. Your feelings will follow your actions.

The Nike Company, maker of athletic shoes and sports equipment, used to express this philosophy in its advertising slogan,

"Just Do It." Don't stop and think about the task ahead, don't let your doubts and fears catch up to you. Whatever you need to do in order to reach your dreams, *just do it*.

Step 3: Be Prepared; Preparation Builds Confidence

The late, great Dallas Cowboys head coach Tom Landry once said, "If you are prepared, you will be confident and will do the job."[21] The logic is inescapable. If you prepare well, your confidence will soar. And the greater your confidence, the better you can focus on the task at hand.

One of the most thoroughly prepared basketball players of all time was Boston Celtics legend Larry Bird. After winning the NBA championship in 1984 against the Los Angeles Lakers, Bird said, "I had all the confidence in the world. When I took a shot, I believed it was going in, every time. I had taken so many shots, I couldn't imagine missing. I only thought in positive terms."

Larry Bird explained his confidence in terms of his intense preparation. "I've always done a lot of shooting on my own in the summer," he said. "I got to the point where I could hit eighty to a hundred in a row without missing. That leads to a feeling of 'Give me the ball. I know I can make it.'"

That kind of confidence enables us to achieve an "in the zone" level of performance, as we explored in Chapter 4. "People talk about being in a 'zone,'" says Larry Bird. "I've been there. It's when you just know you've got control of the whole game. It's hard to explain, but your reactions are quicker, and the rim looks bigger, and your eyes have better focus."

Larry Bird's intense preparation enabled him to extend his career far beyond what anyone thought possible. He played with the Celtics from 1979 to 1992. In one game in 1990, the Celtics played the New York Knicks at Madison Square Garden. Many sportswriters were writing him off as a has-been. Late in the first quarter, Bird received the ball in the right corner and found himself covered by Knicks center Patrick Ewing, who had a three-inch height advantage over him. Holding the ball and grinning fiercely, Bird told Ewing, "I'm going to fake once, drive past you, then put in an underhand scoop layup."

In his defensive stance, Ewing shot back a retort—"Oh, no, you won't," or words to that effect.

Larry Bird rose up, faking a jump shot—that was "fake once." Then he put the ball on the floor, dribbled around Ewing underneath—that was "drive past you." Then he underhanded a scoop shot that rolled over the rim and fell through the net for two points— that was "an underhand scoop layup." He did everything he told Ewing he was going to do, and still Ewing was caught flat-footed.

"If someone said I couldn't do something," Larry Bird said later, "I wasn't going to stop until I did it."

For several consecutive years, Larry Bird dominated the three-point contest at the annual All-Star Game. He dominated the contest through confidence, and he gained his confidence through preparation. He invested hundreds of hours in practice, competing against his teammates Danny Ainge and Scott Wedman, who were excellent three-point shooters. In his practice sessions, he set up conditions to exactly match those of the All-Star Game competition. He made sure that the ball racks were positioned exactly as in the competition, right down to making sure that the seams on the balls were lined up uniformly. Each practice round was timed exactly as in competition. Later, when Larry Bird competed in the All-Star competition, he was totally confident because he was absolutely prepared. And he won, year after year.

Bird's confidence level also enabled him to block out distractions, such as crowd noise. "For some guys, going out and being part of a big event like that with all sorts of people cheering and talking to you and making noise is difficult," he said. "To me, it was nothing. I got out there and focused on the rim and blocked everything else out. When I did that, the basket looked big enough to fit two [balls]."

Near the end of his playing career, Larry Bird was plagued with pain in his heels and back. As a result, he missed a lot of games and workouts. "I lose confidence when I'm not practicing," he said, reflecting on those final few seasons. "When I was out there and I hadn't practiced, I didn't have the same feeling. It was like going in to take a test and you didn't study, and you don't know what's on the test. When you study and you know what's on there, it's a breeze to go through it."

Whatever your dream, whatever your field of endeavor, intense preparation produces confidence, and confidence leads to success. "People think confidence comes from your physical abilities," Larry Bird concludes. "That's partly true. But basketball is a mental game. I always prided myself on being able to convince myself to do whatever it took."[22]

Step 4: Be Boldly Decisive

Gen. Norman Schwarzkopf commanded the Coalition Forces in the Gulf War (1991), one of the most stunningly successful military operations in human history. Gen. Schwarzkopf once described his view of decisiveness as one of the keys to achieving goals and objectives:

> Throughout my early years in the army, I learned that probably the worst leader was one who wouldn't make a decision . . . A bad decision, at least, causes action to occur within an organization, and the organization itself can take a bad decision and turn around and make it a good one. But when you get no decision at all, then the whole organization just kind of sits there . . .

I used to demand a minimum of three courses of action on every major decision . . . We would look at the advantages and disadvantages of each of those courses of action . . . Then it became my job to make a decision . . .

I have always felt that one of my strengths was a willingness to make the decision and then pursue that. Even if it's a bad decision, if you pursue your decision to fruition, you accomplish your mission . . . I would never undertake any task expecting to fail. Once I made the decision, as far as I was concerned, it was going to work.[23]

Does that mean that Gen. Schwarzkopf never agonized over decisions he had made? Of course not. He recalls that during the Gulf War, he didn't sleep well, even after the battle plan was "locked in concrete." Because he cared deeply about his soldiers, he drove himself to make sure that every conceivable contingency was accounted for. "Every night," he said, "I would lie in bed and say, 'What have I forgotten? What have we missed? Is there something more we can do?' And I would go back out and look at the maps again."[24]

It's a good idea to reexamine your plans and refine your strategies, even after you have made your decision. But the important thing to remember is to *make that decision*. Don't allow yourself or your organization to be paralyzed by hand-wringing and vacillation. Decide boldly, then act confidently. Odds are that you will succeed.

Step 5: When You Crash, Get Right Back in the Cockpit

This is a variation on the old cowboy maxim, "When you get thrown from a horse, get right back in the saddle." Bob Hoover is a retired air force test pilot and air show pilot, famed for his broad grin and broad-brimmed straw hat. Born in 1922, Bob has been on a first-name basis with some of the greatest aviators of all time, including Orville Wright, Charles Lindbergh, and Neil Armstrong. He was a combat pilot in World War II and was shot down over southern France. He spent nearly a year and a half in a prisoner-of-war camp in Nazi Germany, then managed to escape. He stole a German Focke-Wulf Fw 190 and flew it safely to the Netherlands and freedom.

After the war, he became an air force test pilot and a close friend of another famed test pilot, Chuck Yeager. When Yeager broke the sound barrier on October 14, 1947, flying the rocket-powered Bell X-1, Bob Hoover was Yeager's handpicked wingman. Journalist Mort Crim said of Bob Hoover that he had "wrestled out-of-control jet fighters back to the ground, fought fires in the air, and crashed more times than he can count." One test flight of an F-100 Super Sabre jet ended in a crash that "broke Hoover's back and almost killed him," wrote Crim. "Just as soon as he recovered, Bob Hoover climbed into the cockpit of another Super Sabre and took it up for another test flight. As he tells it in his easy Tennessee drawl, 'You gotta get back in the cockpit of the bird that bit ya.'"[25]

You can't let one bad experience (or even a string of bad experiences) paralyze you. If your plane crashes, get right back in the cockpit. If your horse throws you, get right back in the saddle. If you go bankrupt, get right back in business. If your dance routine ends in a face-plant, get your face off the floor and keep on hoofing.

Don't let failure stop you. Shrug it off and keep right on going. Let your indomitable courage carry you to your dreams.

Step 6: Be Boldly Who You Are

Don't try to be anyone else. Don't let other people force you into their mold. Break the mold! Be yourself! Be secure in the unique, inimitable person God made you to be.

Playwright Neil Simon gave a commencement address at Williams College in 1984, and his theme was "Be True to Yourself." He said, "Don't listen to those who say, 'It's not done that way.' Maybe it's not, but maybe you will. Don't listen to those who say, 'You're taking too big a chance.' Michelangelo would have painted the Sistine floor, and it would surely be rubbed out by today. Most importantly, don't listen when the little voice of fear inside of you rears its ugly head and says, 'They're all smarter than you out there. They're more talented, they're taller, blonder, prettier, luckier and have connections . . .' I firmly believe that if you follow a path that interests you . . . chances are you'll be a person worthy of your own respect."[26]

Step 7: Have the Courage to Do Good Works

On August 28, 1963, I had the privilege of standing with my mother and sister and thousands of other people on the National Mall before the Lincoln Memorial. It was a hot, humid summer day in Washington, DC, but I'll never forget the moment Dr. Martin Luther King Jr. stood up to speak and delivered his historic "I Have a Dream" speech. Dr. King had a dream of a better world where all people would be judged by the content of their character, not the color of their skin.

In July 2008, I visited Montgomery, Alabama, as a guest of my friend John Merrill. John and Ed Bridges of the State Archives of Alabama took me on a tour of the historic sites of the civil rights struggle. One of the sites we visited was the Cleveland Avenue bus stop where Rosa Parks boarded a city bus on December 1, 1955. A little farther down the line, I saw the place where Ms. Parks was arrested and taken off the bus for refusing to give her seat to a white passenger.

When Rosa Parks boarded the bus one Thursday evening around 6:00 PM, she took a seat in the so-called colored section, behind the seats normally reserved for white passengers. But when a number of white passengers boarded at a stop in front of the Empire Theater, the bus driver ordered Rosa Parks and three other African Americans to leave their seats and move to the back. Three passengers complied. Rosa Parks refused. When the driver asked if she was going to move, she replied, "No, I'm not." So the bus driver called the police, and they arrested her and charged her with a violation of the segregation law of the Montgomery city code. The arrest of Rosa Parks sparked the Montgomery Bus Boycott, which would last for more than a year.

During my 2008 visit to Montgomery, I also got to visit the beautiful white-trimmed, redbrick Dexter Avenue Baptist Church where a twenty-six-year-old Martin Luther King Jr., was pastor. I went into the basement where, on the night of December 2, 1955, King and other community leaders planned the nonviolent protest against the segregated Montgomery bus system. The issues those leaders faced were more complex than simply refusing to patronize city buses. The boycott would require funding and a coordinated public relations campaign and a system of carpools to provide alternate transportation.

In the end, Rosa Parks, Dr. King, and the cause of justice and equality prevailed. The boycott ended on December 20, 1956, when a federal ruling declared the segregation laws unconstitutional.

Retired NBA star Kareem Abdul-Jabbar reflected on the courage of Rosa Parks in his book *Black Profiles in Courage*:

> When I think of Rosa Parks now, I think of the power of an individual act of courage. I am reminded again that when one individual takes a stand, even though the motive in that person's mind might not be heroic at the time, it can affect the lives of other people . . . To me, that is what Rosa Parks' heroism was all about. Here was an incon-

spicuous, private woman, minding her own business, when lightning struck. I believe the lightning struck this particular woman because she had the courage and dignity to command respect, even over the seemingly trivial issue of a seat on a bus.

In November 1995, eighty-two-year-old Rosa Parks was interviewed on the forty-first anniversary of the Supreme Court ruling banning bus segregation in Alabama. She told reporters, with the same modest pride she exhibited back then, "I was willing to risk whatever happened to me to let everyone know that this treatment of our people had been going on much too long."

If anyone epitomizes Jackie Robinson's inspiring statement that "a life is not important except in the impact it has on other lives," it is Rosa Parks.[27]

So take risks to do good for others. Be courageous in doing what is right. Be bold in living out your principles. Demonstrate your character and your courage through doing good works.

Be Boldly Who You Are

In the July 2001 issue of *O, the Oprah Magazine*, Oprah Winfrey told the story of her early years. She said that her journey began "the moment I was conceived out of wedlock to Vernon Winfrey and Vernita Lee, who happened by an oak tree one April afternoon in 1953 in rural Mississippi. Their onetime union, not at all a romance, brought about the unwanted pregnancy that was me . . . There were no baby showers, none of the anticipation of delight that I see in the faces of my expectant friends who rub their swollen stomachs with reverence. My birth was surrounded with regret, shame, and hiding."

Because of her beginnings, Oprah grew up feeling a need to prove her worth—to prove that she belonged in this world. She worked hard in school, earned As in almost every subject, won numerous speaking contests, and was awarded scholarships for her efforts. When she was sixteen, Jesse Jackson spoke at a school assembly, and the words he spoke stuck in her mind and became a mantra that she recited and repeated down through the years: "Excellence is the best deterrent to racism. Excellence is the best deterrent to sexism. Be excellent."

Sometime in her midthirties, Oprah came to the realization that she had nothing to prove. The sheer fact that one has been given life and humanity makes you worthy to be here. And it's up to every individual to make the most of the life that he or she has been given.

"There is one irrefutable law of the universe," she writes. "We are each responsible for our own life—no other person is or even can be. Like me, you might have experienced things that caused you to judge yourself unworthy . . . That is one of the most important challenges of your life—to heal the wounds of your past so you don't continue to bleed. Until you do, you are literally dragging the weight of your past into your present. And that makes it nearly impossible to move forward."

It takes courage to face the wounds of the past, to stop the bleeding, and to step confidently into the future. It takes courage to consider yourself worthy to dream big dreams and then to go out and make those dreams come true. "How can you travel on that road without fear?" writes Oprah. "Whenever I'm faced with a difficult decision, I ask myself: What would I do if I weren't afraid of making a mistake, feeling rejected, looking foolish, or being alone? Remove the fear, and the answer comes into focus."[28]

So my advice to you is this: live courageously. No one lives without fear, but you don't have to obey your fear. Instead, obey your courage. Give yourself permission to make mistakes, and forgive the mistakes you've already made. Don't worry about those who might reject you. Don't worry about looking foolish. There's a dream waiting for you, and it won't wait forever. Pursue it now.

No matter how you got here, you are worthy to be here. Be boldly who you are, my friend, and you will become the person you were meant to be.

8

Focus
on
Commitment

They called him the Ryan Express.

Nolan Ryan played twenty-seven seasons, from 1966 to 1993, and was inducted into the Baseball Hall of Fame on July 25, 1999. A right-handed pitcher, Ryan's pitches were routinely clocked at one hundred miles per hour or more, even when he reached his forties. He played for the Mets, Angels, Astros, and Texas Rangers, and holds a number of Major League Baseball records, including 5,714 career strikeouts, 7 career no-hitters (3 more than his closest competition), and he is tied with Bob Feller for the most career one-hitters.

On August 22, 1989, during his first season with the Texas Rangers, he headed for the stadium, expecting to notch his five thousandth strikeout. He was so deep in concentration, thinking about the game, that he drove right past Arlington Stadium. He made a U-turn and pulled into the lot where he was greeted by baseball commissioner Bart Giamatti. A crowd of 42,869 fans was on hand—the second-largest crowd in the history of the park. At 8:32 PM local time, Ryan hurled the pitch that struck out Rickey Henderson of the Oakland A's for number five thousand. The roar of the crowd and a blast of fireworks hailed his accomplishment.

After the game, Rangers play-by-play announcer Mark Holtz walked through the team dressing room—and there, all alone, was Nolan Ryan on a stationary bicycle. Everyone else had left—but there was the Strikeout King, the Hero, exercising all by himself.

"Nolan," said Holtz, "I can't believe you're not out celebrating!"

"Mark," replied the Ryan Express, "I'm in my forties and if I don't ride this bicycle, I won't get ready for my next start. I've got to ride a bike for forty-five minutes after everybody else." He continued that regimen every day he pitched until he hung up his glove in 1993.[1]

That's called commitment. Nolan Ryan was a talented ballplayer, but talent wasn't the secret to his greatness. Nolan Ryan was great because he was intensely focused on his commitment. He was relentless in his dedication to excellence on the mound.

Power to Persevere and Prevail

One of the most accomplished people I've ever encountered is TV and radio personality Art Linkletter. He hosted two long-running shows that ran on both radio and television, *House Party* (CBS, twenty-five years) and *People Are Funny* (NBC, nineteen years), and was famous for his impromptu interviews with children, which were collected in his book *Kids Say the Darndest*

Things (1957). Born in 1912 in Moose Jaw, Saskatchewan, he was abandoned as a baby and adopted by Fulton Linkletter, an evangelical preacher, and his wife, Mary. He was raised from age five in the United States and became a citizen in 1942.

Linkletter began his career as a radio announcer in San Diego and worked his way up in broadcasting by pioneering new forms of entertainment combining stunts and gags, contests, and audience participation. He was a shrewd investor (he made a fortune investing in everything from real estate to the Hula Hoop), which enabled him to be a generous benefactor to countless charities. Art Linkletter was a close friend of Walt Disney, and I was honored when he agreed to write the foreword to my book on the Disney success principles, *How to Be Like Walt*.

I was saddened when I heard that Art Linkletter passed away on May 26, 2010, just weeks short of his ninety-eighth birthday. There are some people you just wish would go on forever, and he was definitely one of them. Art Linkletter once described his philosophy of life—a philosophy rooted in commitment. He said, "Do a little more than you're paid to; give a little more than you have to; try a little harder than you want to; aim a little higher than you think possible; and give a lot of thanks to God for health, family, and friends."[2]

Commitment is a form of toughness—*mental* toughness. Anyone can make a promise. It takes tough, tenacious character to keep a commitment through trials and opposition. Only those who are truly committed and mentally tough have the stick-to-it dedication to achieve their goals and dreams.

Art Rooney, the founding owner of the Pittsburgh Steelers, once asked a favor of legendary Green Bay Packers coach Vince Lombardi. Rooney had befriended a young man who was trying out for the football team at his prep school, so he asked Lombardi if he would send the boy a few words of advice. Lombardi agreed, and the note he sent was brief yet profound:

Dear Tim,

If you want to make St. Bede's football team, you must be mentally tough.

Best,

Vince Lombardi

Coach Lombardi's son, Vince Jr., observed, "Mental toughness was one of my father's favorite topics. He believed it was the single most important skill leaders could develop in themselves and the people around them. Mental toughness is the ability to hold on to your goals in the face of the pressure and stress of current reality. It's the ability to hold on, and hold on, and *hold on to what you want in the face of what you've got*" (emphasis in the original).[3] In other words, mental toughness is an *extreme focus* on your commitment.

When you are totally committed to your goals, nothing can hold you back. Tough-minded people can't be stopped by failure or setbacks. They are committed to transforming setbacks into learning opportunities. Commitment empowers you to persevere through obstacles and prevail over opponents.

Basketball great Julius Erving, the legendary "Dr. J," defines *commitment* as a determination to give 100 percent of yourself to your goals. He learned the power of commitment at an early age. He once said, "I think as a youngster the work ethic was there—practicing hard and being dedicated and not, by nature, being a complainer. My teammates have always related to me in that way. I think probably the best compliment I've ever received from a teammate was what Henry Bibby told me after we had played together for two seasons in Philadelphia. He said, 'Of all the guys that I've ever played with, I don't know if you're the best that I've ever played with, but I know you come to play every night. And because of that, I feel like we always have a chance of winning.' I thought it was a great compliment."[4]

Juan Marichal grew up playing sandlot baseball in the Dominican Republic and became one of the dominant Major League Baseball pitchers of the 1960s. He began his Major League career in an auspicious way, pitching a one-hitter for the San Francisco Giants, defeating the Philadelphia Phillies 2–0. In that game, he was pitching a no-hitter with two outs in the eighth before the Phillies got their only hit against him.

When he retired from baseball in 1975, he had amassed a 243–142 record over a sixteen-year career. He had completed 244 starts, pitched 52 shutouts, tossed a no-hitter against Houston in 1963, and was selected to ten All-Star teams. He was inducted into the Baseball Hall of Fame in 1983.

Sportswriter Ron Bellamy once described Juan Marichal's pitching style in lyrical terms: "The symbol of his artistry . . . was the windup, with the high, graceful kick that left the San Francisco Giants hurler poised precariously on one leg like a bronzed Nureyev before he swept smoothly forward and propelled the baseball toward the plate." And the great Henry Aaron, who whiffed on more than a few Marichal fastballs, said, "He can throw all day within a two-inch space, in, out, up, or down. I've never seen anyone as good as that."[5]

Juan Marichal himself explained his career in terms of a lifelong focus on commitment. "It was baseball, baseball day and night," he said, "and I dedicated myself to my profession. I think that when you want to be somebody, you have to try hard. You have to work hard, and the more time you put into something that you want and you like, the quicker you can be better. I didn't want to be just a baseball player. When I heard the names Sandy Koufax, Bob Gibson, Warren Spahn, all those big names, I wanted to be the same level as those guys, and to do that you have to work hard. You have to be dedicated to your profession."[6]

Maintain an intense and focused commitment to excellence, to hard work, to continuous improvement. Your commitment is one of the indispensable keys to your dreams.

Steps to Commitment

Let me suggest some specific steps so you can focus on your commitment and remain faithful to your dreams over the long haul:

Step 1: Commit Yourself to Maintaining a Fighting Spirit

Legendary Alabama football coach Paul "Bear" Bryant put it this way: "I have always tried to teach my players to be fighters. When I say that, I don't mean put up your dukes and get in a fistfight over something. I'm talking about facing adversity in your life. There is not a person alive who isn't going to have some awfully bad days in their lives. I tell my players that what I mean by fighting is when your house burns down, and your wife runs off with the drummer, and you've lost your job and all the odds are against you, what are you going to do? Most people just lay down and quit. Well, I want my people to fight back."[7]

To have a fighting spirit is to refuse to give up the fight. A person who is committed to fighting on, even when the battle seems lost, can never be conquered because he will never surrender. If you truly have a fighting spirit, you have already won half the battle. This principle holds true in any endeavor, whether you are in the arts, in business, in the military, or on the field of athletics: if you want to achieve your goals and dreams, never surrender— be committed to the fight.

The great American author, artist, and publisher Elbert Hubbard once wrote, "Genius is only the power of making continuous efforts. The line between failure and success is so fine that we scarcely know when we pass it . . . How many a man has thrown up his hands at a time when a little more effort, a little more patience, would have achieved success? . . . There is no failure except in no longer trying. There is no defeat except from within."[8]

The Rev. Bob Richards competed in the 1948, 1952, and 1956 Summer Olympics as a pole-vaulter. He also competed as a decathlete in 1956. He won the bronze in pole holding in 1948, and won the gold in pole-vaulting in 1952 and 1956. He once wrote about what it means to have a fighting spirit—or as he put it, "It's a will to win, and not just a wish to win . . . I think the greatest thing in life is to be able to dream, to have great aspirations, but I think it equally important that you have a will that can turn that dream into reality. You've got to have something within you that is able to translate into concrete practice the idea in the back of your mind. You've got to dream, yes, but more importantly you've got to have a will that makes that thing come to pass."[9]

Bob Richards goes on to explain that, quite often, the difference between having a *wish* to win and having the *will* to win can be as little as a fraction of 1 percent. The person with a will to win perseveres a fraction of 1 percent longer, pushes himself a fraction of 1 percent further—and that little extra measure of fighting spirit often spells the difference between failure and victory:

> In many a race I have seen that there isn't a gigantic difference between victory or defeat; more often it is simply by the smallest margin that a man is named the winner. This holds true in all of life . . . The difference between a Ph.D. in school and the fellow who didn't quite make it is that little bit more study, that extra page that a man turns every night as he burns the midnight oil. The difference in business is not always that one man is more gifted than

another. It is that one man puts out a little bit more. So often people think that a champion has a tremendous edge over everyone else. They think he is 99 percent perfect as against the other fellow's 50 percent. Actually the difference is more like 98.8 percent over 98.7 percent. It's that small degree of putting out a little bit more that does it.[10]

If you can fight a little bit harder, last a little bit longer, expend a little more effort, endure a little more suffering, and absolutely, positively *refuse to quit*, then you will be a champion. And you will reach your dreams.

Step 2: Commit Yourself to Continuous Improvement, Continuous Growth, and Continuous Learning

In the early part of 2010, I spoke at a convention in Cincinnati, Ohio, and met a man named Jim Serger. Jim is in the ice-hauling business. In my talk, I spoke about the importance of continuous learning and of the crucial role that reading plays in our growth and personal improvement. When Jim approached me, he told me that he had been profoundly challenged by what I had said. Prior to that day, he had never had much enthusiasm for reading, but something I said ignited a spark within him.

A couple of weeks later, I received an e-mail from Jim Serger. He wrote, "I got your book *Extreme Dreams Depend on Teams*, and I read it in ten days. That's the first book I have finished in twenty years. I am now two hundred pages into *How to Be Like Walt*. I have read one hour a day, and I have found myself feeling more upbeat. I've stopped watching pointless TV. Thanks for the jump start."

A short while later, Jim wrote again: "Just finished *How to Be Like Walt*. I had set a goal of reading it in one week, because

I promised a fellow employee that he could have it to read on vacation. Many events in Walt Disney's life remind me of my own family when I was a kid. People predicted Walt would fail, yet he proved them all wrong. People told my mother she would never succeed as an interior decorator, yet thirty years later she is still doing what she loves. These examples teach me that through hard work and commitment, anything is achievable . . . Thanks for inspiring me and making books enjoyable to read."

A month later, he wrote again to tell me he had read my book *It Happens on Sunday*, a book about faith and values in the world of the National Football League. He wrote, "Another excellent book. It explains how, with courage and faith, in good times and bad times, any obstacle can be overcome. This past Sunday, I had a great day with my little girl and my mother-in-law. We went to church, then to lunch, then to a horse show. In the past, I would have stayed home to watch the Masters on TV (it used to be all about me). But in the past six weeks, my attitude has been changing because of the reading I've been doing. I have a whole new understanding of what it means to be a father and a husband, how to put the needs of others first, and how to balance my life. Thanks again. P.S. I just finished reading my fifth book."

A few months later, I heard from Jim again. He had just finished his twenty-eighth book in the six months since we had met. He listed some of the books he had read: *Winning Every Day* by Lou Holtz, *Who Moved My Cheese?* by Spencer Johnson, *The 7 Habits of Highly Effective People* by Stephen Covey, *Lincoln on Leadership* by Donald T. Phillips, and more. He calculated that he was averaging 1.16 books per week.

"Reading has changed my life," he told me. "I see things differently, I listen more, I understand and comprehend material more easily." He added that his reading had even enhanced his TV viewing, as he was now able to come up with many more answers to the questions on *Jeopardy*.

"But," he added in a serious note, "the single most important effect I see is that my daughter is engaged in reading. She started kindergarten two weeks ago. On her first day, she got in trouble with the teacher. She came home and was very quiet, so I got her to open up. It turned out that while her teacher was working with students at the other side of the classroom, our daughter decided to leave the room and walked down to the library and check out a book—the latest Clifford the Big Red Dog book. Wow! I was so glad to see that she loves to read, but I explained to her that she really shouldn't leave class without permission. But really, how many students will leave the classroom to go check a book out of the library?"

Jim concluded, "Pat, I will keep reading for as long as I see it as a positive influence on myself and others. Which means for a *long* time."

As this book was being written, I received one more message from Jim Serger, telling me he was now up to thirty-eight books by authors such as Tom Peters, John Maxwell, Jack and Suzy Welch, Ken Blanchard, and many more. He had also bought a Bible, which he had begun reading.

Jim mentioned one principle that he had read about in one of my books, the concept of having the heart of a servant. As a result, his life was changing in ever-increasing ways. He built the new picnic table for his church ("I never would've done that before I started reading books"). He started volunteering at his daughter's kindergarten, helping the children open their lunch packets and assisting with cleanup ("I never would've done that either"). Jim took his wife, daughter, parents, parents-in-law, and sister-in-law on a family vacation to the lake ("I've never done a big family event like that before"). He also called his brother, whom he hadn't spoken with in more than eight months, and told him how much he missed talking to him ("I never would've done that either").

He helped a twenty-three-year-old man who had a drinking problem get off the streets. The young man said he would like to join the navy, but he knew he would never qualify. So Jim mentored him, helped him get treatment for his alcoholism, and helped him to believe in himself. When the young man took the entrance exam for the navy—a test that required a thirty-five score to pass—he scored a sixty-five.

Jim told me, "You challenged me to be a reader and a servant to others. This has made me a better person at home, at work, and with my neighbors. It has also made me a much happier person. You gave me a start, and that has driven me to higher and higher results. Thanks again."

And the thing that amazes me is that Jim keeps writing again and again to thank me. But what did I do? I just encouraged Jim to read books and commit himself to continuous learning. But all of the changes in Jim's life aren't the result of anything I did. *Jim has done it all.* He took up the challenge. He read the books. He applied what he learned to his everyday life. And he has made the difference. And all I can do is stand in amazement and say, "Jim, my friend—go, go, *GO!*"

Step 3: Commit Yourself to Good Character.

Another indispensable ingredient for success is an intense, daily focus on building our character and strengthening our integrity. Many people are able to gain wealth and power through lying, cheating, stealing, influence peddling, and other unethical shortcuts. But nobody can sustain *genuine success* without character and integrity. I've known wealthy, powerful people who I considered failures as human beings, because they clearly lacked character.

You will know that you have achieved genuine success when

you feel the deep sense of personal satisfaction that comes with achieving your life goals *without sacrificing your soul.*

Several years ago, I shared a speaking stage in Atlanta with Truett Cathy, the founder of the Chick-fil-A restaurant chain. At the time, Truett was well into his eighties, and his net worth was listed by *Forbes* magazine at $1.2 billion.[11] The audience consisted entirely of young people, and despite the gap in their ages, Truett kept his young listeners riveted to every word. I'll never forget one statement he made in his rich Georgia drawl. He said, "Y'all can be honest and successful at the same time." So many people, young and old, think that the only way to get ahead in businesses is to cut corners, to lie and cheat, to compromise one's ethics and integrity. But Truett Cathy is a billionaire entrepreneur who proves that success and integrity go hand-in-hand.

The late *New York Times* columnist William Safire explains why success is impossible without an intense focus on character:

> What's the secret to long-run success?
>
> For a person, it's useful to have the smarts, look great, be lucky, and exude charisma. All that is not enough.
>
> For a political party, it helps to have good organization, articulate candidates, and pollsters to discern a popular set of issues. Not enough.
>
> For a nation, success can seem assured by natural resources, free enterprise, a culture of compassion, and a free press. It can still go under.
>
> For a person, a party, and a nation, the element essential to success is *character,* a word that grew out of the Greek for "to mark, to engrave."[12]

So be a person whose life is engraved by good character. Do the right thing even when no one is watching—and do it all the time. Never lie. Never cut ethical corners. Don't steal—don't even take home a paper clip from the office. Obey the speed laws—and obey the Golden Rule. Do more than people ask of you. Make a commitment to be the best human being you can be. Focus on your character. As journalist Mignon McLaughlin once wrote, "Character is what emerges from all the little things you were too busy to do yesterday, but did anyway."[13]

Step 4: Commit Yourself to Be Accountable to Others

Personal accountability is one of the most powerful ways to build a habit of focused commitment into your life. One of the greatest role models of personal accountability I have ever met is evangelist Billy Graham. I first met Dr. Graham in 1962. I was a student at Wake Forest University in North Carolina, and I hosted my own radio show on the university's radio station. Dr. Graham was on campus as our chapel speaker, so I brought him into the studio and he gave me a great interview, mostly about the sports he loved to play in his boyhood. Years later, I shared my own journey of faith at two Billy Graham crusades, one in Syracuse, the other in Chicago.

In an era when so many religious leaders, political leaders, and business leaders have fallen due to moral, ethical, or legal scandals, Dr. Graham maintained a reputation for honorable and honest leadership. Decade after decade, he topped the pollsters' lists of the most admired people in the world. I believe that the reason for Dr. Graham's sterling reputation is a commitment he made more than six decades ago—a commitment to accountability that has come to be called "The Modesto Manifesto."

In 1948, when Billy Graham was rising to prominence as an evangelist, he noticed that the reputation of Christian evangelism had been tarnished by incidences of sexual immorality, financial impropriety, and fraud. A number of religious leaders had been caught exaggerating the size of their audiences and the numbers of their converts. Some had been accused of mishandling donated funds or betraying their marriage vows. So Dr. Graham called a meeting with his three closest associates—singer George Beverly Shea, music director Cliff Barrows, and associate evangelist Grady Wilson. They met in a home near Modesto, California, to pray for God's direction for the future of their ministry.

As they talked and prayed together, they came up with a plan for keeping their ministry completely above reproach. It was a pact in which all of the Graham team members agreed together to avoid even the faintest whiff of financial or moral impropriety. They committed themselves to absolute integrity in all publicity claims. They pledged that the ministry's finances would be open for inspection.

Throughout his decades of ministry, Dr. Graham never traveled, dined, or even shared an elevator with a woman who was not his wife. He not only guarded the purity of his relationship with his wife, but he made sure that there was not even the remotest possibility that he could even be suspected of impropriety. He was accountable to others for how he spent every hour of his day.

The principle of personal accountability, embodied in the Modesto Manifesto, helped to maintain the sterling reputation of Dr. Graham and the Billy Graham Evangelistic Association through more than six decades of ministry. Those same accountability principles will serve you well today.

One of the best ways to maintain your commitment to your goals and dreams is through an accountability group. Such groups are known by various names, including "mentoring groups," "discipleship groups," "peer success circles," or "mastermind groups." The one thing these groups all have in common is that individual members share their goals and dreams, and the rest of the group holds them accountable for making progress. Accountability groups meet weekly or monthly, and group members often call each other on a regular basis to check in with each other on the steps they are taking toward their goals.

The concept of accountability groups goes back to the Twelve-Step program of Alcoholics Anonymous. I first became acquainted with AA through my father's brother, Worth Williams. Uncle Worth had a major struggle with alcohol throughout most of his adult life. He tried to stop drinking on his own, but he failed repeatedly. Only when he got into AA was he finally able to get sober. In fact, he spent the last years of his life as a counselor and executive with the Alcoholics Anonymous organization. AA saved him, and Uncle Worth remained clean and sober until the day he died.

The Twelve Steps of AA have been adapted to other programs of recovery from addiction, such as Narcotics Anonymous, Overeaters Anonymous, and Debtors Anonymous. The Twelve Steps require the individual to admit that he cannot control his addiction or compulsive behavior, that only a Higher Power can give him the strength to overcome, that he must examine himself for past failures and make amends for those failures, that he must learn to live a new way of life, and he must help others who suffer from similar addictions or compulsive behavior.

Now, what do the Twelve Steps of AA have to do with people who want to achieve their dreams in life? You might say, "I'm not an addict. I don't need this kind of group." But consider this: for the person who is enslaved by alcohol, cocaine, compulsive gambling, or some other self-destructive behavior, their dream is to be free of that enslavement. So what does the addict do to find freedom from his addiction? He goes to a group, and in that group he makes a commitment to follow the Twelve Steps, and the people in that group hold him accountable and help him to keep his commitment. Through that commitment, the addict achieves his dream of recovery from addiction. Novelist William C. Hammond, who once directed the publishing program for the Hazelden Foundation addiction treatment program, has called the Twelve Steps "the most successful program known for changing alcoholics."[14] What makes this program so effective? I believe that, first and foremost, the key ingredient is *accountability*.

Now, what is the dream that *you* want to achieve? Do you want to build a business or a nonprofit organization from the ground up? Do you want to write a novel or a screenplay? Do you dream of running for public office? You may not realize it, but you might have more in common with a helpless alcoholic than you think! You may need to admit that you have been unable to control your addiction to procrastination or lack of discipline or lack of self-confidence. You may need to acknowledge that only a Higher Power can empower you to overcome your self-defeating tendencies. You may need to take a clear-eyed look at your past failures and start making amends for those failures. You may need to live a new way of life and start helping others who are in the same fix you're in.

In short, it may be time for you to go to a group—call it an "accountability group" or a "mastermind group"—and make a commitment to change your habits. You may need to ask the people in that group to hold you accountable for keeping your commitment.

Now do you see the connection? Whether you dream of being free of an addiction or dream of achieving some difficult challenge in life, the key to success is the same: accountability. You need to commit yourself to your dream, then give a small group of people permission to hold you accountable for that commitment. The other members of your accountability group will enable you to focus on your commitment, so that you will keep faith with your dreams. At the same time, you, as a member of the group, will help your fellow group members to achieve their dreams.

Dr. Jeannette Samanen, a professional life coach, calls accountability "one of the most powerful tools for helping people succeed." She explains the power of accountability to enable you to sustain your focus on your goals and dreams:

> Accountability literally means making an account . . . An on-going relationship with someone to whom you make an account helps you stay on track over time.
>
> Involving another person in your behavior-change program helps you strengthen your commitment and maintain your focus. When things go well, you have someone to celebrate with. When problems arise, there's someone to help you identify what went wrong and figure out how to get back on track.[15]

An accountability group can take many forms. It might be a writers' group, a group of business executives, an artists' group, a women's group, a men's group, a college-age group, a seniors' group. It might consist of three members—or two dozen. It could be a group run by a professional leader or coach who requires a membership fee. It could be an ad hoc group of friends who just want to meet and support each other.

Trust is essential to such a group, so there are certain covenants or agreements that you should commit yourselves to in the group. Commit yourselves to absolute confidentiality—nothing shared within the group will ever be mentioned outside the group. Commit yourselves to being honest with each other—not "brutally" honest, but supportively honest. Commit yourselves to holding each other accountable for making progress toward your goals. Commit yourselves to attending every session without fail, unless it is physically impossible to do so.

An accountability group can give you the extra power you need to keep your commitment—and your commitment is the power to keep you on course to your dreams.

That Game-Changing Moment

One of the best recruitment commercials I've ever seen is the U.S. Marine Corps ad that shows quick-cut scenes of marines performing precision drills, marine jets taking off from carrier decks, armed and helmeted marines carrying out a raid in a remote village, marines unfurling an American flag—and then the words, "We don't take applications—only commitments." Whew! After seeing that commercial, I'm ready to join up myself! The U.S. Marine Corps is one place where the word *commitment* still carries full weight.

Winners know that commitment is the engine that powers success. As businesswoman Mary Crowley once observed, "One person with a commitment is worth more than one hundred people who only have an interest."[16] And weight-control expert Judy Wardell Halliday agrees: "Dreams become reality when we keep our commitment to them."[17]

Commitment is the essence of extreme focus, because commitment demands that you be focused on one goal, one purpose, one dream, one destination. There is no such thing as "committing" yourself to twenty things at once. That's not called *commitment*. That's called *multitasking*. Your dream—and your commitment to that dream—must be all-consuming.

The immortal NFL coach Vince Lombardi once said this about commitment: "In a football game, there are approximately 160 football plays. And yet there are only three or four plays that have anything to do with the outcome of the game. The only problem is that no one knows when those three or four plays are coming up. As a result, each and every player must go all out on all 160 plays."[18]

It's true. In football or in life, you never know when that big game-changing moment is going to come, so you have to be committed to going all out on every play. Keep reaching for your dream. Keep fighting, don't give up, never surrender. Be tough, be tenacious. Show the world what you're made of—and you'll find out you're made of sterner stuff than you ever imagined. Never give up, never give in, because you never know when that next half ounce of energy might win the prize.

You're going to make it, my friend. I know you will. You've got the commitment to go all the way.

9

Focus
on
Leadership
and
Influence

A few years ago, I had a phone conversation with Howard Schultz. In 1987, Schultz purchased a little three-store coffeehouse chain called Starbucks and quickly began expanding. By the time of Starbucks's initial public stock offering in 1992, the chain had grown to 165 outlets. Today, there are more than seventeen thousand Starbucks shops around the world. When I had a chance to talk to Howard one-on-one, one of the first questions I asked him was about leadership.

"Howard," I said, "in a company as big as Starbucks, where do your leaders come from?"

"We're opening new stores at a rate of four a day," he said. "That means we need to develop leaders at a rapid clip. So we invest a great deal of time and money in leadership development. You don't find the unique Starbucks culture outside of the company, so we have to train leaders from within."

"How do you identify potential leaders?" I asked.

"People skills," he said. "Customer satisfaction is the key to the growth of our company, so in order to be a leader at Starbucks, you *must* have people skills. That's what our business is all about."

By 2000, Starbucks was booming, and Howard Schultz took a step back from daily operations. He resigned as CEO but remained chairman of the board. In 2008, however, Starbucks fell on hard times, in part because of the global economic downturn. But the shrinking economy wasn't the only problem Starbucks faced. The company was being squeezed by a combination of competition in the marketplace, changes in the culture, and management missteps. Starbucks was in a full-blown crisis.

So Howard Schultz returned as CEO, determined to inject a double shot of espresso into the company he had built. He needed to engineer a turnaround. As he took up the executive reins at Starbucks once again, he faced a company with sharply declining revenues and tumbling stock prices. "When I returned in January 2008," he told *Harvard Business Review*, "things were actually worse than I'd thought."

Starbucks management had missed a major cultural shift, which affected the Starbucks brand. Said Schultz, "For some reason, we seemed to become the poster child for excess." The hip, socially conscious culture that had previously embraced Starbucks now began to view the four-dollar cup of Starbucks as a symbol of wasteful overspending. McDonald's marketed its own espresso-based coffee with ads claiming it is "dumb" to pay four dollars for a cup of coffee. McDonald's quickly ate into Starbucks's market share.

Starbucks's clientele began fragmenting. Some coffee drinkers saw Starbucks as a big corporate intruder, so they turned to local hole-in-the-wall coffee shops. Many of these "support the local merchant" consumers spread their anti-Starbucks opinions around the Internet. "Bloggers were putting holes in the equity of the brand," said Schultz, "and it was affecting consumer confidence, our people, everything . . . The world had changed."

When Howard Schultz took back his old job, he knew he had to make big, sweeping decisions in a short period of time. "The decisions we had to make were very difficult," he said, "but first there had to be a time when we stood up in front of the entire company as leaders and made almost a confession—that the leadership had failed the 180,000 Starbucks people and their families. And even though I wasn't the CEO [at that time], I had been around as chairman; I should have known more. I am responsible. We had to admit to ourselves and to the people of this company that we owned the mistakes that were made. Once we did, it was a powerful turning point."[1]

In the first few months after Schultz's return, there was enormous pressure to abandon the strategy, values, and business model that had built the Starbucks company. There were voices in the marketplace demanding that Starbucks get rid of company-owned stores and franchise the Starbucks brand. Franchising fees would have brought a big cash infusion into the company, which would have stabilized shareholder value. "But," Schultz reflected, "it would have fractured the culture of the company. You can't get out of this by trying to navigate with a different road map, one that isn't true to yourself."

People even urged Schultz to sacrifice quality to save hundreds of millions of dollars. After all, a 5 percent reduction in the quality of the beans would never be noticed, right? But Schultz insisted, "We would never do that."

Schultz was the ultimate insider. He understood the Starbucks corporate culture like no one else. Moreover, he possessed an aura of leadership and authority that no one else could match. Howard Schultz was to Starbucks what Walt Disney was to the Disney Company or Steve Jobs to Apple. So Schultz was able to make risky, expensive decisions that another CEO might not have been able to get away with. He was able to withstand the pressure of those who wanted Starbucks to change its business model and subvert its values.

One of Schultz's most expensive risks was to hold a convention of ten thousand store managers in New Orleans. Why New Orleans? Because Schultz wanted to remind its people—and the world—of the company's humanitarian values. The Starbucks convention took place just three years after the city was devastated by Hurricane Katrina, so the convention began with community service. Starbucks managers invested fifty-four thousand volunteer hours (and the company invested $1 million) in local improvement projects: building playgrounds, painting and landscaping, and restoring entire neighborhoods in some of the hardest-hits parts of New Orleans.

"If we hadn't had New Orleans," Schultz said, "we wouldn't have turned things around. It was real, it was truthful, and it was about leadership. An outside CEO would have come into Starbucks and invariably done what was most expected, which was cut the thing to the bone. We didn't do that . . . We reinvested in our people, we reinvested in innovation, and we reinvested in the values of the company."[2]

As I write these words, the American economy remains weak—but Starbucks is once again strong and growing. The Starbucks story is a prime example of how to achieve success by focusing on leadership and influence.

Leaders Never Say "I"

Swen Nater played for coach John Wooden's UCLA Bruins, and went on to play pro basketball with the Spurs, Nets, Bucks, and Lakers. Today, Nater maintains a website and an e-mail newsletter in which he promotes the insights and principles of Coach Wooden. In one of his e-mail newsletters, Nater said that Coach Wooden often told his players, "Life is the united effort of many."[3] In other words, life was meant to be lived in an environment of teamwork. And the logical extension of this idea is that it takes a *leader* to unite the efforts of the many.

When you get right down to it, even endeavors normally thought of as "solo" accomplishments—writing books, for example—are actually team efforts. I depend on my writing partner to help give shape and structure to my message. I depend on my editors to challenge my thinking, improve the flow of my writing, and clean up my syntax. And where would I be without my able assistants in Orlando, my promotional and marketing experts, and all the bookstore personnel who stock the shelves and ring up the sales? It takes a team to produce a successful book.

Fact is, it's hard to think of *any* successful endeavor that is *not* a team effort! Coach Wooden was right when he said that practically anything we accomplish in this life is the result of the united efforts of many people. So if life is a team effort, then it naturally follows that in order for us to succeed in life, we have to focus on leadership and influence. We have to become leaders and team-builders. We have to inspire the members of the team to add their focus to ours, and to unite their energies with ours, so that *all* of us can reach the dreams we share as a team.

The rewards of leadership often extend far beyond profit and loss statements or getting your picture on the cover of *Sports Illustrated* or *Forbes*. Leadership is not just about success. It's also about influence. John Wooden once told me, "When I was in the service during World War II, I started receiving letters from many young men who had been under my supervision in high school. Reading those letters, I started to realize the kind of impact I'd had on people as a teacher and coach. Many of them were heading off to war themselves, and they expressed appreciation for the values and character traits I had taught. They told me I had helped them accept their situation, and they all wanted to stay in contact with me."

Leadership is not an easy calling. Leaders must make difficult, lonely, and often courageous decisions. Sometimes leaders must put their careers at risk in order to do the right thing. Wooden told me:

> In my third year of teaching, the cocaptains and two best players on my team failed to show up for a game. They told me the following day that they'd both been sick in bed. I showed them a picture of them at a dance. I said, "Obviously, the dance was more important to you than the game." Then I dismissed them from the team.
>
> One of these two young men, whose father was vice principal of the school, said his father would have me fired. I said, "That doesn't change my decision. You're still off the team." His father came to talk to me, and he was definitely disappointed when I told him I had suspended his son for the entire year. But he didn't fire me. In fact, he came back later and thanked me for making a courageous decision. He said it was the best thing that ever happened to his headstrong son. I was a young coach then, and this incident gave me great confidence in standing up for my beliefs.

What is leadership? Simply defined, leadership is the ability to achieve goals through the combined efforts of people. As we focus on our leadership ability, we discover that we can accomplish vastly more through teams and organizations than we ever could through individual effort. We can multiply our efforts and magnify our success by working through others who possess the abilities we lack. By focusing on leadership, we are freed up to focus our time and energies on the things we do best. We stop wasting time on tasks that are beyond our skill set. The more we delegate, the less we have to do ourselves and the more we achieve through others.

"The leaders who work most effectively . . . never say 'I,'" says management expert Peter Drucker. "And that's not because they have trained themselves not to say 'I.' They don't think 'I.' They think 'we.' They think 'team.' They understand their job to be making the team function . . . This is what creates trust, what enables you to get the task done."[4] I once interviewed José Abreu on the subject of leadership. At that time Abreu was the secretary of the Florida Department of Transportation; today he directs the Miami-Dade Aviation Department and oversees operations at Miami International Airport. He told me:

> Whether I'm leading the Florida Department of Transportation or coaching a team of Little Leaguers, my task is essentially the same. My job is to shape consensus and build team unity so that the team can achieve its goals.
>
> I used to coach my son's Little League team in Hialeah . . . Nobody thought our team had the talent to go undefeated, yet there was one season in which we won every game we played. During one of the games that season, I overheard a parent of one of the boys on the opposing team say, "Look at those kids!"—referring to our team.

"Look at the way they follow instructions! I don't know if I would want my son to be on his team. They look more like synchronized sewing machines than real people."

He meant it as a disparaging remark. He saw the kids on our *team* as robots. But they weren't robots. They were a team! They took direction, they were coordinated, they acted as one. I took it as a compliment to my ability to get our team to win games when no one thought they could.

Focus is not just the key to individual success. It's an essential ingredient of *organizational* success. The bigger the dream, the more we need teams to make our dreams come true. And you can't have teamwork without leadership. So if you have a big, audacious dream to achieve, don't go it alone. Focus on leadership and influence—and turn your biggest, most impossible dreams into reality.

Leadership Is Influence

Leadership guru John C. Maxwell once told me, "The benefit of becoming a leader is not that you get to tell people what to do. This is a misconception among adults as well as children. In reality, with leadership comes responsibility. The benefit of being a leader lies in being able to work with others, encouraging and equipping them, and together seeing something great achieved. Although we admire people who seem to be solo achievers—presidents, war heroes, inventors, athletes, and movie stars—the truth is that no individual has ever done anything of significant value on his or her own. Significant accomplishment always requires teamwork. And being a leader means working with a team."

There are many ways to be a leader. Some lead by shouting and throwing fits. Others achieve outstanding results without ever raising their voices (Coach Wooden comes to mind). Some leaders are gifted with eloquence. Others are plainspoken and down-to-earth. Some are even able to influence others without saying a word.

Bill Sharman was head coach of the Los Angeles Lakers from 1971 to 1976. During his playing days with the Boston Celtics, he partnered with Bob Cousy to form one of the most dynamic backcourt duos in NBA history. Cousy would make plays and Sharman would make shots—often shooting .400 or better from the field. Bill shared a story with me about leadership through quiet influence:

> When I was first playing with the Boston Celtics, I would often feel nervous and somewhat lethargic on game days, just sitting around the house or some hotel. So, after a few years I started going to a nearby high school gym to do a little stretching, dribbling, shooting, and so forth for about forty-five minutes in the mornings. Almost immediately, I felt more relaxed, and I had increased confidence for the game that evening. And that became my game day routine.
>
> After doing this for a couple of years, I noticed my game stats and scoring percentage seemed to increase each season. I mentioned this to my teammates, and I soon had a following of players who all went to the gym together on game day. And you know what? Most of them noticed that their proficiency in the game went up.
>
> When I finished my playing career with the Celtics, I coached the Cleveland Pipers in the ABL [All-Star Basketball League]. I used the same routine with the entire team on game day, and we were lucky enough to win the

championship. This increased my confidence in using the game day morning practice throughout my coaching career.

Today, it's called a "game day shoot-around" and it's used by every NBA team and most colleges. And it all began because I felt restless on game day. When I saw that I could have an influence just by my actions, without saying a word, it increased my confidence in my leadership ability. It helped me in other areas, both in and out of sports. You have to have confidence in yourself to be a leader. And there are all kinds of ways to be a leader.

Those are insightful words from a man who is enshrined in the Basketball Hall of Fame as both a player and a coach. Bill Sharman demonstrated leadership, both on the court and on the sidelines. He proved that leadership is influence, and sometimes the most influential leadership of all needs no words.

I once spent a week in Brazil with my friend Vini Jacquery. He is the founder of International Reach, a ministry to the many abandoned street children of Brazil. Vini helped facilitate the adoption of our four Brazilian kids. I once asked him his thoughts on leadership, and he told me, "There are many styles of leadership."

The most common form of leadership, he said, is what he calls a *director*—the kind of leader who gives orders, demands action, holds people accountable, and so forth. But other forms of leadership are less obvious. For example, there is the *persuader*—the person who can challenge, convince, and motivate people through the power of words, either the spoken word or the written word. And there is the *unifier*, the kind of person who generally leads quietly, even self-effacingly, to draw people together, resolve conflicts and differences, and point people toward a common goal. And there is the *perfecter*, the kind of leader who refines and implements ideas; you often find the perfecter in a supportive role, such as an assistant coach, a midlevel manager, or an associate pastor. While the director might define the goals and strategy of the organization or team, the perfecter is the one who fine-tunes and implements that strategy in specific situations. Perfecters tend to be leaders within their own zone of specialization, and they work under the direction and authority of the director.

"All of these different styles," Vini told me, "reflect different personality types, different experience and preparation, different emphases, but they are all forms of leadership. Often, the most effective leaders are the ones who make the least noise and draw the least attention to themselves."

In August 2010, I spoke at a waste management convention near Greensboro, Georgia. My topic was leadership, and I mentioned how important it is to empower and encourage people. Afterward, a man came up to me and said, "My name is Kevin, and I used to live in Birmingham, Alabama, where I worked on the tail end of a garbage truck. One of the homes on our route belonged to Bart Starr, the great Packers quarterback. I'd see him some mornings and he'd always ask me how I was doing and give me a word of encouragement. He became like a second father to me. I never can thank that man enough. I took his motivational insights to heart and applied them to my career. Since then, I've been promoted to management and I've moved to Montgomery. But the impact of Bart Starr on my life will never leave me."

I could hear the emotion in Kevin's voice as he told me that story. Bart's influence had touched this man deeply. I've known Bart Starr for four and half decades, and I couldn't wait to relate that story to Bart himself. When I got back to Orlando, I called Bart and told him what Kevin had said. I expected Bart to say, oh, yes, he remembered Kevin, and all the chats they had, and how is ol' Kevin doing—but Bart didn't say any of that. In fact, I got the distinct impression that Bart simply didn't remember this guy at all. "Isn't it interesting," Bart said, "the impact we have other people even when we don't know it?"

Bart must have had a number of curbside conversations with Kevin years ago, and those conversations lit up Kevin's world. But from Bart's perspective, he was just chatting with the garbageman for a few moments. Then he'd go back inside and read the newspaper and forget all about it. He never had a clue what those chats meant to Kevin.

Mark Freeman was a baseball pitcher who played briefly for the Yankees in 1959. He once said of his teammate, Mickey Mantle, "I think he's basically one of the most decent guys I've ever met . . . He's learned to swap places with rookies, so he understands them, sympathizes with their aspirations. He has a way of making you feel he's really interested in what you're saying. Every day, Mickey would go by [Joe] DiMaggio's locker, just aching for some word of encouragement from this great man, this hero of his. But DiMaggio never said a word. It crushed Mickey. He told me he vowed right then that if he ever got to be a star, this would never be said of him."[5]

We never know what kind of influence we have on others. That's why we need to focus on leadership and influence. We are impacting others all the time. We need to make sure our impact is a positive one, and that we always influence others for good.

The Seven Sides of Leadership

Are leaders born or made? In other words, is leadership a natural gift, or is leadership a set of skills that can be learned? Answer: both! Almost everyone has some capacity for leadership in some arena of life or another. And a few of us are naturally gifted with leadership ability in abundance. But we can all improve the leadership traits we already possess while learning new leadership skills as we go along.

I have made a lifelong study of leadership. I have gone to the best leadership minds in the world for their insights. In the process, I have determined that leadership is a seven-dimensional experience, a seven-sided whole. There is nothing vague or mystical about this concept. It's a clear and practical concept that you can implement immediately. All seven of these dimensions of leadership are learnable skills:

1. Vision
2. Communication
3. People skills
4. Good character
5. Competence
6. Boldness
7. Servanthood

As you focus on all seven dimensions of leadership, you will be fully equipped to achieve your vision and take your organization to the extreme limits of success. Let's take a tour together through these seven sides of leadership.

1. Vision

A vision is a word picture that describes the future in terms that motivate people to work enthusiastically to transform that vision into reality. A vision is a grand, inspiring blueprint of the future. It's the leader's dream of tomorrow expressed in vivid and compelling words. Let me share with you several examples of visions that have been fulfilled in the past—or that are still being fulfilled today:

In 1909, Henry Ford expressed his vision for the future of the automobile—and the future of America: "I will build a motor car for the great multitude. It will be large enough for the family, but small enough for the individual to run and care for. It will be constructed of the best materials, by the best men to be hired, after the simplest designs that modern engineering can devise. But it will be so low in price that no man making a good salary will be unable to own one—and enjoy with his family the blessing of hours of pleasure in God's great open spaces."[6] The next time you pull your car out of the driveway and head for the open road, take a moment to remember Henry Ford and his vision that made it all possible.

In the mid-1950s, Walt Disney—who had already established himself as a maker of family-friendly movies and animated cartoons—described his vision of something that had never existed before. He called it Disneyland. He said,

> The idea of Disneyland is a simple one. It will be a place for people to find happiness and knowledge. It will be a place for parents and children to spend pleasant times in one another's company; a place for teachers and pupils to discover greater ways of understanding and education. Here the older generation can recapture the nostalgia of days gone by, and the younger generation can savor the challenge of the future. Here will be the wonders of Nature and Man for all to see and understand. Disneyland will be based upon and dedicated to the ideals, the dreams and hard facts that have created America . . . It will be filled with the accomplishments, the joys and hopes of the world we live in. And it will remind us and show us how to make those wonders part of our lives.[7]

And I can still recall the thrill and excitement of standing in that vast crowd on the Washington Mall, in front of the Lincoln Memorial on August 28, 1963—because I was there, I was actually there, on that historic day when Dr. Martin Luther King, Jr. expressed this hopeful vision for America: "I still have a dream. It is a dream deeply rooted in the American dream. I have a dream that one day this nation will rise up and live out the true meaning of its creed: 'We hold these truths to be self-evident: that all men are created equal.' . . . I have a dream that my four little children will one day live in a nation where they will not be judged by the color of their skin but by the content of their character . . . In the words of the old Negro spiritual, 'Free at last! Free at last! Thank God Almighty, we are free at last!'"[8]

Vision is the foundation of everything you do as a leader. Your vision is your dream, the grand destination you are working for and moving toward. All of your communication, people skills, character, competence, boldness, and servanthood are focused on transforming that dream, that vision, into reality. The retired president of Notre Dame University, Father Theodore Hesburgh, put it this way: "Vision is the essence of leadership. Knowing where you want to go requires three things: having a clear vision, articulating it well, and getting your team enthusiastic about sharing it. Above all, any leader must be consistent. As the Bible says, no one follows an uncertain trumpet."[9] To focus on leadership and influence, first focus on your vision of the future.

2. Communication Skills

It's not enough to have a vision. You must persuade and motivate the people on your team to help you build your dream. And that means you must *communicate*. You're not just a leader—you're a marketer of dreams! It's your job to persuade your followers to buy into *your* dream and adopt it as *their own* dream. You have to convince them that it is not just "my vision" but "our vision."

Great leaders radiate enthusiasm, encouragement, and an irrepressible confidence. Optimism is contagious.

The best leaders are great storytellers. Stories are powerful channels of emotion, and when you link a strong vision to strong emotions, you have a winning combination. People forget principles and charts and bullet points, but great stories stick in the mind forever.

Ernest Hemingway once had lunch with a circle of writer friends at a New York City restaurant. The table talk was about writing: is it possible to write a story that evokes real emotion in as little as a page or two? Most of the writers at the table claimed it couldn't be done. How could you tell a story, convey a character, and tug at your reader's emotions in just two or three hundred words? But "Papa" Hemingway stunned them all, saying, "I can tell a story that will break your heart in six words." Hemingway challenged them to a bet, which his colleagues accepted.

Everybody put a ten-dollar bill on the table, and Hemingway opened his wallet and matched the pot. Then he pulled out his fountain pen, wrote six words on a napkin, and showed it to his colleagues. The six words read: "For sale: Baby shoes. Never worn."

Hemingway won his bet. Words are powerful, my friend. Learn to use them effectively and persuasively as a leader.

The ability to communicate effectively and persuasively is a leadership skill we can learn, practice, and continually improve. Former Detroit Tigers executive Don Miers once told me how he learned at an early age that communication skills are indispensable to leadership:

> When I was in the eighth grade, I ran for student council treasurer. I was the class clown and I played all sports, so I was not your typical student council material. But I capped my campaign with a hilarious speech in the auditorium in front of the whole student body and faculty, and I won in a landslide.

I learned from that experience that even at the tender age of thirteen, I could get people to listen to me and see me as a leader if I exhibited confidence as a public speaker. And because I was now a leader in the student government, and in charge of student council funds, I had influence. Students started coming to me with questions, asking for advice, and sharing problems. I was amazed. It was a sobering responsibility. I realized that people looked up to me as a role model, and I needed to conduct myself in a proper manner. That was the beginning of my leadership journey.

Later, my high school soccer team voted me cocaptain. I realized that my teammates appreciated the way I conducted myself on the field, they respected me for the way I communicated my values and competitive spirit, and they saw me as a role model. After college I got into hotel management, and later moved into sports management with the Houston Astros and Detroit Tigers. I also got involved in local politics. And it all goes back to the speech I gave in middle school and the early lessons I learned in communication skills.

So practice your public speaking and writing skills. Learn to communicate effectively and persuasively. Communication skills are essential to leadership and influence. (For a more thorough discussion of public speaking skills, read *Turn Boring Orations into Standing Ovations* by Pat Williams and Ruth Williams with Mike Kocolowski).

3. People Skills

Industrialist and philanthropist John D. Rockefeller once said, "I will pay more for the ability to deal with people than any other ability under the sun."[10] It's true. People skills are an essential asset for anyone seeking to focus on leadership and influence.

Great leaders wield their authority lightly. They praise in public and criticize in private. They never shame their people or force them to choke down their pride. Leaders with people skills know how to boost morale and motivate peak performance.

A leader with strong people skills is visible and available to the members of the team or organization. Leaders should be close to the front lines—visiting the shop floor, the locker room, the lunchroom. They should be out walking around, asking questions, and building relationships. No one ever demonstrated leadership by holing up in an office behind closed doors. A leader who is isolated from the people is a leader in trouble.

I had the privilege of being mentored by the great baseball owner and innovator Bill Veeck—a man who had some of the best people skills I have ever witnessed. He owned and presided over some of the storied teams of professional baseball: the minor league Milwaukee Brewers, the Cleveland Indians, the St. Louis Browns, and the Chicago White Sox. As an owner, he mixed and mingled with the players and the public, he never had a door on his office, and he answered his own phone and his own mail. He was generous in donating his time and advice to a young minor-league baseball executive named Pat Williams, and his example left a deep imprint on my life. To this day, I try to run my own office as he ran his.

I once interviewed Dr. Hal Urban, author of *The 10 Commandments of Common Sense*, and asked him about the key role models in his early life that helped shape his leadership philosophy:

> **The key people in my development as a leader were my best teachers in high school, college, and graduate school.**

My favorite teachers all had certain traits in common, such as a total commitment to teaching and mentoring, an infectious enthusiasm for learning, an eagerness to help, and the ability to inspire and influence others. I was blessed with teachers who consistently modeled these leadership qualities. They had excellent people skills.

I also remember two coaches I had when I played basketball in college. One was an excellent role model in terms of people skills. He was supportive, encouraging, and never missed a chance to give positive feedback.

The other coach was a negative role model. He was always angry, he had a foul mouth, he humiliated his players, and he yelled and never gave positive feedback. I played much better for the first coach because he built my confidence. I played worse for the screaming coach, because his anger and belittling shook my confidence and made it hard for me to focus on my game. I learned that when you are a leader—whether as a parent, teacher, coach, or business executive—you have a responsibility to bring out the best in the people you lead. You do that by practicing good people skills.

Zig Ziglar once said something that I quote all the time: "Be a good finder." Always try to find the good in people. And Dale Carnegie put it this way: "Give the other person a good reputation to live up to." That's excellent advice for leadership. As leaders, we need to focus on catching people doing something right, then build on that. People thrive on positive feedback.

4. Character

I once asked Coach Wooden the secret to success in sports and in life. Without hesitating, he replied, "The secret, in a word, is *character*. Ability can get you to the top, but it takes character to keep you there." He added that leaders must be people of unimpeachable character themselves, and they must continually instill character in the people they lead. "I required my players and students to treat everybody with respect," he added, "whether it be the custodian or the president of the university. I told them I expected them to always be considerate of others, and I never permitted profanity."

On one occasion, as coach of the UCLA Bruins, John Wooden was in the process of recruiting one of the best high school players in the nation. When that player and his mother came on campus for a visit, Coach Wooden changed his mind and scratched this player off his list. Why? Because Coach saw this young man treat his mother with disrespect. He knew that any player who would behave disrespectfully to his mother would be a bad character risk on the team. In fact, a player with a disrespectful attitude might infect the entire team and ruin the team chemistry.

Some people confuse character with reputation. But a reputation is only what other people think of you. Your character is your inner reality, the real you, which many people keep hidden behind a false reputation. A minister may have a sterling reputation for good character—until he is caught in a love nest with the church organist. A student may have a great reputation as a person of character—until she is caught plagiarizing a term paper. A banker may be thought of as a pillar of the community, a man of unimpeachable character—until an audit exposes him as an embezzler. Your reputation is your external image, but character is your innermost reality.

If your character is hollow, your facade will eventually

crumble. When the whole world sees your ethical corruption or immorality, it will cost you dearly. It may cost you your marriage, your family, and your career. It will certainly destroy any chance of achieving your dreams. Don't let that happen to you. Guard your character at all costs.

As one of the greatest of all American leaders, George Washington once said, "I hope I shall always possess firmness and virtue enough, to maintain, what I consider the most enviable of all titles, the character of an 'Honest Man.'"[11] And another great American military leader, Gen. Matthew B. Ridgway, said this about the crucial importance of character to any leadership role:

> During a critical phase of the Battle of the Bulge, when I commanded the 18th Airborne Corps, another corps commander just entering the fight next to me remarked: "I'm glad to have you on my flank. It's character that counts." I had long known him, and I knew what he meant. I replied: "That goes for me too." There was no amplification. None was necessary. Each knew the other would stick however great the pressure; would extend help before it was asked, if he could; and would tell the truth, seek no self-glory, and everlastingly keep his word. Such trust breeds confidence and success.[12]

There are many important character traits we could focus on, but let's just look at three—integrity, humility, and diligence:

Integrity. The character quality of integrity is the state of being complete and unified. A person of integrity is one whose actions are consistent with his words. There is no duplicity or hypocrisy in his character. People of integrity do not compartmentalize and tell themselves, "I can still be a good person even if I cheat a little on my wife, or cheat a little on my taxes, or cheat a little in my business ethics." People of integrity do what is right even when no one else can see them. They have nothing to hide—and that's why they have nothing to fear.

My friend Gil Peterson has a great definition about integrity in leadership. He says that when leaders demonstrate integrity, "Their life supports what their lips purport."

Humility. The greatest leaders are always humble. One of the pitfalls of leadership is that a position of power and influence often leads to arrogance. We easily confuse leadership with importance, and we begin to think that we are "better people" than our "underlings." Such arrogance can destroy our leadership and authority—and it can lead to the destruction of our dreams.

I once heard a story about Don Keough, the former president of Coca-Cola, who—in spite of his position—was a humble and unassuming man. One day, he took part in the grand opening of a new McDonald's restaurant. He didn't just make an appearance and give a speech. He actually waited on customers. His job was to dispense Coca-Cola. After an hour or so of filling cups with ice and Coke, he asked the young lady in the McDonald's uniform next to him, "How am I doing?"

"Well, Mr. Keough," she said, "you're a very nice man, but you're kind of slow filling those cups."

Arrogance makes leaders look small. Humility is a key to leadership greatness.

Diligence (a strong work ethic). Great leaders set a good example of hard work—and a strong work ethic is infectious. I once spoke at a Martin Luther King Day luncheon in Orlando. One of the other speakers that day was an African American woman, Clara Walters, who worked for the Orange County School Board. She told a story about her life that has lodged in my memory ever since.

I grew up in DeLand, Florida, and during the summers I

was a cabbage cutter. They would put you out in the field on a cart between the cabbage rows with a machete in your hand. As you were pulled along on that cart, you'd lean out and whack the cabbage stems at ground level. Then other people would come along behind you and pick them up. I hadn't been working in that field too long before I learned a little secret. If I put a machete in each hand, I could lean out of the right side of the cart, then the left side, and I could whack two rows of cabbages in one pass. So when the day was over, I had cut twice as many cabbages as everybody else. It was piecework, so I earned more than everybody else.

Ever since then, I've been a cabbage cutter. So whenever they make budget cuts in the Orange County School system, I'm the last one to be cut. They can't afford to get rid of me, because it would take two people to replace me—because I am a cabbage cutter.

This world needs more cabbage cutters—more people who are so diligent, who have such a strong work ethic, that they're absolutely irreplaceable. We need leaders who set an example of cabbage cutting and followers who learn from that example and become hardworking cabbage cutters themselves.

Self-help author Dale Carnegie once placed an advertisement in the newspaper for an administrative assistant. Within days, he received several hundred replies. Most of the letters began with words like these: "I wish to apply for the position you offered . . ."

But one letter caught Carnegie's attention: "You will probably receive two or three hundred letters in reply to your ad," a woman wrote. "You haven't time to read all of them. If you will just reach for your telephone right now and call me at the number below,

I'll gladly come over, sort through the letters, and place on your desk the ones that are worth your attention. I have fifteen years' experience . . ." Dale Carnegie didn't need to read any further. He picked up the phone, called the woman, and told her he wanted to hire her on the spot.

"Oh, I'm sorry," she said, "but after I mailed that letter, I received another job offer and I accepted."[13] People with a strong work ethic rarely have trouble finding employment.

I once heard Gen. Schwarzkopf speak to a business audience in Orlando. In the course of his talk, he said these words, which I wrote down on the spot: "People choose their leaders based on character. I admire men of character. I judge character not by how men deal with their superiors, but by how they deal with their subordinates. That's how you find out what the character of a man is. Leaders have to lead by example."

5. Competence

To be a person of leadership and influence, you must inspire confidence in your team or organization. Your followers must trust you to be a competitive and competent leader. They must believe you have the skills, the savvy, the experience, and the fighting spirit to lead them into the winner's circle.

In the late 1990s, Ken Carter, the proprietor of a sporting goods store, accepted a part-time coaching position at nearby Richmond High School. Richmond is a poor, crime-ridden city across the bay from San Francisco. Coach Carter had been a star basketball player with the Richmond High Oilers in the 1970s, and he wanted to give something back to his old school.

Carter began by sitting his players down and having them sign an academic contract. Among other things, his players agreed to maintain a 2.3 GPA, study ten hours a week, maintain a perfect attendance record, and sit in the front row in all their classes. Every player signed, including Coach Carter's son, Damien.

The 1998–99 season got off to a great start. The team went undefeated in its first thirteen games. But Coach Carter wasn't happy. As the season progressed, he received troubling reports from teachers. About a third of his players were habitually late for class. A few weren't showing up at all. Many performed poorly on homework and tests. At first, Coach Carter thought he could bring his team in line by making them run laps and do push-ups. But their academic performance showed no improvement.

So Coach Carter took drastic action. When his players showed up for practice a few days before the big game against Fremont High, they found the gymnasium doors chained and padlocked. A handwritten sign on the door read, "No Practice Today— Report to the Library."

At the team meeting in the library, Coach Carter told his players that fifteen of them were not living up to their agreement. As a result, the *entire team* would be barred from competition until *every player* was in compliance. "I'm prepared to forfeit the rest of the season, if that's what it takes," he said—and he meant it.

It was a painful decision for Coach Carter. Those most hurt by the decision were the ones who were totally innocent. Carter's own son, Damien, was not only a star point guard but a model student with a 3.7 GPA. But Damien knew what his father was trying to accomplish. "Education comes first," Damien said. Then he added, speaking for the team, "We haven't been handling our business in the classroom."

Coach Carter's decision infuriated players and parents alike. Even school officials left angry messages on his answering machine. Someone egged his car. "I got calls at home, at school, at my job, and they were all negative," he told a reporter. "People wanted a state championship, and I know we sacrificed that. But my goal was to get these boys into college, where they could learn to become leaders and come back to this community as productive citizens."

When people saw that Coach Carter would not back down from his position, they began focusing on what the players needed to do. The academic achievers sat down with the struggling students and tutored them. The underachievers began changing their habits, showing up for class and improving their grades. After the Oilers had forfeited two games, Coach Carter agreed to let the team start practicing again in preparation for an important game against Oakland's St. Elizabeth High.

By this time, Coach Carter's actions had attracted statewide media attention. One of those who came to show support for Coach Carter was California governor Gray Davis. The governor and the coach sat together before the game and chatted. "Coach," Governor Davis asked, "could some of these young men play at a pro level one day?"

"Governor," Coach Carter replied, "now that they've seen you here, maybe one of them will even become governor. They might have great careers in politics or business. It's fine to be like Michael Jordan—but why shouldn't they be like the person who *pays* Michael Jordan?"

The Oilers defeated St. Elizabeth High that day, 61–51, and went on to finish the season with a strong 19–5 record. The team lost in the second round of the district play-offs. Even after the season was over, some parents and school officials continued to criticize Coach Carter's methods, saying it was unfair to punish the whole team for the sins of a few. But the critics didn't understand the true nature of teamwork.

Coach Carter said, "We rise as a team, and we fall as a team." Not every player makes baskets, yet all share in the thrill of victory. If a few players break their contract, then all must share in the pain. From a teamwork point of view, the lockout was totally fair—and it achieved the results Coach Carter was after. He wasn't focused primarily on winning basketball games. He was teaching his players life skills so that they would be competent to lead successful lives.

Every senior on Coach Carter's team that year went on to either junior college or a four-year college. One of his players had come to Richmond High with an academic record of straight Fs, because he lost his motivation after his older brother was killed in a street shooting. "I was on a bad path," this young man said—but Coach Carter turned him around. He went to junior college, then attended university on a basketball scholarship.

Coach Carter taught his team competence, not just on the basketball court, but in life. He taught them to be not just players, but leaders. He showed them how to lift their eyes beyond basketball and see a wide horizon of opportunities awaiting them. He taught them the importance of competence.

What is competence? I would suggest that competence is the sum of five ingredients: 1. Knowledge: a competent leader is well educated and well read, and committed to lifelong learning. 2. Experience: a competent leader has gained the kind of firsthand knowledge that only comes from practical experience. 3. Confidence: a competent leader is self-assured and optimistic, even under pressure. 4. Commitment to excellence: a competent leader always wants to be the best and never tolerates a second-rate effort. 5. Competitiveness: a competent leader always wants to win.

These five qualities make up the character trait called competence, and competent leaders inspire trust. When your people have confidence in your competence, they will follow you anywhere—and they will enable you to achieve your leadership dreams.

6. Boldness

"Boldness" is another way of saying "courage and confidence." It's a willingness to take prudent, calculated risks in order to achieve big goals and dreams. You might also call it a "pioneering spirit," or a "spirit of adventure." It is the courage to blaze new trails, to take a lonely stand in the face of criticism or ridicule, or to risk one's self and one's possessions in order to do what is morally and ethically right.

We already devoted an entire chapter to boldness (see Chapter 7), so I won't dwell on it here—except to say that there is no success without boldness. Only those who are willing to act courageously will see their dreams come true. Boldness is an essential character trait of those who achieve success by focusing on leadership and influence.

7. Servanthood

The seventh and final side of leadership is servanthood. Those who think that leadership is about being a boss have missed the point of leadership. In reality, genuine leadership is all about serving others, not about being served. As James M. Strock wrote in *Theodore Roosevelt on Leadership*, "A leader should aim to build a life based on service, not a career based on advancing up a series of positions."[14]

In a real sense, the theme of service is woven throughout all seven sides of leadership. If leadership was simply about being "the boss," you wouldn't need the first six sides of leadership. As a "boss," you wouldn't need to communicate your grand vision in a persuasive way. You could simply bark orders and make people do your bidding. As a "boss," you wouldn't need people skills, because you wouldn't need to care how people feel or what motivates them. You wouldn't need good character; you could simply exploit your workers and dispose of them when they are no longer useful to you. As a "boss," competence wouldn't matter because you wouldn't need to set an example or inspire anyone. A "boss" exists to be served.

But a leader needs all seven sides of leadership precisely because a leader is not a "boss." A leader is a servant. If you don't grasp the concept of servitude, then you don't grasp leadership, period. A well-led team or organization is not just a collection of individuals. When a genuine servant-leader practices these seven sides of leadership, odds are that the team or organization will become a true *community*, even a *fellowship*. Through the example you set, the environment you create, and the character traits you display, you will generate an atmosphere in which everyone pulls together to fulfill your vision, your dream. Your followers will be motivated and inspired to pull together and work together to win.

John Kotter, a professor at Harvard Business School, formulated what I think is the most succinct definition of leadership I've ever heard: "Leadership is mobilizing people to make great and challenging things happen."[15] It all starts with you. It starts with the way you treat your people and the way you inspire them to treat the public and each other. It starts with the attitude you display every morning when you come to work. It starts with the character you display in a crisis. It starts with your dedication to winning and your passion for excellence.

When *Harvard Business Review* asked Starbucks CEO Howard Schultz about the legacy he would leave as a leader, he replied, "Our role as leaders is to celebrate the human connection that we have been able to create as a company, and to make sure people realize the deep level of respect we have for the work they do and how they act. That is the legacy of the company. It's not to get bigger or to make more money."[16]

In other words, Schultz defined his leadership legacy in terms of servanthood. Then he told a story to illustrate the point. "A woman barista in Tacoma, Washington, sees a customer every day," he said, "and they become friendly as a result of her work. She begins to see that the woman looks ill. Finally she gets up the courage to say, 'You just don't look well—what's wrong?' The woman says, 'If I don't get a kidney transplant, I am going to die.' A miracle occurs: The barista is a match for the customer, and she gives her a kidney. It's incredible. I drove to Tacoma to see her, and I said, 'Who are you? I've never heard a story like this.' There are a lot of really great companies out there, and wonderful cultures, but something like this doesn't happen very often."[17]

Howard Schultz is right. It doesn't happen very often. But these kinds of random acts of servanthood are most likely to occur whenever the people at the top focus on true leadership and influence. These stories happen when leaders dream big dreams and practice true seven-sided leadership.

There's power in poetry. I think of my friend Swen Nater as the poet laureate of America. I recently asked him to summarize in verse my teaching on the seven sides of leadership, and he graciously penned these memorable lines:

Seven things one must do
To be a leader right and true:
Have a vision, strong and clear;
Communicate so they will hear;
Have people skills based in love;
And character that's far above;
The competence to solve and teach;
Boldness that has fearless reach;
A serving heart that stands close by
To help, assist, and edify.

These are the seven keys to effectiveness as a leader. Make them the seven keys to your leadership success.

10

Focus
and
Finish
Strong

When I came to Florida in 1986 to help build the
Orlando Magic from the ground up, one of the
earliest supporters of our efforts was Jacob Stuart, then executive vice president of the Orlando
Regional Chamber of Commerce. Jacob is a physically imposing
man with a dynamic, upbeat personality. He came alongside our
efforts early on and was a wonderful coach and door-opener for
me. We couldn't have built this dream without him.

In September 1986, I led a delegation from Orlando to the
NBA owners' meeting in Phoenix. Accompanying me were two
key investors, the Hewitt brothers, Jimmy and Bobby, accountant
Stewart Crane, and Jacob Stuart. Six cities were vying for potential

expansion franchises. Each city would get a chance to make a thirty-minute oral presentation to all of the NBA owners as to why it should get the nod. I have never been more focused in my life. I felt the future of central Florida weighing on my shoulders. The other members of the delegation were there for moral support, but I would do the talking. Thousands of jobs, millions of dollars, worldwide publicity, and the future of the region were riding on what I would say during that brief pitch.

I didn't sleep the night before the presentation. I was keyed up all night long. I was still keyed up as the delegation was ushered into the room to face the panel of NBA owners. We handed out our white three-ring binders printed with the words "Orlando Believes in Magic!" The binders contained our marketing data, financial projections, architectural renderings of the arena, newspaper clippings, and more.

But I knew it was passion and persuasion, not charts and graphs, that would determine our fate. This was the moment—and I seized it. I launched into my pitch, speaking with every ounce of energy and enthusiasm in my being. I told stories about the people in our community and how all of central Florida was in an absolute tizzy over NBA basketball. I told them how the people of Orlando were so eager to see the Magic become a reality that they had already purchased 14,046 season ticket reservations—even though there was as yet no franchise, no arena, and no team!

As I spoke, I was "in the zone." I delivered that presentation at the absolute maximum of my abilities. When I had finished, I felt great—wrung out, but great. I did it! It was over! And from the expressions around the room, I was sure it had gone over well. (One of the owners was my friend Norm Sonju of the Dallas Mavericks; he later told me that the owners were impressed that I did the entire talk without notes—but I was so passionate about this dream that I could have delivered that pitch in my sleep!)

After my thirty-minute pitch, our delegation headed for a session with the media. Each of the groups representing the six prospective cities had to face questioning from national sportswriters. As I walked into the media room, Jacob Stuart ran up to me, seized me by the shoulders, and with his nose practically touching mine, he barked, "Stay up! Stay up! You can't let down, Pat! Stay up!"

Perhaps Jacob could see in my posture that I had started to slump inside. I had been so focused on my presentation to the owners that I was just relieved to have it over and done. But Jacob knew that the media session was every bit as important as the session with the owners. He knew I needed to maintain my extreme focus. So he literally grabbed me by the shoulders, got right in my face, and poured the energy of his personality into my weary, sleep-deprived brain: "Stay up! Stay up!"

Instantly, I sprang back to life. I was revitalized. And as I stepped up onto the platform to face those reporters, I felt the energy come back into my footsteps, my limbs, my posture, my facial expression, and my voice. And throughout that session, I kept hearing those words in my mind—*Stay up! Stay up!* And the media session went just as well as the pitch to the owners— thanks to the *extreme focus* of Jacob Stuart.

The city of Orlando received very favorable press coverage, and in April 1987, when the owners made their decision, Orlando got a thumbs-up! Our dream had come true!

The moral of this story is simple: *focus—and finish strong!*

As you reach for your dreams, don't let your guard down. Don't let your passion run hot and cold. Never stop focusing on today, never stop focusing on tomorrow. Maintain your self-discipline. Hold fast to your commitment. Be courageous and confident. Stay up! Finish strong!

That's what Jacob Stuart was saying to me, and it was good advice. In fact, his words may have spelled the difference between success and disaster. What if I had gone out on that platform to face the press feeling spent and depleted? What if I had lost my focus at the very moment the national media turned its spotlight on me? We could have lost everything we had worked for in that moment.

But Jacob Stuart saved the day. He had just the right words to bring me back into focus. To this day, whenever I'm tempted to let down my guard, I can hear Jacob Stuart say, "Stay up! Stay up!"

Press On and Finish the Race!

Randy Pausch was a father of three and a much-respected professor of computer science at Carnegie Mellon University. At age forty-seven, he was diagnosed with pancreatic cancer. Once he adjusted to the reality that he had six months to live, he set a goal of creating memories for his three young children, so they would always know their father. He also committed himself to a goal that became known as the "Last Lecture," an answer to the difficult question, "What message would you leave to the world if you knew you were about to die?"

On September 18, 2007, he delivered a lecture that the university recorded and posted to YouTube.com. The lecture quickly went viral and more than ten million people viewed it. ABC news anchor Diane Sawyer conducted a series of interviews with Randy Pausch, in which he was thought-provoking, funny, and inspiring. His lecture and the Sawyer interviews also brought attention to pancreatic cancer, the fourth-leading cause of cancer death in America and one of the few forms of cancer that has seen very little progress in treatment, prognosis, and cure.

In his "Last Lecture," Randy Pausch talked about the hard work that's required in order to achieve our dreams. He spoke of what it takes to overcome seemingly insurmountable obstacles, which he spoke of as "brick walls" of opposition. "The brick walls are there for a reason," he said in his "Last Lecture." He added, "The brick walls are not there to keep us out; the brick walls are there to give us a chance to show how badly we want something. The brick walls are there to stop the people who don't want it badly enough. They are there to stop the *other* people!"[1]

Let me underscore that. Let me put it up in neon lights: the brick walls in your life are *not* meant to keep you out. They are there to stop *other* people—not you. So don't let anything keep you from your dreams. Stay up! Keep going! Finish strong!

When Randy Pausch died on July 25, 2008, his book, *The Last Lecture* (cowritten with Jeffrey Zaslow), topped the *New York Times* bestseller list. Randy Pausch stayed focused and finished strong. After his heart stopped beating, his unconquerable spirit continued to inspire millions.

I'll never forget one profound moment I experienced during a running of the Boston Marathon more than a decade ago. As I reached the seventeen-mile mark, I knew there were nine punishing miles left to go. At that point, my motivation failed me. I was totally spent, and I knew I could never make it to the finish line. I was right on the cusp of giving up.

Then, out of the corner of my eye, I glimpsed a woman on the sidewalk holding a sign. Every runner passing that point could see her sign, because she had printed across it in bold, black capital letters, this one word: *FOCUS!*

That was what I needed! That one word breathed new life into my running shoes. I heard these words in my mind: *Stay up! Keep going! Finish strong!* I picked up my stride and I focused on the road immediately in front of me. I pressed on. I finished the race.

How do you maintain your focus on your dreams and goals over the long haul, day after day after day? David E. Rye, in his book *1,001 Ways to Inspire Your Organization, Your Team, and Yourself,* suggests three exercises for keeping yourself motivated and focused on your goals in just minutes a day. Each exercise is only two minutes long, but packs a big motivational wallop:

> *Idea: The Two-Minute Morning Motivational Exercise:* Spend two minutes every morning reviewing your routine goals and what you'll do that day to help meet those goals. Routine goals are a continuation of what you are already doing or are expected to do; they are typically work-related, but they can also be personal.

> *Idea: The Two-Minute Midday Motivational Exercise:* Spend two minutes every afternoon reviewing your problem-solving goals and what you will do that day to help meet those goals. What problems have been solved so far today? What new problems do you want to add to your list?

> *Idea: The Two-Minute Evening Motivational Exercise:* Spend two minutes every evening reviewing personal goals and what you've done today to help meet tomorrow's goals. Also review all of the goals you have accomplished during the course of the day and congratulate yourself.[2]

So take a few minutes to remind yourself of your goals every day—and to check on your progress toward your goals. The six minutes you spend each day focusing on your goals and renewing your motivation could be the six most powerful minutes of your day. Keep your eye on your dreams!

Stay up! Keep going! Finish strong!

Don't Let Success Ruin You

Comedian Conan O'Brien had a successful run as host of *Late Night with Conan O'Brien* from 1993 to 2009, before taking a tumultuous and short-lived stint hosting TV's late-night classic, *The Tonight Show*. At the desk once held by Steve Allen, Jack Paar, Johnny Carson, and Jay Leno, Conan O'Brien departed after a brief seven-month run. In his parting monologue in January 2010, O'Brien thanked his fans for supporting him and offered a word of wise advice.

"To all the people watching," he said, "I can never thank you enough for your kindness to me, and I'll think about it for the rest of my life. All I ask of you is one thing: please don't be cynical. I hate cynicism—it's my least favorite quality, and it doesn't lead anywhere. Nobody in life gets exactly what they thought they were going to get. But if you work really hard and you're kind, amazing things will happen."[3]

It's true. Nobody gets exactly what they thought they were going to get—not even the most successful among us. In my own case, my boyhood dream was to become one of the great catchers in Major League Baseball and to end up enshrined in the Baseball Hall of Fame. I never realized that dream, and I never will. My life took a different direction. I worked hard—and just as Conan O'Brien said, amazing things have happened in my life. Fact is, I've had the most amazing and exciting life anyone could imagine!

Here's the point: don't let success ruin you. As Conan O'Brien said, if you work really hard *and you're kind*, amazing things will happen. Pursue your dreams—but be kind. Many people become rich and famous by trampling other people on their way to the top. That's not success. What good are wealth and fame if you had to cheat or backstab people to achieve it? What good will it do to gain the whole world but lose your soul?

Be focused and finish strong—but keep your balance. Don't let success change you. Don't lose your marriage, your family, your friends, your reputation, or your self-respect on your way to your dreams.

Coach Mike Krzyzewski is the men's college basketball coach at Duke University. Over a thirty-season career, he has coached the Duke Blue Devils to four NCAA championships, eleven Final Fours, twelve Atlantic Coast Conference (ACC) regular season titles, and twelve ACC championships. I have always admired Coach K because he seems to have found that elusive balance between finishing strong as a coach versus finishing strong as a husband and father. Mike Krzyzewski and his wife Carol "Mickie" Krzyzewski have three married daughters and five grandchildren. Mike and Mickie celebrated their thirty-fifth wedding anniversary in June 2004 by renewing their wedding vows in the Duke Chapel.

In his book *Leading with the Heart*, Coach K explains how he maintains a balance between success as a basketball coach and success as a family man. He writes:

> I constantly ask myself the question: "What's your job, knucklehead?"
>
> Answer: "I'm the Duke basketball coach. My job is to be the leader of my basketball program. My job is to be the husband and father of my family. Do your job, Mike. Do your job."
>
> A person has to take care of his core. And my core revolves around my family and coaching basketball. It always has . . . [I'm] doing right now what I wanted to do when I was nine years old. I'm a lucky guy. I'm living my dream. And in my case, reality is better than the dream itself.
>
> Today, I try to keep a balance with all the people and

things I love in my life. There are many games to be played and, hopefully, they're not just basketball games. There are dances to be danced, pianos to be played, and cheers to be cheered. I want to play those games, too. I don't want to be one-dimensional and have my whole life revolve around a series of screens and picks to produce a basket.[4]

Balance! Coach K knows—there is no genuine success without balance. In order to maintain your focus and finish strong in the things that matter most, you must keep your balance. Success in life is only meaningful if you can share it with the ones you love. If you lose your family on your climb to your dreams, who will be with you to celebrate your success?

Gail Goodrich played for Coach Wooden when the UCLA Bruins won their first two national championships in 1964 and 1965. He went on to a successful career with the Los Angeles Lakers. He recalled that one of the recurring themes of Coach Wooden's teaching and coaching was *balance*.

Coach Wooden, he said, "always talked about balance: body balance, scoring balance, team balance, and most of all, mental and emotional balance. Your feet have to be balanced. Your body has to be in balance over your feet. Your head needs to be in balance with your body and your arms. He said if you're not in balance, you'll eventually fall over, and he meant it in more ways than one . . . I came to see balance as one of the keys to success not only in basketball, but in life. . . . Everything needs balance."[5]

Gen. Colin Powell is a retired four-star general who has held several of the most powerful and prestigious jobs in government. In his illustrious career, Gen. Powell has served as national security advisor (1987–89), commander of the U.S. Army Forces (1989), chairman of the Joint Chiefs of Staff (1989–93), and secretary of state (2001–5). In an interview with *Success* magazine, Gen. Powell spoke of the importance of keeping your balance in life, no matter how great your responsibilities or your level of success.

"I have a family," he said, "that understands the army had to come first, but that my family wasn't last. I had to go to Vietnam and Korea. I was blessed with a wife and family that understand." Because of overseas deployments, Powell had to miss a lot of events in the lives of his children—but he made sure he never missed a holiday celebration or school performance when he was home on leave. During the times he couldn't be there, he said, "My wife supplied most of the balance."

As a leader, Powell impressed the concept of balance on his subordinates. After he became secretary of state, he gave a speech in which he said, "I am sixty-three going on sixty-four. I don't have to prove to anybody that I can work sixteen hours a day if I can get it done in eight. If I'm looking for you at 7:30 at night, eight at night, and you are not in your office, I will consider you to be a very, very wise person. If I need you, I will find you at home. Anybody who is logging hours to impress me, you are wasting your time."[6]

Bobb Biehl agrees. Biehl is the founder of Masterplanning Group International and an executive mentor. He once said, "Life is a constant struggle for balance. Balance is a result of one word: schedule. Typically, you determine your own schedule. Therefore, you schedule your own balance or imbalance."[7]

Monica Wofford, leadership speaker and author of the book *Contagious Leadership*, puts it this way: "Balance can be described in one sentence, as those who've worked with me can attest: 'If you don't have a life, get one.'"[8]

The Ten Keys to Your Dreams

In the closing pages of this book, let me review a few key insights of *Extreme Focus*. If you will live by these principles day by day and week by week, if you will turn these principles into habits, and those habits into a way of life, you *will* reach your dreams. In fact, if you follow these principles, I don't see how anything could ever stop you.

These are the same principles by which I lived my life as I was pursuing the dream of an NBA championship in Philadelphia and the dream of an NBA expansion team in Orlando. Every success habit I've recommended to you in these pages has served me well in my own life. These principles have been proven again and again in the lives of hundreds of successful people I've known. So let's look at these success principles once again. Let's put these principles together and see how they make it possible for us to live a lifestyle of *extreme focus*.

Key No. 1: *Extreme Focus* Is the Key to Achieving Your Dreams

Get started—just do it! Then stay focused until you finish. Learn to say no to distractions and time-wasters, so you can focus on what is most important in life.

The ability to focus with intensity is a key to success in every field, from athletics, to business, to the arts, to the sciences, and to mathematics. *Extreme focus* is not merely the ability to think the right thoughts, but also the ability to screen out the *wrong* thoughts—the distractions, doubts, and fears that interfere with our best performance. To those who are truly focused, time disappears. Distractions fade away. People of *extreme focus* see nothing but the goal—and that is why they succeed.

Key No. 2: Focus on Your Passion in Life

Passion is an intense and compelling emotional drive. It is the energy that powers us as we reach for our dreams. Nothing great was ever accomplished without passion.

Focus on the one thing in life that you are truly passionate about—then pursue it with all your might. Be a doer, not a dabbler. Remember the phrase, "This *one* thing I do!" Focus on *your* dreams, *your* goals, *your* passion—not on pleasing other people.

Key No. 3: Focus on Tomorrow

Goals are dreams with deadlines—so set deadlines for your goals and keep faith with your dreams. Don't put your dreams on hold—take time *today* to brainstorm and visualize a brighter tomorrow. Write down your short-range, medium-range, and long-range goals. Post your goals where you can see them and be inspired by them every day. Review and recalibrate your goals on a regular basis. Focus on tomorrow by preparing today.

Key No. 4: Focus on Today

This day belongs to you. Seize it. Own it. Use it well. Ask yourself, "What am I trading for this twenty-four-hour period called 'today'?" Practice effective time-management techniques. Cut big tasks down to small steps. Group related actions together for maximum efficiency. Prioritize your goals. Meet your deadlines. Use the power of the Grab 15 Principle to magically add more time to your life.

Get "in the zone." Prepare yourself mentally so that you can overcome self-doubt, self-limiting assumptions, laziness, fear, and lack of focus. Meditate on positive beliefs. Spend time around positive thinkers, and feed your mind on positive thoughts. Relax. Stay in the moment—and stay "in the zone."

Key No. 5: Focus on Self-Discipline

Good habits and hard work are the stuff dreams are made of. Self-discipline isn't a shoe you put on and take off. It's a lifestyle. Commit yourself to lifelong, year-round self-discipline. Be disciplined in the small things, and the big things will take care of themselves. Strive for quality; "good enough" is never good enough. Maintain a disciplined work ethic. Everyone dreams—but those who are disciplined make their dreams come true.

Key No. 6: Focus on Things You Can Control—and Let Go of Everything Else

You can't choose your level of talent, but you can control your effort. You can't control the weather, but you can control your attitude. Don't be a control freak. Instead of obsessing over the things you can't control, meditate on the Serenity Prayer.

Do what you can to guard your health—but accept the fact that we all get sick from time to time. You can't control the questions, but you can control the answers. You can't control the advance of time, but you can control your schedule. You can't control the marketplace or the regulatory environment, but you can control the performance of your organization. You can't control your feelings, but you can manage how you respond to your feelings. If you control what you can control and let go of the rest, you are well on your way to achieving your dreams.

Key No.7: Focus on Your Courage and Confidence

Fortune favors the bold, so take calculated risks. Focus on your courage, not your fears. Do the thing you fear, and the death of fear is certain. Don't fear ridicule or criticism or what other people may think; just do what you know is right. Keep advancing toward your dreams, no matter what others say. Don't be a spectator—*live the adventure!*

Give yourself permission to fail. Be prepared; preparation builds confidence! Be boldly, courageously decisive—a bad decision is better than no decision at all. When you crash, "get right back in the cockpit of the bird that bit ya." Don't try to be someone you're not—be boldly who you are. Be courageous in doing good works.

Key No. 8: Focus on Commitment

When you commit yourself to a goal, you empower yourself to prevail over obstacles and opposition. Be mentally tough! Commit yourself to a fighting spirit—never give up the fight! Commit yourself to continuous growth and learning. Commit yourself to good character. Allow others to hold you accountable for keeping your commitments. Never give up, never give in—because the next few seconds, the next ounce of energy you expend, may make the difference in achieving your dreams.

Key No. 9: Focus on Leadership and Influence

If you dream of success on a grand scale, then *think teamwork*. The bigger the dream, the more we need teams to make our dreams come true. You can't have teamwork without leadership, so be a leader!

The seven sides of leadership are: vision, communication skills, people skills, character, competence, boldness, and servanthood. As you focus on all seven dimensions of leadership and build these traits into your life, you will be fully equipped to lead your team to the extreme limits of success.

Key No. 10: Focus—and Finish Strong!

Brick walls are there to stop other people—not you. They are there to stop those who don't want success badly enough. I know you want it. So stay up, stay focused, keep going, finish strong! Even while you work hard to achieve success, be kind to others.

Above all, keep your balance. Don't become so obsessed with your dreams of success that you lose your spouse, your children, your reputation, or your self-respect. To maintain your balance, control your schedule.

These are the principles of *Extreme Focus*. These are the keys to your dreams.

Turning a Nightmare into a Dream Come True

On the evening of December 15, 1997, a Philadelphia woman, Luz Cuevas, was enjoying a quiet evening at home in the two-story row house she shared with her common-law husband, Pedro Vera, and her children. Luz had just put her ten-day-old baby girl, Delimar, to bed in the upstairs bedroom when she heard a knock at the door. Luz answered the door and found a woman on her doorstep who introduced herself as Carolyn Correa, a distant stepcousin of Pedro's.

"I heard you just had a baby girl," Carolyn Correa said. "I just had a baby myself, so we have something in common. I thought it would be good for us to know each other." With that, Correa produced a small gift for the baby.

So Luz sat down and talked for a while with the woman. Then, hearing a noise from upstairs, Luz left the woman and went upstairs to check on the baby. At the door of the bedroom, she smelled smoke. She flung the door open and found the room in flames. She screamed and dashed to the crib—but the crib was empty. The baby was gone! She looked up and saw that the window was open, and cold air blew in from outside.

Panic-stricken, Luz ran downstairs calling for Pedro and her two sons, ages four and five. She shouted in Spanish, "My baby's not in the room! My baby is gone!" In her panic, Luz wondered if she had been mistaken. Her baby *had* to be in the crib—and the crib was surrounded by flames! She tried to run back up the stairs, but strong hands grasped her and pulled her out the front door, into the cold December air.

Soon the fire trucks arrived, and the firefighters entered the house. Luz, Pedro, and their two sons were out on the sidewalk— and so was the woman, Carolyn Correa. Above them, the open window to Delimar's bedroom spewed billows of flame. Several times Luz broke free from her husband's grasp and tried to run back into the house to save her baby, but the firefighters held her back.

Luz screamed. She wept. The grief-stricken mother was inconsolable. Where was her baby? What had happened to her baby?

Less than fourteen minutes after the firefighters arrived, they had the flames extinguished. The fire was confined to the one room, which was charred and filled with rubble. Two firefighters found a blackened, misshapen mass among the smoldering ruins of the crib, and they decided that it must be the remains of the baby. They wrapped it in a blanket and took it away before the mother could see it.

When Luz Cuevas tried to tell the police and fire officials that her baby was gone, they shook their heads and chalked up her story to hysteria. She insisted that someone had stolen her baby and had taken her out through the open window. Whoever took the baby must have set the fire to conceal the evidence of a kidnapping. But fire investigators concluded that the blaze was started by a space heater plugged into a faulty extension cord.

When the coroner's office examined the "body" the firefighters had brought back from the gutted bedroom, it turned out to be nothing more than a mass of melted mattress filler. The inspectors combed through several hundred pounds of rubble, but they found no body, no bones, no teeth, nothing. They decided that the fire had consumed the baby's body. Yet, because no human remains were found, the coroner could not issue a death certificate.

Luz Cuevas was convinced that her daughter was not dead, but *kidnapped*. She could not prove it, however, and she could not get the police to listen to her suspicions. And what about Carolyn Correa? It didn't seem possible that she had anything to do with the baby's disappearance. After all, Correa had been standing on the sidewalk with Luz and her family, trying to comfort them.

Luz suspected that Correa had something to do with the disappearance of her daughter—but she couldn't explain her suspicions. And she had no evidence. No one would listen to her. Even her husband, Pedro, said she was just being hysterical. When Pedro suggested they hold a funeral for the baby, Luz angrily refused. There would be no funeral. Her baby was not dead.

Time passed. A year, then two years, then three. Wherever Luz went—to the grocery store, the mall, or around the neighborhood—she looked at the faces of the little girls she passed. Was one of them Delimar? Finding her lost daughter became Luz's passion, her obsession, her *extreme focus*—even though she didn't have a scrap of evidence to base her suspicions on.

In January 2004, when Delimar would have been just over six years old, Luz attended a birthday party for the child of a friend. As chance would have it, Carolyn Correa was also there along with her child—a six-year-old girl named Aliyah. When Luz

Cuevas saw the dark-haired Aliyah, she couldn't stop staring. Aliyah had exactly the same dark brown hair, dark brown eyes, and dimpled chin that her two boys had. In fact, Luz had looked much like Aliyah when she was six.

Luz was certain: Aliyah was Delimar. But how could she prove it? Luz recalled a trick she had seen on a TV detective show—so she decided to try it herself. She sidled up close to the girl, pretended to find chewing gum in Aliyah's hair, then combed her fingers through the girl's hair, coming away with a few strands. She placed the hair sample in a napkin and hid it in her purse.

She wanted to hug Aliyah and take her away—but she knew she had to be patient. So she left the party, went home, and placed the hair sample in a plastic bag, which she hid in a safe place. Luz didn't know much about DNA testing, but she knew that a sample of hair could prove a person's identity.

Luz contacted the office of congressman Angel Cruz, who represented her district. He was a busy man, and Luz had a hard time getting through to him. But she was persistent and passionate, and she refused to let anything stand in her way. When she finally was able to sit down in his office and explain her suspicions to him, Congressman Cruz was frankly skeptical. Her claim was utterly bizarre, and she had no evidence.

But Luz insisted that she *did* have evidence. She had a sample of hair.

Congressman Cruz contacted the police and had them look into the background of Carolyn Correa. The police found that Correa had pled guilty to arson for a fire she had set in 1996. Carolyn Correa had stolen checks from a medical office where she worked, then had set the fire to destroy evidence and conceal the theft. She had struck a plea deal—five years probation plus community service.

Suddenly, Luz Cuevas's suspicions no longer seemed far-fetched. The police asked for the hair sample and conducted DNA tests. The hair sample proved that "Aliyah" was in fact Luz Cuevas's long-lost daughter Delimar.

The police took Carolyn Correa into custody, and six-year-old Delimar finally came home to her mother and to her family. With the help of counselors from family services, Delimar continues to adjust to her new family and her real mother.

Carolyn Correa pled no contest to charges that included kidnapping, arson, interfering with the custody of a child, burglary, criminal trespass, and conspiracy, and she was sentenced to a term of nine to thirty years in prison. Police say she had to have help in order to steal the baby—but no one has ever been charged as an accomplice. Luz Cuevas says she dreads the day when her daughter's kidnapper comes up for parole, but she will deal with that when the time comes. For now, all that matters is that her daughter is alive—and she is home.

Luz Cuevas had a dream of being reunited with her little girl. She was totally focused on that dream, even though no one would believe her, not even her baby's father. She was focused on her passion for her little girl. She was focused on tomorrow, focused on today, focused on controlling what she could control, focused on her courage to stand alone, even when everyone thought she was delusional and hysterical. She was focused on her commitment. She refused to give up the fight.

Mother and daughter were reunited for one reason only: the *extreme focus* of Luz Cuevas. The police had given up. Luz's own husband had given up. Only a mother's love and unquenchable commitment could turn this nightmare into a dream come true.[9]

What is your dream? What is the passion that drives you and motivates you and won't let you go? Take a lesson from Luz Cuevas. Believe in your dream. Don't let anyone take it from you.

Follow it with an intense passion. Pursue it with relentless focus. Never give up. Never let go. Never stop fighting for the things that truly matter.

Dreams really do come true—through the power of *extreme focus*.

ACKNOWLEDGMENTS

With deep appreciation I acknowledge the support and guidance of the following people who helped make this book possible: Special thanks to Bob Vander Weide, Rich DeVos, and Alex Martins of the Orlando Magic.

Hats off to my associate Andrew Herdliska; my proofreader, Ken Hussar; and my ace typist, Fran Thomas.

Thanks also to my writing partner, Jim Denney, for his superb contributions in shaping this manuscript.

Hearty thanks also go to my friends at Health Communications, Inc., and especially to publisher Peter Vegso, who believed in the message of this book, and to my skilled and insightful editor, Allison Janse. My thanks to the entire HCI team for their vision, professionalism, and skill in helping me to shape this message for publication.

And, finally, special thanks and appreciation go to my wife, Ruth, and to my wonderful and supportive family. They are truly the backbone of my life.

NOTES

Introduction: Focus! Focus! Focus!

1. Jerry Braza, *Moment by Moment: The Art and Practice of Mindfulness* (Boston: Tuttle, 1997), 66.

1. Turning Dreams into Reality

1. Harvey Araton, "News Analysis: A Chance to Re-Examine Hank Aaron," *New York Times*, August 5, 2010, http://www.nytimes.com/2010/08/06/sports/baseball/06aaron.html.

2. John Cook and Leslie Ann Gibson, *The Book of Positive Quotations* (Minneapolis, MN: Fairview Press, 2007), 606.

3. Ruth Stevens, "Wiles Selected to Receive Shaw Prize," News at Princeton, June 3, 2005, http://www.princeton.edu/main/news/archive/S11/78/32K43/index.xml.

4. David G. Myers, *Psychology* (New York: Macmillan, 2003), 428–29.

5. Nancy Gondo, "Benoit Ran Ahead of Her Time," AlphaImports.com, September 26, 2006, http://www.alphaimports.com/benoit-ran-ahead-of-her-time-a-123.html.

6. Donald Honig, *The Fifth Season* (Chicago: Ivan R. Dee, 2009), 206–7.

7. Kendall Gammon, *Life's a Snap* (Overland Park, KS: It's a Snap, 2008), 79.

8. Kara Leverte Farley and Sheila M. Curry, *Get Motivated! Daily Psych-Ups* (New York: Simon & Schuster, 1994), entry for January 14.

9. Warren G. Bennis, *Managing the Dream: Reflections on Leadership and Change* (New York: Perseus, 2000), 7.

10. H. Jackson Brown and Robyn Spizman, *A Hero in Every*

Heart: Champions from All Walks of Life Share Powerful Messages to Inspire the Hero in Each of Us (Nashville, TN: Thomas Nelson, 1996), 88.

11. Thomas E. Ricks, *Making the Corps* (New York: Simon & Schuster, 1998), 187–88.

12. Tim Calkins, "A Marketing Plan for Turbulent Times," *Ivey Business Journal*, March/April 2009, http://www.iveybusinessjournal.com/article.asp?intArticleID=818.

13. Daily Mail Reporter, "Celebrity Plastic Surgeon Dr. Frank Ryan 'Was Texting' When His Car Went Off a Cliff," Mail Online, August 18, 2010, http://www.dailmail.co.uk/tvshowbiz/article-1303850/Heidi-Montags-plastic-surgeon-Dr-Frank-Ryan-killed-car-crash.html; Tom McCarthy and Luchina Fisher, "Heidi Montag Plastic Surgeon Frank Ryan Texting Before the Fatal Crash," ABCNews.com, August 18, 2010, http://abcnews.go.com/Entertainment/heidi-montag-plastic-surgeon-frank-ryan-texting-car/story?id=11427497.

14. Tom Vanderbilt, *Traffic: Why We Drive the Way We Do (and What It Says about Us)* (New York: Random House, 2009), 74.

15. Bob Gibson and Reggie Jackson with Lonnie Wheeler, *Sixty Feet, Six Inches: A Hall of Fame Pitcher and a Hall of Fame Hitter Talk About How the Game Is Played* (New York: Random House, 2000), 180.

16. B. Eugene Griessman, *The Achievement Factors: Candid Interviews with Some of the Most Successful People of Our Time* (San Francisco: Pfeiffer, 1993), 142.

17. Jim Denney, *Quit Your Day Job: How to Sleep Late, Do What You Enjoy, and Make a Ton of Money as a Writer* (Sanger, CA: Quill Driver Books, 2004), 88.

2. Focus on Your Passion in Life

1. Sharon Levine Waldman, "Tribute to Katharine Hepburn: Special Thoughts for Films for Two," Films for Two, http://www.films42.com/tribute/hepburn.asp; Jone Johnson Lewis, "Katharine Hepburn Quotes: Katharine Hepburn (1907–2003)," About.com Guide, http://womenshistory.about.com/cs/quotes/a/qu_k_hepburn.htm.

2. "Having Passion, Faith & Determintion Quotes," BestInspirational Quotes4u.com, http://www.bestinspirationalquotes4u.com/Success/Passion/passion.html.

3. Eileen Collins, "The Best Advice I Ever Got," Fortune, April 30, 2008, http://money.cnn.com/galleries/2008/fortune/0804/gallery.bestadvice.fortune/20.html.

4. Martin Woodside, Thomas Edison: The Man Who Lit Up the World (New York: Sterling, 2007), 52.

5. Carol Cramer, Thomas Edison (Farmington Hills, MI: Greenhaven Press, 2000), 195.

6. Blaine McCormick, At Work with Thomas Edison (Irvine, CA: Entrepreneur Press, 2001), 63.

7. Robert E. Conot, Thomas A. Edison: A Streak of Luck (Cambridge, MA: Da Capo Press, 1986), 458.

8. Theodore Dreiser, "A Photographic Talk with Edison: A Quiet Interview in His Laboratory; The Story of 52 Years of Manficent Work," Success, February 1898, http://nationalhumanitiescenter.org/pds/gilded/progress/text6/dreiser.pdf.

9. Gregory K. Morris, In Pursuit of Leadership: Principles and Practices from the Life of Moses (Longwood, FL: Xulon Press, 2006), 99.

10. Herb Miller, Leadership is the Key: Unlocking Your Effectiveness in Ministry (Nashville, TN: Abingdon Press, 1997), 59.

11. Dotson Rader, "Why He's Coming Home," *Parade*, December 16, 2001, 6.

12. Jim Valvano, "Espy Awards Acceptance Speech," March 4, 1993, the V Foundation for Cancer Research website, retrieved at http://jimmyv.org/remembering/jim/espy.cfm.

13. Justin Spizman with Robyn Spizman, *Don't Give Up . . . Don't Ever Give Up* (Naperville, IL: Sourcebooks, 2010), 53–54.

14. Patrick O'Brian, *Pablo Ruiz Picasso: A Biography* (New York: Norton, 1976), 72.

15. Ted Goodman, *The Forbes Book of Business Quotations: 10,000 Thoughts on the Business of Life* (New York: Black Dog & Leventhal, 2006), 158.

16. "Yastrzemski, Carl," National Baseball Hall of Fame and Museum, http://baseballhall.org/hof/yastrzemski-carl.

17. Peter G. Peterson, "The Best Advice I Ever Got," *Fortune*, April 30, 2008, http://money.cnn.com/galleries/2008/fortune/0804/gallery.bestadvice.fortune/3.html.

18. Larry Page, "The Best Advice I Ever Got," *Fortune*, April 30, 2008, http://money.cnn.com/galleries/2008/fortune/0804/gallery.bestadvice.fortune/2.html.

19. Andrea Guerra, "The Best Advice I Ever Got," *Fortune*, April 30,2008, http://money.cnn.com/galleries/2008/fortune/0804/gallery.bestadvice.fortune/22.html.

20. Michael Mink, "Leaders & Success: Pete Sampras, Tennis' Smash Hit," *Investor's Business Daily*, August 20, 2010,http://www.investors.com/NewsAndAnalysis/Article/544486/201008201740/Pete-Sampras-Tennis-Smash-Hit.aspx.

21. Steve Deger, *The Boy's Book of Positive Quotations* (Minneapolis, MN: Fairview Press, 2009), 8.

22. Bob Iger, "The Best Advice I Ever Got," *Fotune*, April 30, 2008, http://money.cnn.com/galleries/2008/fortune/0804/gallery.bestadvice.fortune/11.html.

23. Mike Miller, "My Amazing Journey," 2007–8 Season Preview, NBA.com, http://www.nba.com/preview2007/journey_miller.html.

24. John Edmund Haggai, *How to Win Over Worry* (Eugene, OR: Harvest House, 2009), 138.

25. Neal Gabler, *Walt Disney: The Triumph of the American Imagination* (New York: Random House, 2005), 50.

26. Westville High School, "Johnny Unitas Just Kept on Working," iHigh.com, May 19, 2010, http://www.ihigh.com/school11707/article_28306.html.

3. Focus on Tomorrow

1. Hal Urban, *Life's Greatest Lessons: 20 Things That Matter* (New York: Simon & Schuster, 2003), 102, 104.

2. Michael Bergdahl, *The Ten Rules of Sam Walton: Success Secrets for Remarkable Results* (Hoboken, NJ: Wiley, 2006), 23.

3. Bob Ortega, *In Sam We Trust*, book excerpt published in the *New York Times* online, 1998, http://www.nytimes.com/books/first/o/ortega-sam.html.

4. Brian Tracy, "Success Through Goal Setting," *Innovative Leader*, November 2000, http://www.wistonbrill.com/bril001/html/article_index/artcles/451-500/article498_body.html.

5. Ibid.

6. Brian Tracy, "Seven Steps to Success," Brian Tracy International, January 9, 2009, http://www.briantracy.com/blog/personal-success/seven-steps-to-success/.

7. Associated Press, "Pilot's Life Prepared Him for 'Miracle' Flight," MSNBC.com, January 16, 2009, http://www.msnbc.msn.com/id/28683246/.

8. Transcript, Jeffrey Brown speaks with Capt. Chesley "Sully" Sullenberger, "Sullenberger: Lifetime of Preparation Led to 'Miracle,'" PBS *NewsHour*, October 23, 2009, http://www.pbs.org/newshour/bb/transportation/july-dec09/sully_10-23.html.

9. John C. Maxwell, *Talent Is Never Enough: Discover the Choices That Will Take You Beyond Your Talent* (Nashville, TN: Thomas Nelson, 2007), 99.

10. Gary Mack with David Casstevens, *Mind Gym: An Athlete's Guide to Inner Excellence* (New York: McGraw-Hill, 2002), 157.

11. Eddie Lampert, "The Best Advice I Ever Got," *Fortune*, April 30, 2008, http://money.cnn.com/galleries/2008/fortune/0804/gallery.bestadvice.fortune/9.html.

12. Linda Picone, *The Daily Book of Positive Quotations* (Minneapolis, MN: Fairview Press, 2008), 51.

13. Tony Dungy with Nathan Whitaker, *Quiet Strength: The Principles, Practices & Priorities of a Winning Life* (Carol Stream, IL: Tyndale, 2007), 267.

14. Dick Weiss, "Irish Stay Afloat, Sink Navy with Late Field Goal," *New York Daily News*, November 9, 2003, http://www.nydailynews.com/archives/sports/2003/11/09/2003-11-09_irish_stay_afloat_sink_navy_.html.

15. Eric Uyttewaal, *Dynamic Scheduling with Microsoft Project 2002: The Book By and For Professionals* (Boca Raton, FL: J. Ross, 2003), 39.

16. Peter Gammons, "Forever a Kid," *Sports Illustrated*, April 30, 1990, http://sportsillustrated.cnn.com/vault/article/magazine/MAG1136931/5/index.htm.

17. Rubén González, "Focus, You Won't Succeed Without It," Rubengonzalez.Wordpress.com, August 15, 2006, http://ruben gonzalez.wordpress.com./category/motivational-stories/.

18. Connie Robertson, *Dictionary of Quotations* (Ware, Hertfordshire, England: Wordsworth Editions, 1998), 193.

19. Rick Hansen, "Rick's Journey Overview," Rick Hansen Foundation, http://www.rickhansen.com/code/navigate.aspx?Id=164; Rick Hansen, "Early Years," Rick Hansen Foundation, http://www.rickhansen.com/code/navigate.aspx?Id=15.

4. Focus on Today

1. Story of Dru Scott Decker and her friend Margaret was personally related by Dru Scott Decker to my writing partner, Jim Denney.

2. John C. Maxwell, *Leadership Gold: Lessons I've Learned from a Lifetime of Leading* (Nashville, TN: Thomas Nelson, 2008), 115.

3. John Wooden with Steve Jamison, *Wooden on Leadership* (New York: McGraw-Hill, 2005), 153.

4. Al Browning, *I Remember Paul "Bear" Bryant: Personal Memories of College Football's Most Legendary Coach as Told by the People Who Knew Him Best* (Nashville, TN: Cumberland House, 2001), xxii.

5. David Roper, "Time Flies," *Our Daily Bread*, entry for Saturday, January 31, 2004, http://www.mail-archive.com/parablenet@jesusyouth.org/msg01773.html.

6. Wayne Teasdale, *The Mystic Hours: A Daybook of Inspirational Wisdom and Devotion* (Novato, CA: New World Library, 2004), 293.

7. Pat Williams with Karen Kingsbury, *Forever Young: Ten Gifts of Faith for the Graduate* (Deerfield Beach, FL: Faith Communications, 2005), 77.

8. Lalitha V. Raman, "Your Time is Limited, So Don't Waste It Living Someone Else's Life! Aren't These Amazing Quotes?," Associated Content, April 20, 2010.

9. Diane Yendol-Hoppey and Nancy Fichtman Dana, *Powerful Professional Development: Building Expertise Within the Four Walls of Your School* (Thousand Oaks, CA: Corwin, 2010), 41.

10. Barry Stanton and Margaret Sinclair-Hunt, *Management Skills* (Harpenden, Hertfordshire, England: Select Knowledge Limited, 2006), 2.

11. Lou Holtz, *A Teen's Game Plan for Life* (Notre Dame, IN: Sorin Books, 2007), 60–62.

12. Phil Jackson, *Sacred Hoops: Spiritual Lessons of a Hardwood Warrior* (New York: Hyperion, 1995), 4.

13. Kirsten A. Holmstedt, *Band of Sisters: American Women at War in Iraq* (Mechanicsburg, PA: Stackpole Books, 2007), 27–34.

14. Swen Nater, "The Long Bus Ride," e-mail newsletter, September 12, 2010.

15. Bob Highfill, "Athletes Find Focus in 'The Zone,'" *Stockton Record*, August 15, 2010, http://www.recordnet.com/apps/pbcs.dll/article?AID=/20100815/A_SPORTS/8150309.

16. Pat Williams, *Extreme Dreams Depend on Teams* (Nashville, TN: Center Street, 2009), 147.

17. Kenneth Schuman and Ronald Paxton, *The Michelangelo Method: Release Your Inner Masterpiece and Create an Extraordinary Life* (New York: McGraw-Hill, 2006), 177.

18. Michael Cassutt, "The Cassutt Files: In the Zone," *Sci Fi Weekly*, October 23, 2006, retrieved at http://www.scifi.com/sfw/column/sfw13949.html.

19. Mihály Csíkszentmihályi, *Beyond Boredom and Anxiety: Experiencing Flow in Work and Play* (San Francisco: Jossey-Bass, 2000), 65–66.

20. Kara Leverte Farley and Sheila M. Curry, *Get Motivated! Daily Psych-Ups* (New York: Simon & Schuster, 1994), entry for January 14.

21. Paul Mason, *A World-Class Swimmer* (Chicago: Heinemann Library, 2004), 29.

22. Brett Rutledge, "How Does a Champion Think?," BrettRutledge.info, http://brettrutledge.info/Champthink.html.

5. Focus on Self-Discipline

1. Brian Tracy, "Seven Steps to Success," Brian Tracy International, January 9, 2009, http://www.briantracy.com/blog/personal-success/seven-steps-to-success/.

2. Kara Leverte Farley and Sheila M. Curry, *Get Motivated! Daily Psych-Ups* (New York: Simon & Schuster, 1994), entry for March 1.

3. Bob Richards, *The Heart of a Champion: Inspiring True Stories of Challenge and Triumph* (Grand Rapids, MI: Baker, 2009), 12–14; Roger Bannister, "The Four Minute Mile!," Tom Michalik, professor of physics (retired) faculty webpage, RandolphCollege.edu, http://faculty.randolphcollege.edu/tmichalik/4min.htm.

4. Jeff Fletcher, "Buster Posey Already Carrying Giants," MLB.Fanhouse.com, July 27, 2010, http://mlb.fanhouse.com/2010/07/27/buster-posey-already-carrying-giants/.

5. Tyler Kepner, "Posey Starts Even Better than Giants Had Hoped," *New York Times*, August 11, 2010, http://www.nytimes.com/2010/08/12/sports/baseball/12posey.html.

6. Kara Leverte Farley and Sheila M. Curry, *Get Motivated! Daily Psych-Ups* (New York: Simon & Schuster, 1994), entry for June 12.

7. Donald Norfolk, "How to Write Successful Novels," Donald Norfolk.co.uk, October 1, 2009, http:/www.donaldnorfolk.co.uk/228/writers-corner/how-to-write-successful-novels/.

8. Gary Graves, "Mike Shanahan Offers Yet Another Fresh Start for Redskins," *USA Today*, August 13, 2010, http://www.usatoday.com/sports/football/nfl/redskins/2010-08-12-washington-redskins-shanahan-mcnabb-eagles_N.htm.

9. John C. Maxwell, *The 21 Indispensable Qualities of a Leader: Becoming the Person Others Will Want to Follow* (Nashville, TN: Thomas Nelson, 1999), 127.

10. Venus Williams, *Come to Win* (New York: HarperCollins, 2010), 122.

11. Will Friedwald, "Lena Horne Gave Her All to Her Songs," *Wall Street Journal*, May 11, 2010, http://onlinewsj.com/article/SB10001424052748703880304575236233315241878.html.

12. Oren Harari, *The Powell Principles: 24 Lessons from Colin Powell, Battle-Proven Leader* (New York: McGraw-Hill, 2004), 31.

13. Fred McMane, *The 3,000 Hit Club* (Champaign, IL: Sports Publishing LLC, 2000), 186.

14. Ibid.

15. Russ Volckmann, *Insights on Leadership, Volume 3: Executives* (San Francisco: Integral Leadership Review, 2002), 129.

16. William C. Roberts, M.D., "Organizational Philosophy of Paul 'Bear' Bryant," Baylor Health Care System, *BUMC Proceedings*, January 2000, http://www.baylorhealth.edu/proceedings/13_1/13_1_roberts.html.

17. Bill Bradley, *Values of the Game* (New York: Workman, 1998), 7–9.

18. Steve Deger, *The Boy's Book of Positive Quotations* (Minneapolis, MN: Fairview Press, 2009), 193.

19. Bob Knight with Bob Hammel, *Knight: My Story* (New York: Macmillan, 2003), 173–75.

6. Focus on Things You Can Control

1. John R. Wooden with Steve Jamison, *The Essential Wooden: A Lifetime of Lessons on Leaders and Leadership* (New York: McGraw-Hill, 2006), 32.

2. Daniel Schorn, "Comeback Kid James Blake: James Blake Talks to Mike Wallace About Life's Challenges," CBS News 60 *Minutes*, November 27, 2005, http://www.cbsnews.com/stories/2005/11/22/60minutes/main1066081.shtml?tag=contentMain;contentBody; Pat Williams, *The Pursuit* (Ventura, CA: Regal Books, 2008), 35.

3. Mark Goldhaber, "History of the World, Part 1," MousePlanet.com, January 28, 2004, http://www.mouseplanet.com/7107/History_of_the_World_Part_1.

4. Phil Taylor, "The Joint Is Jumping," *Sports Illustrated*, December 11, 1995, http://sportsillustrated.cnn.com/vault/article/magazine/MAG1007534/index.htm.

5. Stephen Fox, *Big Leagues: Professional Baseball, Football, and Basketball in National Memory* (Lincoln: University of Nebraska Press, 1994), 399.

6. Marilyn Pincus, *Boost Your Presentation IQ* (New York: McGraw-Hill, 2005), 42.

7. Pete Carroll with Yogi Roth, *Win Forever* (New York: Portfolio, 2010), 96–97.

8. Chellie Campbell, *The Wealthy Spirit: Daily Affirmations*

for Financial Stress Reduction (Naperville, IL: Sourcebooks, 2002), 264.

9. Colonel James H. Benson, Sr., *So You Want to Be a Leader? Advice and Counsel to Young Leaders* (Bloomington, IN: Trafford, 2007), 63.

10. Alexander Wolff, "The Coach and His Champion," *Sports Illustrated*, April 3, 1989, http://sportsillustrated.cnn.com/vault/article/magazine/MAG1068223/2/index.htm.

11. Pat Williams, *Mr. Littlejohn's Secrets to a Lifetime of Success* (Grand Rapids, MI: Fleming H. Revell, 2000), 108.

12. Kara Leverte Farley and Sheila M. Curry, *Get Motivated! Daily Psych-Ups* (New York: Simon & Schuster, 1994), entry for June 15.

13. Rubén González, "How to Condition Your Mind to Succeed," Rubengonzalez.Wordpress.com, August 15, 2006, http://ruben gonzalez.wordpress.com/category/motivational-stories/.

14. Economics Academy 101, "The Super Bakery Story," WesternReservePublicMedia.org, http://westernreservepublicmedia.org/economics/images/bakery1.pdf; Barry J. Farber, *Diamond in the Rough: The Secret to Finding Your Own Value—and Making Your Own Success* (New York: Berkley Books, 1995), 60.

7. Focus on Courage and Confidence

1. Author uncredited, "Howard Cosell," Sports Broadcasting Hall of Fame, http://www.sportsvideo.org/portal/hof/articles/publish/Howard_Cosell.shtml.

2. Thomas Lane Butts, *Tigers in the Dark* (Nashville, TN: Abingdon Press, 1978), 15–16.

3. Brian Tracy, *The 21 Success Secrets of Self-Made Millionaires* (San Francisco: Berrett-Koehler, 2009), 67.

4. Matt James Mason, *The Pirate's Dilemma: How Youth Culture Is Reinventing Capitalism* (New York: Simon & Schuster, 2008), 40.

5. Steve Deger, *The Boy's Book of Positive Quotations* (Minneapolis, MN: Fairview Press, 2009), 8.

6. Taylor Hicks with David Wild, *Heart Full of Soul: An Inspirational Memoir About Finding Your Voice and Finding Your Way* (New York: Random House, 2007), viewed online at www.books.google.com, unnumbered pages.

7. Robin Roberts and C. Paul Rogers III, *The Whiz Kids and the 1950 Pennant* (Philadelphia: Temple University Press, 1996), 88.

8. Ibid.

9. Ibid., 89.

10. Ibid.

11. Swen Nater, "Condition: The First Key to Your Team Never Beating Itself," Collaboration Is a Win-Win blog, July 29, 2009, http://blog.coachswen.com/2009/07/29/condition-the-first-key-to-your-team-never-beating-itself.aspx.

12. Michael Jordan, "Michael Jordan on Fear," TeamArete: Coach Dreiling Basketball Website, http://www.teamarete.com/mjonfear.html.

13. "Inspirational Quote from Motivation in a Minute," Multidimensional Man, June 22, 2010, http://multidimensionalman.grouply.com/message/24264.

14. David M. Campbell, *Do You Really Need an MBA? The Way of an Entrepreneur* (Vancouver, BC: Douglas & McIntyre, 2004), 13.

15. Greg Morris, "The Rewards of Risk," Greg Morris Ministries, Ministry Health website, 1998, http://www.ministryhealth.net/mh_articles/214_gm_rewards_of_risk.html.

16. Andy Serwer, "Larry Page on How to Change the World,"

Fortune, May 1, 2008, http://money.cnn.com/2008/04/29/magazines/fortune/larry_page_change_the_world.fortune/index.htm.

17. Bill O'Hanlon, *Write Is a Verb: Sit Down. Start Writing. No Excuses* (Cincinnati, OH: Writer's Digest Books, 2007), 13.

18. William Safire and Leonard Safir, *Words of Wisdom: More Good Advice* (New York: Simon & Schuster, 1990), 335.

19. Marty Angelo, *Strategic Studies e-News*, page 3, August 1999, http://www.e-tutor.com/eNews/issue0899/.

20. Stephen King, *On Writing: A Memoir of the Craft* (New York: Pocket Books, 2000), 210.

21. "Tom Landry Quotes," IWise Wisdom On-Demand, http://www.iwise.com/hufpt.

22. National Basketball Association, *The Perfect Team: The Best Players, Coach, and GM—Let the Debate Begin!* (New York: Doubleday, 2006), excerpt from Chapter 1, "Larry Bird," Powell's Books website, http://www.powells.com/biblio?show=HARDCOVER:USED:9780385501460:8.95&page=excerpt.

23. Edgar F. Puryear, *American Generalship: Character Is Everything; The Art of Command* (New York: Random House, 2001), viewed online at www.books.google.com, unnumbered pages.

24. Ibid.

25. Mort Crim, *Second Thoughts: One Hundred Upbeat Messages for Beat-Up Americans* (Deerfield Beach, FL: Health Communications, 1998), 45–46.

26. William Safire and Leonard Safir, *Words of Wisdom: More Good Advice* (New York: Simon & Schuster, 1990), 102; Rebecca Gibbon, *Graduation* (Philadelphia: Running Press, 2000), 108.

27. Kareem Abdul-Jabbar with Alan Steinberg, *Black Profiles in Courage: A Legacy of African-American Achievement* (New York: Morrow, 1996), 246–47.

28. Fr. Dennis McBride, "The Circumstances of Our Birth: John the Baptist's, Oprah's, Yours and Mine," Reflection for the Nativity of John the Baptist, Ascension Catholic Church, http://www.ascensioncatholic.net/lectionary/AllCycles/reflection/JohnBaptist.html.

8. Focus on Commitment

1. Curt Smith, *Storied Stadiums: Baseball's History Through Its Ballparks* (New York: Carroll & Graf, 2003), 452.

2. A. S. Damiani, *Creative Leadership: Mining the Gold in Your Workforce* (Boca Raton, FL: CRC Press, 1998), 148.

3. Vince Lombardi, Jr., *What It Takes to Be #1: Vince Lombardi on Leadership* (New York: McGraw-Hill, 2003), 119.

4. Julius Erving interview, "The Great and Wondrous Dr. J," Academy of Achievement, December 13, 2007, http://www.achievement.org/autodoc/page/erv0int-2.

5. Fay Vincent, *It's What's Inside the Lines That Counts: Baseball Stars of the 1970s and 1980s Talk About the Game They Loved* (New York: Simon & Schuster, 2010), 27–28.

6. Ibid., 38.

7. Brad Winters, "Coach Paul Bear Bryant Quotes," Leadership Quotes by Coach Bear Bryant, http://www.coachlikeapro.com/coach-paul-bear-bryant.html.

8. Daniel Diehl and Mark P. Donnelly, *Elbert Hubbard: The Common Sense Revolutionary; A Business Vision for Our Times* (London: Spiro Press, 2003), 119.

9. Bob Richards, *The Heart of a Champion: Inspiring True Stories of Challenge and Triumph* (Grand Rapids, MI: Baker, 2009), 10.

10. Ibid., 113.

11. Forbes, "The World's Billionaires: No. 799 S. Truett Cathy," Forbes.com, March 8, 2007, http://www.forbes.com/lists/2007/10/07billionaires_S-Truett-Cathy_AARY.html.

12. William Safire, "Character Is Destiny," *New York Times*, January 12, 2005, http://www.nytimes.com/2005/01/12/opinion/12safi.html.

13. Kellie Johnston, "Meet Your Facilitator: Favorite Quotes," Alabama Clean Water Partnership, http://www.cleanwater-partnership.org/pages/?pageID=19.

14. William C. Hammond, 12 *Step Wisdom at Work: Transforming Your Life and Your Organization* (Dover, NH: Kogan Page, 2001), xi.

15. Jeannette Samanen, Ph.D., "Accountability Will Help You Achieve Your Goals," Make Your Good Life Better: Tips to Help You Achieve Your Goals, December 15, 2009, http://goodlife.achieveyourgoals.com/accountability-achieve-your-goals/25/.

16. Lee J. Colan, *Orchestrating Attitude* (Dallas, TX: Corner-Stone Leadership Institute, 2005), 33.

17. John C. Maxwell, *Talent Is Never Enough: Discover the Choices That Will Take You Beyond Your Talent* (Nashville, TN: Thomas Nelson, 2007), 133.

18. Donald T. Phillips, *Run to Win: Vince Lombardi on Coaching and Leadership* (New York: St. Martin's Press, 2001), 26.

9. Focus on Leadership and Influence

1. Howard Schultz interviewed by Adi Ignatius, "The HBR Interview:'We Had to Own the Mistakes,'" Harvard Business School Publishing, July 26, 2010, http://www.eiu.com/indexasp?layout=ebArticleVW3&article_id=597286844 &channel_id=788114478&category_id=1168152916&refm=vw Cat&page_title=Article&rf=0.

2. Ibid.

3. Swen Nater, "Life Is the United Effort of Many," e-mail newsletter, September 19, 2010.

4. Hans Finzel, *The Top Ten Mistakes Leaders Make* (Colorado Springs, CO: David C. Cook, 2007), 103.

5. Jane Leavy, *The Last Boy: Mickey Mantle and the End of America's Childhood* (New York: HarperCollins, 2010), 239-240.

6. Gerrylynn K. Roberts and Philip Steadman, *American Cities & Technology: Wilderness to Wired City* (New York: Routledge, 1999), 61.

7. Stephen Denning, *The Leader's Guide to Storytelling: Mastering the Art and Discipline of Business Narrative* (San Francisco: Jossey-Bass, 2005), 233.

8. Dr. Martin Luther King, Jr., "I Have a Dream," U.S. Constitution.net, http://www.usconstitution.net/dream.html.

9. Pat Williams with David Wimbish, *Secrets from the Mountain: Ten Lessons for Success in Life* (Grand Rapids, MI: Revell, 2001), 135.

10. John C. Maxwell, *Be All You Can Be: A Challenge to Stretch Your God-Given Potential* (Colorado Springs, CO: David C. Cook, 2007), 105.

11. John Frederick Schroeder, ed., *Maxims of Washington: Compiled for Use in Schools, Libraries, and All of American Homes* (New York: D. Appleton, 1894), 309.

12. Robert Lewis Taylor and William E. Rosenbach, eds., *Military Leadership: In Pursuit of Excellence* (Boulder, CO: Westview Press, 2000), 7.

13. Dale Carnegie and Associates, Oliver Crom, and Michael Crom, *The Sales Advantage: How to Get It, Keep It, and Sell More Than Ever* (New York: Simon & Schuster, 2003), 59.

14. James M. Strock, *Theodore Roosevelt on Leadership* (New York: Random House, 2001), 44.

15. Lan Liu, *Conversations on Leadership* (San Francisco: Jossey-Bass, 2010), 154.

16. Howard Schultz, ibid.

17. Ibid.

10. Focus—and Finish Strong!

1. Randy Pausch, Carnegie Mellon University, "Last Lecture: Achieving Your Childhood Dreams," YouTube.com, http://www.youtube.com/watch?v=ji5_MqicxSo.

2. David E. Rye, 1,001 *Ways to Inspire Your Organization, Your Team, and Yourself* (Franklin Lakes, NJ: Career Press, 1998), 73–74.

3. Lynette Rice, "Conan O'Brien's Final Monologue," *Hollywood Insider,* January 22, 2010, http://hollywoodinsider. ew.com/2010/01/22/conan-obriens-final-monologue-nobody-in-life-gets-what-they-thought-they-were-going-to-get/.

4. Mike Krzyzewski with Donald T. Phillips, *Leading with the Heart: Coach K's Successful Strategies for Basketball, Business, and Life* (New York: Warner Business Books, 2000), 274.

5. John R. Wooden with Steve Jamison, *Wooden on Leadership* (New York: McGraw-Hill, 2005), 134.

6. Mary Vinnage, "Points from Powell," *Success Magazine*, February 2009, 56.

7. Daniel S. Harkavy, *Becoming a Coaching Leader: The Proven Strategy for Building Your Own Team of Champions* (Nashville, TN: Thomas Nelson, 2007), 130.

8. Monica Wofford, *Contagious Leadership* (Austin, TX: Presentersplus, 2004), 41.

9. Associated Press and other sources, "Delimar Vera Cuevas Articles," posted by Tracy Curry-Reyes, August 2008, http://delimarveracuervas.blogspot.com/.

INDEX

CONTACT

You can contact Pat Williams at:

Pat Williams
c/o Orlando Magic
8701 Maitland Summit Boulevard
Orlando, FL 32810
phone: 407-916-2404
pwilliams@orlandomagic.com

Visit Pat Williams's website at:

www.PatWilliamsMotivate.com

If you would like to set up a speaking engagement for Pat Williams, please call or write his assistant, Andrew Herdliska, at the above address, or call him at 407-916-2401. Requests can also be faxed to 407-916-2986 or e-mailed to aherdliska@orlandomagic.com.

We would love to hear from you. Please send your comments about this book to Pat Williams at the above address. Thank you.

Other Books by Pat Williams

The Takeaway $14.95 • item #3892
(and Karyn Williams with Peggy Matthews Rose)

How to Be Like Women of Influence $12.95 • item #0545
(and Ruth Williams with Michael Mink)

How to Be Like Mike $12.95 • item #9551
(with Michael Weinreb)

How to Be Like Coach Wooden $14.95 • item #3919
(with David Wimbish)

**How to Be Like Women Athletes
of Influence** $14.95 • item #6772
(with Dana Pennett O'Neil)

How to Be Like Jackie Robinson $14.95 • item #1738
(with Mike Sielski)

How to Be Like Jesus $14.95 • item #0693
(with Jim Denney)

How to Be Like Rich DeVos $16.95 • item # 1584
(with Jim Denney)

How to Be Like Women of Power $14.95 • item #6500
(and Ruth Williams with Michael Mink)

How to Be Like Walt $13.95 • item #2319
(with Jim Denney)

Winning with One-Liners $14.95 • item #057x

Read for Your Life $14.95 • item #5458
(with Peggy Matthews Rose)

Forever Young $14.95 • item #253x
(and Karen Kingsbury)
